TEACHING JEWISH HISTORY

Julia Phillips Berger
Sue Parker Gerson

A.R.E. Publishing
An Imprint of Behrman House, Inc.
Springfield, New Jersey
www.behrmanhouse.com

Historical Consultant: Rabbi Martin S. Cohen
Project Editor: Terry S. Kaye
Editorial Assistant: Sam Weinreich
Cover art: Lydie Egosi
Cover design: Devorah Wolf

Copyright © 2006 by Behrman House, Inc.
Springfield, New Jersey
ISBN 10: 0-86705-183-3
ISBN 13: 978-0-86705-183-4

Manufactured in the United States of America

Library of Congress Cataloging-in-Publication Data

Berger, Julia Phillips.
  Teaching Jewish history / Julia Phillips Berger, Sue Parker Gerson.
    p. cm.
  Includes bibliographical references.
  ISBN-13: 978-0-86705-183-4 (pbk.)
  ISBN-10: 0-86705-183-3 (pbk.)
  1. Jews—History—Study and teaching. 2. Judaism—History—Study and teaching. I. Gerson, Sue
Parker. II. Title.

DS115.95.B47 2006
909'.04924071—dc22

                                                                                    2006016602

Dedicated to my parents, Howard and Sheila Phillips, who taught me that while I may not have landed at Plymouth Rock, I most certainly stood at Sinai; and to my husband, Adam Berger, for his enthusiastic support of this project and all of my endeavors — **Julia Phillips Berger**

Dedicated to my wonderful family: to my husband, Rabbi Bernard Gerson, and our children, Elliot and Jennie, for their continuous love and support; and to my parents: my father, Judge Ronald I. Parker, for his lifelong guidance, and in loving memory of my mother, Adrienne Parker *z"l*, my first and best teacher. — **Sue Parker Gerson**

CONTENTS

CHAPTER ONE

AN INTRODUCTION TO TEACHING JEWISH HISTORY

Shira walked out of the religious school director's office feeling both elated and anxious. She was thrilled that she had been hired to teach religious school for the coming year, but Jewish history? What did she know about teaching Jewish history? In her last teaching job she had taught Jewish holidays and Hebrew. At least those were things she understood. How was she supposed to make Jewish history interesting and exciting?

If you have ever felt like Shira, you are not alone. The sheer span of Jewish history is enough to intimidate many an experienced teacher, let alone a brand-new teacher. Even if your goal is teaching just a slice of Jewish history, making all those names and dates relevant to modern American Jews, especially kids, may seem impossible. Relax. It doesn't matter if you know the names and dates. It doesn't matter if you've never taught history before. The information, activities, and resources in this book will help you on your way. If, on the other hand, you have taught Jewish history for years, this book will help you find new ways to look at "old" topics and a variety of teaching activities that will help you keep history alive in your classroom.

THE IMPORTANCE OF TEACHING JEWISH HISTORY

One of the first questions many people ask is, "With so little time and so many important subjects to teach, why should we include Jewish history in our curriculum?"

One compelling reason to make sure our students have a grasp of Jewish history is that Judaism is a historical religion. Each year, we relive our history through the holiday cycle as participants—just consider the Passover seder. It is not just our ancestors who lived through these events, but each one of us today. We follow Moses out of Egypt, sing with Miriam at the crossing of the Sea of Reeds, stand in awe at the base of Mount Sinai, build and dwell in booths on the festival of Sukkot, and celebrate the rededication of the Temple after its desecration by the Greeks on Ḥanukkah.

So aware are we of the significance of history in Jewish ritual life that two major Jewish events of the twentieth century— the Holocaust and the birth of the State of Israel—have been added to the Jewish religious calendar. Judaism celebrates not only an individual's relationship with God, but with the entire Jewish people across the generations. One doesn't have to be born Jewish to be a part of the family, because every Jew by Choice becomes the son or daughter of Abraham and Sarah, thus joining our family tree.

Although biblical history is a critical touchstone of our tradition, we do ourselves a disservice when we focus only on the biblical period and fail to take into account subsequent generations of our family's history. To understand ourselves fully as Jews requires a knowledge of our history from Abraham's time to the present day. Teaching history to our children adds a foundational layer to their ritual lives. It helps them better understand where they came from and where they are going—developing a stronger Jewish identity along the way. And, like all knowledge, it will deepen and acquire a different focus as we grow older and have the benefit of life experience and wisdom. That's why we hope this book will be useful not only for teachers of children, but also great for educators working with adults in synagogues, community centers, family education, and other learning environments—both formal and informal.

When taught well, Jewish history allows each individual to form an emotional connection to the past and thus a stronger connection to Judaism. Learning about the struggles, choices, convictions, inventions, and artistic creations of the Jews who came before us can help us better travel the roads of our own Jewish lives. The big questions of history are the same questions we deal with today and will continue to deal with tomorrow. In learning from the past, we can better answer those questions for ourselves in the future.

Given that Jewish history is central to Jewish identity, we consider it vitally important for Jewish educational institutions to make studying the Jewish past an ongoing part of the curriculum. In this book we strive to provide teachers of Jewish history with theoretical ideas as well as practical suggestions for presenting the Jewish past to those living in the Jewish present. Throughout the book, teachers will find numerous resources, including examples of activities to be used in the classroom. More important, teachers will find tools to help their students personalize the historical experience by learning how to interpret

information—such as documents, photographs, facts, and dates—through the lens of "big ideas." In addition, we have provided ideas for helping students to develop their own historical narratives.

WHAT DO WE MEAN BY "JEWISH HISTORY"?

The term "Jewish history" may seem self-evident, but the meaning varies depending on the community in which it is discussed. Each teacher's working definition of Jewish history—that is, the underlying assumptions in one's teaching about what constitutes historical truth about the Jewish past—is usually influenced by one's personal view and the philosophy of the educational or religious institution. Quality teaching requires personal reflection.

The following section examines two common perspectives on Jewish history, the sacred and the academic. This issue may be particularly sensitive for those teaching the biblical and rabbinic periods.

Sacred History

Sacred history is the traditional, Jewish religious interpretation of historical events. It is the story Jews have always told themselves about the past through their sacred texts including the Tanach, or Hebrew Bible, Talmud, and other religious writings, as well as oral traditions passed down over the centuries. Observant Jews have understood their history as true because the sacred texts are authoritative for them as Jews; most traditional Jews believe that the Torah was disseminated to the Jewish people directly by God. From a religious perspective, archaeological evidence is not needed to prove that miracles happened, or that the Patriarchs actually existed—that these events occurred as they are written in the Torah is taken, literally, on faith. For traditional

Jews, the central relevant part of history from a sacred perspective is the relationship between God and the Jews, and how that relationship has unfolded over the centuries. This perspective on Jewish history has shaped both the experience of Jews and the Jewish response to historical events.

Academic History

The academic approach to history is not concerned with religious truths, but rather with historical accuracy. The historian relies on a range of materials to determine historical truth: religious texts (analyzed as historical, not sacred, literature), ritual objects, archaeological ruins, artifacts, and documents of all types written by Jews and non-Jews of the time period under study, for example, contracts, diaries, and inscriptions). Historical records are not taken at face value; they are authoritative only insofar as they can be authenticated through scientific methods of analysis. In addition, the secular academic historian does not necessarily accept God as a legitimate actor in human history. A variety of factors might help to explain a historical event, but, in a purely academic setting, God is not one of them.

Both sacred history and academic history contain truths that we need for self-reflection as a people and as individuals. The sacred history of the Jews has shaped the Jewish experience and kept Judaism alive for over five thousand years. However, if we teach Jewish history only from a sacred perspective, we deprive our

students of the skills to analyze Jewish life in the past and in the present. Conversely, teaching only the academic approach takes away a core purpose of Jewish education: to pass on Jewish thought and traditions through the lens of our sacred experience as a people connected to God. While a critical historical analysis of the political, economic, and social realities of the Jewish past is indispensable for under-standing contemporary Jewish life, we lose our essence as a people if we do not teach our children the sacred perspective as well.

AD versus CE

In thinking about Jewish history as Jews, from a sacred or academic perspective, it is helpful to strip away some of the layers of terminology commonly used by histori-ans that are actually grounded in a Chris-tian perspective of the world. Many otherwise secular historians commonly use the abbreviations BC (Before Christ) and AD (Anno Domini—"in the year of the Lord," i.e., in the time of the Christian era) to divide earlier and later periods of history. In this book, the more secular abbreviations BCE (Before the Common Era) and CE (Common Era) will be used to indicate similar divisions of historical periods.

CHAPTER TWO

AN INTEGRATED APPROACH TO TEACHING JEWISH HISTORY

Teachers and students often find that the most effective learning occurs within a multilayered approach: one that organizes units of study around big ideas, and allows students to encounter the evidence of history directly. Based on this model, there are three primary elements to consider when teaching any unit of Jewish history:

- What are the big ideas of the period of history in question?
- What historical evidence is available for the students to engage with directly?
- What activities enrich the encounter with historical sources and allow students engaging ways to create their own responses and analyses?

To examine each of these unit elements, showing how they work together and complement each other, we will begin with a vignette:

While Mrs. Adler has taught at the Temple Shalom religious school in California for three years, this is the first year she is teaching American Jewish history to fifth graders. Over the summer, she reviewed the textbook, which primarily examines the experience of Jewish immigrants on the East Coast. Mrs. Adler knows that many of her students have family living back East, but otherwise it is a distant place to most of them. So, an American Jewish history unit concentrating on the Northeast probably will not capture the imagination of her California students. Therefore, Mrs. Adler chooses specifically to focus on the experience of American

Jews in the West during the late nineteenth and early twentieth centuries. The textbook discusses this topic in only two paragraphs, so she sets aside the book and searches the synagogue library and the Internet for other possible sources. As she researches, Mrs. Adler realizes that there are many ways she could approach her topic. She could focus on the dates and places of famous events or the biographies of famous Jews such as Levi Strauss. But the more research that Mrs. Adler does, the more she realizes that many of the dilemmas Jews faced a century ago are related to those her students currently experience and those they will one day encounter. Some of these dilemmas include whether or not to move, whether or not to marry a Jewish spouse, where to find a Jewish spouse, and how to practice Judaism in communities in which there are few Jews.

And so Mrs. Adler selects the core concept of "choices," and creates the following "big idea" statement: "The choices made by the Jewish men and women who moved West, and many others like them, would change their lives and the lives of those who came after them." Each lesson in her unit will contribute to the "unpacking," or parsing out, of this statement. By the end of the unit, her students will be able to defend or challenge this big idea.[1]

---

[1] For more on "big ideas" and Understanding by Design, see "Curriculum Planning: A Model for Understanding," by Nachama Skolnik Moskowitz in *The Ultimate Jewish Teacher's Handbook*, Denver: A.R.E., 2003, pp. 278–291.

Mrs. Adler begins the unit by asking, "How many of you have ever moved to a new city?" The class works together to make a list of reasons why people might decide to move elsewhere. When possible, she highlights issues that will be relevant in the historical material. In the next few classes, Mrs. Adler introduces primary sources—reproductions of advertisements and articles from period newspapers, and letters written by Jews in the West to their families in the overcrowded cities back East—as a way of examining why American Jews chose to move West. The students read these materials and analyze them using questions Mrs. Adler provides. They make a list of reasons that Jews chose to move out West. As background, they watch a video about this topic and read a short piece Mrs. Adler found in a collection of essays.

After the presentation of the background material and the analysis of the primary sources, a process that has taken several weeks, Mrs. Adler returns to the very first activity in the unit. She asks the class to compare their own lists of reasons to move with the historical reasons for why Jews actually did move. She poses several questions:

- What are the similarities and differences between the two lists?
- What different historical realities influenced each group's decision to move?
- Which of the reasons for moving on the two lists were influenced by the participants being Jewish?
- Which of the reasons were influenced by the fact that the Jews were American?

Mrs. Adler concluded this unit with a discussion of what defines "Jewish" and "American" values, asking her students to reflect on the extent to which they separate the two in their lives.

BIG IDEAS

In the above vignette, Mrs. Adler's topic is "Jews in the American West in the Nineteenth and Twentieth Centuries." Within that topic, she chooses one core concept, an axis around which to organize the important names, dates, and events of that period. By highlighting the theme of the choices Jews made in their journey out West, she is able to raise several levels of questions for her students. Some of the questions relate to their current lives, for example, What dilemmas do they presently face? Some relate to questions they will encounter later in life, for example, Should they marry a Jew? Some relate to the material itself, for example, Why did Jews move West? These questions allow students to explore the topic on a variety of levels.

"Big ideas" are the basic yet sophisticated concepts that lie at the heart of any academic discipline; they are the perennial ideas that make the discipline intriguing. Facts alone do not generate discussion; big ideas do. For example, a traditional approach to teaching Mrs. Adler's unit on the experience of American Jews who moved to the West might be: (1) follow a standard history textbook, which may only barely cover the experience of the Jewish move west; (2) leave the textbook, but focus on the timeline of the Jewish move to the West, including how they managed the move, what life was like for Jews when they arrived, and even how little the history of the Jews of the west is understood today—all the "hard data." Mrs. Adler, however, chose (3) a big idea as the organizing principle of the unit, a statement to be explored on many levels.

One example of a big idea for this unit might be "Building Community." A key statement for students to explore might be

"The choices made by the Jewish men and women who moved West, and many others like them, would change their lives and the lives of those who came after them." To "unpack" this statement, that is, truly to understand it, Mrs. Adler's students would need to explore the following issues: (1) What dilemmas did the Jews of that period face, and why? (2) What choices did they make in the face of those dilemmas? (3) Why did they make those particular choices? (4) How did these choices affect the lives of the people in the time period? (5) How did these choices affect future generations? (6) Do the students feel the effects of these choices in their lives today? Through this complex series of questions—questions that involve facts as well as meaning—a big idea serves to connect students to the past by giving them the opportunity to explore issues that are also relevant for them in the present.

Basing a Jewish history unit on a big idea shifts the attention from the rote memorization of dates, names, and other facts. Instead, the emphasis becomes an exploration of the dilemmas, struggles, and experiences of the Jewish people. History comes alive for students through a deeper and focused study of these experiences, because such an exploration allows the students truly to relate to the material at hand, and to their place in the sacred history of the Jewish people.

Available Historical Evidence

Teaching through big ideas enables students to see the big picture, but that larger perspective can be vague and sometimes confusing if students are not offered the opportunity to explore those ideas in a specific context. Thus, while big ideas serve as organizing principles of any given period of Jewish history, primary sources provide the details—the who, what, where, when, why—that make those concepts come to life. Without big ideas, history can all too easily be reduced to a list of names, dates, and facts. Without primary resources, big ideas can be ephemeral and difficult to grasp.

What falls under the category of "primary source"? A primary source is any object or written document from the time period under study—historical evidence that students can experience directly. Secondary sources are scholarly works that interpret primary sources.[2] Some of the primary sources a teacher might use in a lesson include: artifacts, diaries, contracts, sacred texts, paintings, sculpture, audio and videotapes (of a historical event), to name just a few. Some examples of secondary sources are textbooks, articles, scholarly writings about the period of history under discussion, and documentaries.

The ways in which primary sources are used in the classroom depends, of course, on the age of the students. For younger students, primary sources might include pictures, artifacts and artwork, while older children, teens, and adults are also able to read and analyze historical documents.[3] No matter what primary sources are chosen for the lesson, there are several important steps to follow when using them. A good general rule to follow is that a primary source is only as good as its

---

[2] Monica Edinger, *Seeking History: Teaching with Primary Sources in Grades 4–6*, Portsmouth, NH: Heinemann, 2000, p. 25.
[3] This section emphasizes the structure of the primary source activity as a way to help students analyze objects and documents. Students with learning disabilities will need further assistance, particularly with documents that might contain difficult language. Reading the text out loud, providing a vocabulary list, and continuous reinforcement of the context in which the text is being read might be helpful.

setup and analysis. That is to say, by itself a primary source teaches very little. However, with the proper presentation, both before and after actually encountering the primary source itself, an object or document can change the way students think of history. Below are some general guidelines to follow when using primary sources:

Provide context for the primary source— All students, from young children and teenagers to adults, need a context in which to place the primary source they are about to encounter. Some background considerations might include the following: Where did the object come from? Who is the author of the document? What role did he or she play in history? Why do you think we are reading (looking at, exploring) this piece? Clear introductions give students the tools they need to analyze the object or document on their own.

Work in small groups—While the teacher-student ratio dictates to what extent small group work is possible with younger children, with older students we highly recommend working in pairs with a primary source whenever possible. This allows each student to wrestle with the problems presented through objects or documents, actively engaging in under-standing history. The teacher facilitates group work by checking in with each group, answering questions, and ensuring that students are on the right track.

Provide basic questions—Students usually do not know what to look for when presented with a primary source. Guideline questions serve two purposes: they help the students get as much as possible from the document or artifact, and they train students to read a primary

source. Clearly, younger children will need the guidance of the teacher, but older children and adults also need prompting. With objects or documents, the goal of the basic questions is to ensure that each student understands the fundamentals of the primary source. Here are some basic questions to be answered:

Objects as Primary Sources
- What is the object?
- What is the object used for?

Documents as Primary Sources
- Who wrote the document? When was it written? For whom was it written?
- Are there any words in the document you don't understand? (Look them up.)
- What are the main points of the document? (It is crucial that every student in the class understands the basic meaning of the document—even a story—before proceeding to analyze it.)

Provide Analysis Questions—"Students don't learn from experiences upon which they don't reflect."[4] Encountering a primary source will have only a temporary impact unless the students reflect on its meaning in a larger context. Thus, after every student in the class understand the basic meaning of the primary source, a critical part of the educational process is for them to analyze the object or document. The questions guiding them in their analysis will, of course, be determined by the big idea you choose and the reasons you selected the primary source in the first place. Here are a few analysis questions to consider:

---

[4] "Better Endings for Classes and Courses," *ClassWise*, May/June 1997.

Objects as Primary Sources

- What can the object tell us about the life of the person that used it? About the times in which it was used?
- How can the above information help us understand the big idea of this unit? (Phrase this question in terms understandable to the students.)

Documents as Primary Sources

- Why was the document written? (Is the author trying to solve a problem? Presenting a viewpoint on an important issue?)
- Is the author a reliable source on the issue at hand? How can you find out?
- Are there any contradictions in the document? If so, why do you think they are there?
- In what way(s) does this document shed light on the larger issues being discussed in this unit?

Post-analysis—In the best of circumstances, students often have a hard time recalling what they encountered in a previous class. So, in order to maximize the learning from a primary source, be very aware of the time and end a few minutes early in order to wrap up the day's work (yes, even if they are going to continue with the document or object the very next day). Whether a brief verbal summary that ties together what the students have learned so far, or an activity in which students themselves pull together the various elements of the lesson, every examination of a primary source should include some sort of concluding reflective exercise.

If you have not used primary sources before, you may be surprised at how much time it takes to elucidate the basic meanings of the texts (depending on their difficulty). This challenge may be due to several factors: (1) Students are not used to engaging actively with the material—they are usually told what is important to know; (2) If reading primary sources from earlier periods of history, the language of the texts is sometimes difficult and the ideas may be quite foreign; (3) Part of the process of using primary sources includes teaching students how to think like historians—this does not come naturally. For all these reasons, successful use of primary sources always includes appropriate setup and concluding discussions or activities.

MEGA ACTIVITIES

Mega activities are strategies that enrich the encounter with the historical sources and allow students to create their own responses and analyses.

Small groups of sixth graders moved around the exhibit on the Jews of Yemen. Each student had a clipboard and pencil and was writing down answers to questions on a worksheet as they looked at display cases and read labels. Mr. Rothman moved among the groups, answering questions and helping the students with unfamiliar vocabulary. The students were trying to determine what their own lives might be like if they had lived in Yemen rather than twenty-first-century America. What would be the same? What would be different? How would they have learned about Judaism? Where would they have prayed? What would that structure look like?

These were just a few of the questions the students had come up with before the trip. They already knew that they would be using the answers to these questions that they found at the exhibit, plus information from their textbook back in the classroom, to write two to three journal entries for a

Yemenite Jew of their own age. They would also compare this Jewish community with Jewish communities in other parts of the world that they had already studied.

In science classes, students use the scientific method in order to propose hypotheses, analyze data, and form conclusions. They learn by doing, and in the process become scientists themselves. Thanks to new and exciting theories about how students learn and retain information, teachers in many disciplines, including history, are increas-ingly incorporating into their lessons activities that engage students on the experiential level and allow them to enter into the same processes used by professionals in the field.

As with lab work, experiential activities teach nothing in and of themselves. To be effective—and to do more than just provide a fun time—these activities must be part of a very structured unit or lesson plan and clearly tied to big ideas. Activities as learning tools allow students to build their own knowledge from the experience, but only when they are properly guided. When well constructed, activities tap into student creativity, helping them retain their learning longer. Given the opportunity to be actively engaged in the learning process, students find added relevance and meaning in the Jewish past. Below are a few suggested activities.

Field Trips
Purposes of this activity: To take the learning out of the classroom; to utilize local resources for the teaching of Jewish history; and to provide links between students and local Jewish history.

Goals of this activity: At the conclusion of a field trip activity, students should be able to (1) describe and discuss the site or objects they visited; (2) connect information about the site or objects studied in light of the historical background studied in class; and (3) produce a reflective piece about their experience.

Depending on your community, there may be museums, historic synagogues, Jewish cemeteries, or other local sites that might add to a unit on American, Canadian, or local Jewish history. These sites offer opportunities for students to use historical objects (headstones, buildings, ritual objects) to experience history in the same way that historians use such materials to research the past. Of course, it is important to spend time introducing any field trip before students embark, and to follow up when the students return to class in order to frame the experience within the context of the unit of study. Field trips are appropriate for all ages. Follow-up projects will differ depending on the age of the students. Some of these are described briefly below.

Some Preparations before the Trip
- Create in-class lessons that will help the students put what they will see on the field trip in a larger context.
- Provide information about what the students will see, especially anything you think will be of special interest to them. Some museums will supply slides, catalogs, or written material that you can use with your class before your visit.
- Give the students things to look for or questions to think about while they are on a trip. This can be done through a student activity sheet that students work on during the trip.

Some Wrap-Up Ideas for the Classroom
Here are some suggestions for processing the field trip when you return to the classroom:

- Ask students to share highlights from the trip, verbally or in writing. These might form the basis for writing thank-you notes to anyone who helped during the visit.
- Discuss the questions students were assigned during the visit, or go over information collected on their student activity sheets.
- Develop a project that uses information from the trip.

Creating Your Own Museum

Purpose of this activity: To engage students in the research, construction, and presentation of history.

Goals of this activity: To provide students with the opportunity to (1) research a time, person, or event in Jewish history; (2) make decisions regarding how history is under-stood through its presentation; and (3) use their creativity to tell a story.

One of the many things that historians do is to use objects, documents, and art to tell a story. Student historians can also develop museum exhibits in their classroom or for the whole school. Give the class a topic to research that will become the basis for the exhibit. After some general reading on the subject, possibly from the textbook, have the class generate ideas for different aspects of the topic to be covered in its exhibit. Break the class into small groups, with each assigned the task of researching a particular aspect of the main topic. Groups might use the Internet, books in the library, primary documents that have been prepared by the teacher, and/or objects that they have at home or can be found in the synagogue. After a certain amount of

research has been done, each group should choose items to put in their part of the exhibit. As a class, you might want to discuss the order of the exhibit and legends. Exhibits can range from the traditional poster board displays or trifold science project boards to costumed student presentations and interactive Web sites created by the students.

Exhibits are appropriate for students in third grade and up. The younger the children, the more direction and structure you will need to provide. In younger grades the teacher may want to provide the packets of materials available for the children to use in their research. Older children can take more of a role in developing their own research questions and determining where best to find the information.

Reenactments

Purpose of this activity: To provide students with experiential learning about an event or time in Jewish history.

Goal of this activity: For students to understand the emotions, struggles, and dilemmas of Jews during a particular moment in Jewish history.

One way to illustrate a big idea or core concept is for students to relive part of the experience. This experience can either become the basis for discussion and further study, or the culmination of what the students have been studying. Reen-actments are often used in camp settings, and they also can be effective in a classroom setting. For example, Julia remembers how every year for Shavuot she and the students in the religious school became a group of wandering Jews following Moses to Mount Sinai. One of the teachers appeared in costume and played Moses, leading the students to Mount Sinai (the rabbi's house, a quarter-mile from the synagogue). Once there, Moses climbed Mount Sinai (the back porch), while students built a Golden Calf (in the backyard). To this day, it is one of her most vivid religious school memories.

Reenactments often take a lot of planning on the teacher's part and may require additional people to carry them out in the classroom. The main reason for organizing such reenactments is for the students to experience something akin to the actual historical event. It could be following Moses to Mount Sinai, arriving at Ellis Island, or being a pioneer on an early Israeli kibbutz. It is hard to generalize about how to plan such activities because they vary so much according to the time and place you are trying to re-create, but here are some things to consider when planning your reenactment:

Before you begin, determine whether the reenactment will be used as the introduction to a new unit or the conclusion. If used as an introduction, think about what activities will be used to lead away from the reenactment into further study. If used as a conclusion, consider what information students will need to have already in order to get the most from the reenactment. Either way, it is important to remember that a reenactment works best if it is not left to stand on its own and relates to the core concept or big idea you are teaching.

Research the event—Before deciding what to reenact, read books, check Web sites, and review videotapes to find out as much as possible about what happened. (With older grades, you can involve your students in this step.) Take special note of challenges or conflicts involved in the situation.

Incorporating these will make your reenactment more interesting and can give rise to follow-up discussion and study.

Plan the activities—Once familiar with the information surrounding the event or time period, decide which aspects to re-create. These decisions should be based on how the experience can further support the core concept or big idea being taught, as well as taking into consideration issues of time, space, and personnel.

Develop materials and find props—Some of the activities will require worksheets or props to be used by the students or by the facilitators.

Find people to portray historical characters or be group leaders—One advantage of reenactments in camp settings is that there are usually lots of counselors around to assign different roles. In a school setting, you may need to call upon adult volunteers or parents. Since your volunteers may not be familiar with the events being reenacted, it is important to provide them with background information ahead of time.

Conclusion: While reenactments are likely to be memorable events simply because they are a change from the ordinary school or camp routine, what the students learn from them also depends on what happens when the reenactment is over. Have the students reflect on the reenactment and think of issues that the experience raised for them. Have them think of things about which they would like to know more; then, consider where they could find answers to their questions. This can lead to further study during the rest of the unit.

Object Reading or "You Are the Detective"

Purpose of this activity: To engage students in the process of analyzing objects and pictures to create an understanding of the past.

Goals of the activity: Children should leave this activity understanding: (1) that people make assumptions based on what they see; (2) how to use objects and pictures to put together a story of the past; and (3) history is constructed by people.

As with the other activities, this one works best when part of a larger unit, particularly as an introduction or conclusion. Be sure you set up the activity by providing students with the background information they will need to make appropriate analyses.

Invite a guest—perhaps an older member of the community—a well-respected local Jewish leader, or a famous Jewish person connected to the school—and ask him or her to bring a bag or box of objects and pictures that represent important parts of the guest's life. The students should not be told very much about the guest. Instead, they are to examine the contents of the bag or box, either in small groups or as a group, guided by the teacher. The immediate goal is for the students to ascertain what they can about the person who brought in the objects.

By choosing objects that are not obvious to the children, the teacher and guest deliberately challenge the students to question their assumptions. For instance, if the guest brings in a picture of herself with some children, students might reasonably assume the guest has children, and it is they who are in the picture. However, if the picture actually shows the guest with her nieces and nephews, or the children of a close friend, students learn to question their assumptions about what they see. Either through discussion or some other activity, the class comes to conclusions about who the guest is (likes, dislikes, religion, marital status, sense of humor—whatever is indicated by the objects).

Next, get the children to reflect on what they can and cannot learn about a person through a random collection of objects. Ask them to draw or list what they would want to put in a bag so someone could learn about them. (What objects might convey the most information, if there was no one to explain them? What pictures would tell a story that is essential to their place in the world and what is important to them?)

Alternatively, bring in a large picture or painting of an event or moment in Jewish history and have students discuss what they can learn from the picture. Particularly if you have already studied a period of history that the picture reflects, this exploration can serve to reinforce the analytical skills of the initial part of the activity. The long-term success of this activity depends on the conclusion you set up for the students. A creative activity that allows students to discuss or analyze their experience of constructing history can serve as a wonderful concluding exercise. Creative ideas might include writing a diary entry of the people seen in the photograph or painting or, for older students, writing and performing a skit based on what they learned from the painting or picture.

Trials

Purpose of this activity: To engage students actively in investigating and understanding a particular historical figure and/or event in history.

Goals of this activity: At the end of this activity, students should: (1) understand the moral issues present in the event under investigation; (2) have developed the skills to build an argument; and (3) understand the historical context relevant to the event or person under question.

Putting a historical figure on trial for his or her actions engages students in learning about a particular event, person and/or period of history. Trials are probably most useful for students in the sixth grade or older. Examples of historical figures to put on trial would be Moses (for killing the Egyptian—Exodus 2:11–15), King David (for stealing Bathsheba from Uriah and having Uriah killed—II Samuel 11:2–27), and the first-century military figure and historian Josephus (as a traitor to the Jews). The students often get carried away with the dramatics, but creating a clear structure for them ensures that there is solid educational value to this activity. There are many ways in which you might organize the preparation for the trial. Below is one example used by Lauren Granite in her sixth-grade supplementary school class studying the stories of King David.

Learning the material—A successful trial is grounded in a thorough understanding of the facts, so the first step is for students to read texts, watch a video, or otherwise learn the material. Consider having the students read the stories or primary sources in small groups, followed by questions that will get them thinking about the key issues of the trial. Follow their independent learning with a class discussion to make certain that every student is clear about the main issues and facts.

Building a prosecution and defense—Divide the class into two groups, assigning one group to be the prosecution and the other the defense. Each group must decide how to build their case and, in the process, what witnesses they want to bring to the stand. The students must not only develop an argument for their side of the case, but also determine what witnesses they need to support their argument. (Supervise this process to ensure that there is not more than one student playing each character.)

For greater creativity, allow the students to include characters that might not clearly be part of the story as told in the sources. For example, when this class put King David on trial for adultery with Bathsheba and the death of her husband, Uriah, one student wanted to play Michal, David's first wife, who is not at all mentioned in the Bible in the context of the David and Bathsheba story. The student beautifully reflected on the life of Michal in her testimony, providing the defense with an important character reference for King David. (In fact, fictionalized accounts of the biblical period, such as *Queenmaker* by India Edghill and *The Red Tent* by Anita Diamant, are good secondary sources for different perspectives that might be used in a trial activity.)

Preliminary questions—An optional element, preliminary questions help in trial preparation by allowing everyone to hear what each witness will say at the trial. Both prosecution and defense ask the same number of questions, and the witnesses must be warned that they cannot change their testimony between the preliminary questioning and the trial. Each side should then have more time to tighten their arguments.

The trial—Invite people from outside the class to be the jury. The teacher or another authority figure can serve as the judge to ensure that the trial keeps moving and order prevails. Encouraging appropriate costumes for all students lends excitement to the activity.

Sentencing—If the jury in the trial finds the defendant guilty, you may want to include a sentencing phase. In a trial of David, the judge could sentence David as he is sentenced in the Bible. Then students could discuss whether they think David's punishment is just or not.

Wrap-Up—Ask students to write some sort of reflective statement in the character of the person they portrayed (prosecutor, defense lawyer, character in the story), or work in small groups to answer a few analytical questions about the trial. Whatever activity you create, the students must reflect on the larger issues and themes that emerged in the course of the trial.

Oral Histories

Purpose of this activity: To engage students actively in the process of investigating history.

Goals of this activity: By the end of the unit, students should: (1) understand the broader historical context of the life of the person they interviewed; (2) have improved their ability to ask pertinent questions of a source; and (3) have a clearer understanding of their own family's history (if the students interviewed a relative).

Within the context of Jewish education, oral histories are usually interviews of older people conducted by students as a way of learning about the immigrant or Holocaust experiences of the older generations. Oral histories are often used as a way for a student to understand his or her family's history and Jewish heritage. We want to emphasize the importance of

placing these historical accounts in a larger historical context. While conducting an oral history may be an enriching experience for the child, the educational impact is greatly increased if the student is encouraged to make connections between what he or she learned in the interview and the broader themes of the historical period under question.

Within the context of a history course, it is not enough for Rivka to interview her grandmother who emigrated from Czechoslovakia to the United States in the 1920s and end the exercise there. Rivka should learn that her grandmother's experience was part of a larger trend that took place at that time and why these events are central to Jewish history. In the process, Rivka should develop questions about why her grandmother settled in Ohio instead of New York and, perhaps, hear the story of someone who went to New York at the same time.

The activities above are just a few examples of how you can make history come alive in your classroom and give your students the opportunity to reflect on the past in ways similar to those used by historians. These activities can be adapted for use in the study of different time periods, and you will find some more specific examples of these mega activities throughout the book.

The Use of Textbooks in the Classroom

The use of Jewish history textbooks that are intended specifically for the classroom, such as *The History of the Jewish People: A Story of Tradition and Change* by Jonathan D. Sarna and Jonathan B. Krasner, can enhance a student's study of the subject and help the teacher organize the curriculum. This book is intended to be used either in conjunction with a textbook or separately. When a particular unit of study or activity might be enhanced by using the two books together, you'll find specific references and suggestions on how to do so.

Resources

"Better Endings for Classes and Courses." *ClassWise*. May/June 1997.

Diamant, Anita. *The Red Tent*. New York: Picador, 1997.

Edghill, India. *Queenmaker*. New York: Picador, 1999.

Edinger, Monica. *Seeking History: Teaching with Primary Sources in Grades 4–6*. Portsmouth, NH: Heineman, 2000.

Sarna, Jonathan D., and Jonathan B. Krasner. *The History of the Jewish People: A Story of Tradition and Change*. Springfield, NJ: Behrman House, 2006.

What?! This Old Thing? How Objects Can Tell Us Who We Are. New York: Museum of Jewish Heritage: A Living Memorial to the Holocaust.

CHAPTER THREE
ABOUT THIS BOOK

In planning and writing this book, we have taken the basic ideas expressed in the previous chapters and used them to show how they can apply to teaching different periods of history. In order to provide a consistent framework for these basic concepts, we have outlined certain "big ideas" that appear again and again throughout Jewish history; used these big ideas to tell the stories of each period; provided connections to other areas of Judaism; and offered a selection of learning activities designed to engage your students even further. We hope this book becomes a useful resource for anyone teaching Jewish history in any setting.

BIG IDEAS

There are certain big ideas that appear again and again throughout Jewish history. Here we would like to introduce you to a few of the big ideas that you will find in this book.

Diaspora

Since our people were first exiled from Eretz Yisrael—the Land of Israel— centuries ago, much of the Jewish population has remained dispersed throughout the world. Once scattered, we did not stay in one place but continued to move from country to country. Some of our moves were forced; others were chosen. This dispersion has allowed the growth of a variety of Jewish cultures, but it has also left Jewish communities vulnerable to larger powers under which they lived.

Related Discussion Question:
How has the existence of a vibrant Diaspora contributed to the survival of the Jewish people while so many other ancient civilizations have disappeared?

Acculturation

Judaism and the Jewish people have survived through centuries of change, but they have not remained the same. At different times and in different places, Jews have adapted to the cultures within which they found themselves. This adaptation has brought new traditions, rituals, and cultural elements into Judaism. In some cases, Judaism has also left behind elements of itself in the dominant culture.

Related Discussion Question:
What are some of the unique cultural elements of Judaism today and where did they come from?

Assimilation

The people with whom Jews have lived have often held Jews at arm's length, even when not persecuting them. However, throughout history there have been times when Jews have been allowed to enter the mainstream society. The survival of Judaism and the Jewish people has been most threatened when Jews have been free to determine as individuals how much and to what extent to keep traditional religious rituals and values.

Related Discussion Question:
What are the pros and cons of assimilation's effect on Judaism?

Although not a separate big idea, there has often been a tension between acculturation and assimilation. Exploring this tension within certain periods of history can also help students gain a different perspective on these issues, both historically and in their own experience.

Building Community
Regardless of the reasons for Jewish migration, when a few Jews settled somewhere, they sought one another out and established communal institutions to help support a Jewish way of life.

Related Discussion Question:
How have Jewish institutions helped to preserve a Jewish way of life in communities throughout the world?

Jewish Culture and Thought
Despite repeated devastation to Jewish communities over the centuries, a creative, rich Jewish culture and religious life have always continued to flourish. The flexible and resilient nature of that rabbinic-based religious system has enabled Jews to successfully respond to and thrive in new places and circumstances.

Related Discussion Question:
Many cultures that developed at the same time as Judaism no longer exist. How has the flexibility of Jewish culture and thought helped Judaism remain relevant today?

Covenant
Jews have traditionally understood the events that befell them to be the will of God, part of God's overarching plan for Jewish history in particular and human history in general. Intrinsic to this view is the understanding that Jews are God's chosen people, singled out for a special covenant that promised us the Land of Israel, as well as growth and prosperity for the Jewish people throughout the ages.

Related Discussion Question:
What impact has the idea of "covenant" had on Jewish history?

CHAPTER ORGANIZATION
In each of the "Major Periods of Jewish History" chapters you will find the following information:

Big Ideas—This section will highlight one or more of the big ideas described above and how it relates to the period of history discussed in the chapter.

Background Information—This section will provide a brief description of the period of history as interpreted through the lens of the big idea.

Connecting to Our Tradition—Here you will find some basic Jewish values that may have been important to the people of this period and helped them persevere, make choices, and live their lives Jewishly. You may want to integrate some of these values into your lessons.

Important Terms—Key terms that are relevant to the study of this period of history will be listed and/or defined.

Names, Places, and Events—A suggested list related to the period of history under study is provided; you may want your students to be able to identify the items on the list.

Discussion Questions—These are questions that will help the students "unpack" the big idea related to this period of history. Examples of how to use these questions may also be provided.

Activities—This section provides a variety of activity ideas that can be used with students of different ages. To help determine which activities would be best suited for your students, we have also included a code with each activity:

E—activities best suited for elementary
    school students
S—activities best suited for secondary
    school students (middle and high school)
A—activities best suited for adults

In many cases, the activities provided can be adapted for use with younger or older audiences. You should also feel free to skim through the suggested activities in other chapters to find additional ideas that can be adapted.

Did You Know?—These sections include nuggets of interesting information that may help spark your students' interest.

Timeline—The timeline for each chapter presents some of the important dates and events related to the historical period in chronological order.

Resources—Here you will find books, articles, and videos to use for your own edification or with your students as part of a lesson. Keep in mind that artifacts, documents, photographs, and knowledge-able individuals are also terrific resources.

Visit www.behrmanhouse.com/booklinks for links to Web sites that offer additional resources for each chapter.

As you travel through the history found in this book, we hope that you become caught up in the journey and the many possibilities for igniting the imagination and curiosity of your students—and yourself.

Biblical Period

CHAPTER FOUR
OUR MATRIARCHS AND PATRIARCHS

WHAT'S THE BIG IDEA?
Covenant

The idea that the Jews are God's chosen people begins with an agreement, or covenant, between Abraham and God. God's promise to Abraham and his descendants is central to the traditional Jewish view of history. The belief that God has a plan for us as a nation, both in terms of our connection to the Land of Israel and our mission among the nations of the world, is a cornerstone of traditional Jewish belief and philosophy.

BACKGROUND INFORMATION

The pivotal figure of Avram first appears in the Torah in Genesis, chapter 12. In the biblical narrative, God appears to Avram, a wealthy Mesopotamian tribal leader from Ur of the Chaldees in the Fertile Crescent, and commands him to leave his native land and go to the place that God will show him. In return, God promises to make of him a great nation, to bless him, and to give the Land of Israel to his descendants. Taking his wife Sarai and his nephew Lot, Avram left his home in Haran, settled in Canaan, and the rest, as they say, is history.

The Torah paints a picture of Avram as a wealthy patriarch with substantial movable goods, servants, and a cadre of fighting men. Descriptions of his military and political exploits in the land of the Philistines, Egypt, and locally with other Canaanite leaders throughout the narrative further support the view of him as a man of power and means. By choosing Avram to be the founding father of a new religion, God shows confidence in Avram as a national leader and spiritual messenger. God changes the name of Avram to Abraham ("father of multitudes") and slightly modifies the name Sarai by changing it to Sarah (both mean "princess") in recognition of their connection to God and their role in history (Genesis, chapter 17).

In order to seal this covenant, God commands Abraham to circumcise himself and all the males in his household. The fact that God refers to the covenant as an "everlasting pact" (Genesis 17:13) connects the Jewish people to God throughout the generations. In fact, our term "brit milah" literally means "covenant of circumcision." The word "brit" or "bris," which in modern parlance refers to the ritual of circumcision and celebration that takes place eight days after the birth of a Jewish boy, means "covenant" in Hebrew.

The obstacles that Abraham must overcome in meeting God's challenge include being asked to banish the concubine Hagar and her son Ishmael (Genesis, chapter 21), sacrifice his son Isaac (chapter 22), and, after the death of his wife Sarah, choose an appropriate wife for Isaac (chapter 24). Abraham's fortitude in these situations as well as in his rescue of Lot (chapter 14) and his argument with God as to the fate of Sodom and Gomorrah (chapter 18) give evidence of his strong character and leadership qualities as well.

The line of Abraham and Sarah continues in the Book of Genesis with that of Isaac and Rebecca, who gives birth to the twins Jacob and Esau. Although the legacy of Isaac in Torah is a quiet one, the covenant is further cemented with his son Jacob. Later named Israel in recognition of his struggle with God (Genesis, chapter 32), Jacob, along with his wives Rachel and Leah and his two concubines, becomes the parent of twelve sons and a daughter, insuring that the legacy of the covenant would continue. (In fact, the Jewish people is named B'nei Yisrael—the children of Israel—in honor of Jacob and his legacy because Jacob is also referred to by the name "Israel" in the biblical narrative.) All the patriarchs establish altars and places of worship to God, and the text is clear about naming and locating them.

Once Jacob's son, Joseph, goes down to Egypt (abandoned by his brothers and then sold as a slave to a passing caravan), the covenant of the Jewish people with God encounters two new challenges: surviving in a foreign land and sustaining the Israelites' relationship with God under adverse circumstances.

The Middle East of the Patriarchs' and Matriarchs' Time

Interestingly, no separate historical account exists of the early history of the Jewish people outside of the Torah text. Archaeological evidence suggests the appearance of a people called the Hapiru (or Hebrew) in the region of Egypt and southern Canaan sometime between the years 2000 and 1200 BCE, when Jacob and his descendants would have been moving to and from the area. We know that Egypt controlled Canaan during much of the second half of this millennium, and the manner of rule was to leave local governors and native rulers in place. In addition, the culture of the region was such that—as today—many people were constantly moving from one area to another; Babylonians moved to Canaan to farm and vice versa, foreign mercenaries came to Egypt to join the army needed to fight continuous wars with the Hittites, and so on. Therefore, the archaeological and other historical evidence of the period is consistent with the information we find included in the Torah text.

Sarah, Rebecca, Rachel, and Leah

From the Torah text, we get the sense of these four matriarchs as strong women and leaders in their own right. God speaks to Sarah (Genesis, chapter 18) and backs her up when Abraham questions her judgment over banishing Hagar and Ishmael (Genesis, chapter 21). God also speaks to Rebecca during her difficult pregnancy (Genesis, chapter 25). In both instances, God affirms the covenant with the matriarchs in the context of promising that their children-to-be would inherit both the greatness and responsibility originally promised to Abraham. In addition to bearing the sons (along with their husband's concubines) who would ultimately be the ancestors of the twelve tribes of Israel, Rachel and Leah act decisively in helping Jacob to leave Laban's household and establish his own community (Genesis, chapter 31).

There is evidence that, sociologically, the Middle East of the time was undergoing a change from a matriarchal culture to a patriarchal one. In the early biblical period, it was usual for a groom to go and live with the bride's family. This pattern changes gradually beginning with Rebecca being asked her permission to return with Abraham's servant to marry Isaac (chapter 24) and shifting back with Jacob's flight to live with Rachel and Leah's family. One might note as well that both Isaac and Jacob marry women from their mother's extended family; Rebecca was Sarah's niece, and Rachel and Leah were Rebecca's nieces. The custom of cousins marrying each other was typical of the period, and also served to help influential families to consolidate their property, wealth and power.

Human Beings with Human Flaws

Many have commented that our ancestors do not always act in a manner that we find especially appealing. Even as we recognize their many strengths and qualities, it's not hard to find instances that are, well, unsavory. Although acting on God's orders, Abraham does banish Hagar and Ishmael following his wife's insistence that he do so, and binds his son Isaac to an altar, holding a knife to slay him. Jacob tricks his brother Esau into giving up his birthright in exchange for a bowl of lentil soup, and he deceives his father Isaac (with his mother's complicity) into giving him the blessing for the firstborn son, reserved for Esau. Jacob's sons slaughter the inhabitants of the town of Shechem as a revenge killing over the rape of their sister, Dinah.

Although there are alternative readings and understandings for all these incidents that make them understandable—even necessary—within the context of God's plan for the Jewish people, it is crucial to note that like us, our ancestors and heroes were human beings with flaws. And still, we strive to emulate them and their good qualities. It's possible to emulate these types of heroes precisely because they are representative of our best possibilities and our worst faults, and therefore we can wholly relate to them as individuals and as role models.

The Legacy of the Matriarchs and Patriarchs

Abraham, Isaac, Jacob, Sarah, Rebecca, Rachel, and Leah serve as the pioneers for the Israelite people and the covenant with God as we still know it. Through their values, leadership, and actions, the patriarchs and matriarchs are God's partners in the challenge of bringing the covenant from its origins to the next stage in our history.

CONNECTING TO OUR TRADITION

The time when our matriarchs and patriarchs lived and forged their connection to God through the covenant is the formative period for many of the Jewish values that we take as "given" now, four thousand years later:

Engaging in Our Relationship with God

To our ancestors in the Torah, God wasn't just a far-off figure with little connection to their lives. Our matriarchs and patriarchs conversed with God, followed God's commandments, and strove to make the covenant an enduring legacy for generations to follow.

Standing Up for the Rights of Others

When told that God planned to destroy the towns of Sodom and Gomorrah, Abraham didn't just say, "Okay, whatever You think is best." Instead, Abraham went to the mat to argue with God about what it would take to save innocent lives even in the face of overwhelming odds.

Through this process of struggling with God, Abraham was instrumental in not only setting an example for generations to follow about standing up for the rights of others, but he helped to clarify the terms of what a community needs (ten righteous individuals) in order to remain viable. (It's interesting that Abraham chose *not* to engage in an argument when it came to saving the life of his own son, Isaac.)

Pursuing Peace

Even after many years, Jacob and Esau—sworn enemies—find a way to make peace with each other. It is worthy of note that not only Jacob and Esau, but Isaac and Ishmael, too, come together to bury their fathers. It's no coincidence that later in the Psalms the Jewish people are commanded to "seek peace and pursue it" (Psalm 34:15).

Brit Milah (Bris)

Thousands of years later, Jews today still circumcise their male children as a sign of the covenant between God and the Jewish people.

IMPORTANT TERMS

Covenant
Brit milah (bris)
Matriarch
Patriarch
B'nei Yisrael (children of Israel)

Names, Places and Events

Mesopotamia	Rachel
Ur of the Chaldees	Leah
Fertile Crescent	Ishmael
Abraham	Hagar
Isaac	Esau
Jacob	Lot
Sarah	Laban
Rebecca	

DISCUSSION QUESTIONS

- Can a leader do questionable things and still be considered a role model? Give examples both from the Torah and modern life.
- Do you think the matriarchs are portrayed in the Torah as equal partners in the covenant? Give examples from the Torah text.

- How do we know that God's covenant wasn't just for our matriarchs and patriarchs, but for us as well?
- Would you have stood up to God in order to save the people of Sodom and Gomorrah? Why or why not?

ACTIVITIES

Reminder: Feel tree to adapt these suggestions to your particular situation. For example, activities that are described here for younger students can be expanded for older students, and those suggested for more advanced classes can be simplified for elementary school groups.

Game: Jewish Jeopardy (E, S)

Jewish Jeopardy is a standard and easily manipulated game that can be used for many units of study in endless ways.

Buy a large piece of poster board and several library card pockets (or, cut off the tops of invitation-size envelopes). Glue the library pockets onto the board in rows of five across and five down.

Create (or have your students create) five different categories for your game with several questions written on index cards for each category. For example, if this game is "Matriarchs and Patriarchs," the categories could be Name That Person (with the answer "Hagar" for the question "What was Ishmael's mother's name?"); Biblical Places ("Haran" as the answer to "What city was Abraham from?"); Hospitality ("Cakes, curds, milk and calf" as the answer to "What foods did Abraham serve to the angels?"); Travels ("Laban" as the answer to the question "To whose home did Jacob go when he fled from Esau?"); and Events ("Two servants" as the answer to the question "Whom did Abraham take with him when he brought Isaac up to the mountain?").

Time Travel (E, S)

Invite the students to travel back in time to visit the homes of Abraham and Sarah, Rebecca and Isaac, and the camp of Jacob, Leah, Rachel, and their children. Focus your "visit" on times when God interacts with the patriarchs and matriarchs in order to reiterate God's covenantal promises. For example, you might have your students research God's visit to Rebecca in Genesis 25 or Jacob's wrestling with the angel in Genesis 32. This activity can be acted out in costume, with an art activity, for example, create a mural depicting the incident, or as a writing activity.

Biography (E, S)

Assign each student to research an important figure from the time period, dress up as his or her chosen character, and address the class.

Sodom on Trial (S, A)

Assign teams to take the sides of Abraham and God in a courtroom drama or debate the fate of Sodom and Gomorrah. Character witnesses can include Lot, Lot's wife, and the townspeople. Each side should prepare for the debate by focusing on the issues of covenant (How does Abraham's relationship with God allow Abraham to debate with God?) and community (What impact does our covenant with God have on our responsibility to help communities in need?).

Abraham Act-Alike Contest (E, S)

Look up people who live in your community or in the world at large who have stood up for the rights of others. Create a museum exhibit that presents through pictures and words how these people acted like Abraham.

Biblical Treasure Hunt (E, S)

How many times does God express the covenant with our ancestors through words or actions in the Book of Genesis? How many times does God send an angel or angels to fulfill this task? Split up into teams and see how many references or biblical verses you can find. This activity can be turned into a race by specifying a set amount of time. Have the teams present their findings to the larger group.

Bibliodrama (S, A)

Did Isaac know where he was going when Abraham led him up the mountain? What was Rebecca thinking as she helped her son Jacob deceive his father Isaac into giving him Esau's blessing? Through guided questions, encourage students to put themselves in the place of these biblical characters. This activity can be accomplished with questions alone, or with costumes and settings for a more complete experience.

Midrash Maven (S, A)

Many of the stories we think we know from the biblical text aren't in the Bible at all—they are additional rabbinic teaching stories called midrashim. Explore one or two of these famous stories, for example, Abraham breaking the idols, from a collection of midrashim such as *The Book of Legends* (*Sefer Ha-Aggadah*; see bibliography) along with the biblical text. Have the students compare the biblical text with the midrash and write their own midrashic interpretation.

History Quest (E, S)

World history at the time of the matriarchs and patriarchs was a fascinating mix of old and new, rural and urban, class warfare and military warfare (sort of like today). Have students look at life in Mesopotamia and Egypt between 2000 and 1500 BCE, by reading an encyclopedia article, watching a video, or searching the Internet. What similarities are there between life in these areas of the world and that described in the biblical text?

DID YOU KNOW?

- The beginning of the alphabet is dated to the period of the patriarchs and matriarchs. The early Semitic alphabet (the forerunner of Hebrew), the Egyptian alphabet of twenty-four signs, and the first Hittite cuneiform inscriptions were all developed between 2000 and 1500 BCE.
- Babylon became the capital of the Mesopotamian Empire due to a shift in the course of the Euphrates River. Abraham's journey from Ur to Canaan follows the path of the Euphrates River all the way north to Haran, where Abraham and Sarah settle before continuing according to God's instructions to Canaan.

TIMELINE

Because of the difficulty of accurate dating during the early biblical period, dates are of necessity approximate.

c. 20th century BCE
  Abraham leaves Ur to travel first to Haran, and then to Canaan

18th century BCE
  Reign of Hammurabi in Babylon; Hammurabi writes major law code

16th century BCE
  Hittites invade Babylon and end the Hammurabi dynasty

16th century BCE
  Joseph goes down to Egypt

16th–14th century BCE
  Hittites war with Egypt

RESOURCES
Books and Articles

Barnavi, Eli, ed. *Historical Atlas of the Jewish People: From the Time of the Patriarchs to the Present.* New York: Schocken Books, 1992.

Bialik, Haim Nahman, and Yehoshua Hana Ravnitsky. *The Book of Legends/Sefer Ha-Aggadah: Legends from the Talmud and Midrash.* New York: Schocken Books, 1992.

Gilbert, Martin. *The Routledge Atlas of Jewish History,* 6th ed. London: Routledge, 1995.

Grun, Bernard. *The Timetables of History: A Horizontal Linkage of People and Events.* New York: Simon & Schuster, 1979.

Pasachoff, Naomi, and Robert J. Littman. *Jewish History in 100 Nutshells.* Northvale, NJ: Jason Aronson, 1995.

The Rabbinical Assembly and The United Synagogue of Conservative Judaism. *Etz Hayim Torah and Commentary.* Philadelphia: Jewish Publication Society, 2001.

Sarna, Jonathan D., and Jonathan B. Krasner. *The History of the Jewish People: A Story of Tradition and Change.* Springfield, NJ: Behrman House, 2006 (see especially pp. vi–5).

Teubal, Savina J. *Sarah the Priestess: The First Matriarch of Genesis.* Athens, OH: Swallow Press Books, 1984.

Internet

Visit www.behrmanhouse.com/booklinks for links to Web sites that offer additional resources for this chapter.

CHAPTER FIVE

BECOMING A PEOPLE: MOSES AND THE EXODUS

WHAT'S THE BIG IDEA?
Covenant
After four hundred years of slavery in Egypt, God's covenant with the Jewish people is reinvigorated through the actions of one of the most pivotal figures in our history—Moses. In the midst of the Israelites' oppression under a cruel Pharaoh, the Jews cry out to God to remember the promise that was made to their matriarchs and patriarchs—and God *does* remember. Through the miracles that make the Exodus possible, through the giving of the Torah at Mount Sinai, through the wandering in the wilderness, the national plan that God has for the Jewish people comes to fruition as the Israelites strive toward and eventually reach the Promised Land.

The message of the Exodus—that God's covenant remains in force even when things seem impossible—has served as a rallying cry and cornerstone of belief for Jews in difficult times throughout our history.

BACKGROUND INFORMATION
According to the Torah, the Israelites—who had enjoyed relative security in Egypt during the time of Joseph—were ultimately enslaved by a pharaoh "who knew not Joseph" (Exodus 1:8). Although the exact dating of the Exodus is open to debate, most scholars agree that the Jews left Egypt sometime between 1500 and 1250 BCE. The Torah describes their plight: "The Israelites were groaning under the bondage and cried out; and their cry for help from the bondage rose up to God. God heard their moaning, and God remembered God's covenant with Abraham and Isaac and Jacob. God looked upon the Israelites, and God took notice of them" (Exodus 2:23–25).

The early chapters of the Book of Exodus detail Moses's origins as a Hebrew child destined for the death decreed by Pharaoh for all Jewish boys at the time. Miraculously, he is saved through the actions of his sister and Pharaoh's daughter, and although he lives in his parents' home as an infant and young child, Moses spends the rest of his childhood and adolescence in Pharaoh's palace.

Moses sees the plight of the Israelites and acts by killing a brutal taskmaster. When the matter is discovered, he runs away, marrying the daughter of the priest of Midian. Sixty years later, God appears to Moses and instructs him to free the Israelites, with the help of his brother Aaron. The story of the Exodus from Egypt is detailed in chapters 3–15 of that book of the Torah, and is rich with examples of God's intervention in the course of human affairs in order to effect the covenant with the Jewish people.

Moses
One of the most complex characters in all of Torah, Moses is at once impetuous, controlled, organized, distracted, over-whelmed, caring, angry, pleading, and distant. In that, he serves as a role model for Jews throughout history—a leader with an almost supernatural connection to God who is, in the end, still a fallible human being.

Moses is well placed to act as a guide for the Jewish people in their deliverance from slavery. Much of his early childhood is spent living in his parents' home in the Jewish enclave near the palace. The Torah tells us that after finding him in the basket floating in the river and recognizing that he must be a Jewish baby, Pharaoh's daughter hires Moses's own mother to nurse him at his sister Miriam's behest.

Upon weaning, "when the child grew up, she [Moses's mother] brought him to Pharaoh's daughter, who made him her son" (Exodus 2:10). The text makes it clear in the Hebrew words "*va'yigdal hayeled*" ("and the child grew up") that Moses spent his earliest formative years in his parents' Jewish home, and rabbinic tradition expounds upon this upbringing.

It would be a mistake, however, to underestimate the value of growing up in Pharaoh's palace, where Moses would most likely have had access to an unsurpassed education as well as all the privileges of royal society. That Moses's formative years gave him an understanding of both the oppressed Jews and the Egyptian rulers must have helped to foster in him a critical set of leadership skills and knowledge that helped him become an influential leader himself.

Primarily, however, the sages refer to Moses as "Moshe Rabbeinu"—Moses our Teacher. As God's representative, Moses serves the Jewish people as rescuer in both a physical and a spiritual sense. Because Moses delivered the Jewish people in body to the edge of the Land of Israel, he helped God fulfill the promise to give the land to the Jewish people as an inheritance. Because Moses brought the Jewish people the Torah, he is seen by rabbinic tradition as the quintessential teacher.

Behind Every Successful Man . . .

It's clear from the beginning of the Book of Exodus that the ability of the Jews to survive in Egypt depended on the actions of a handful of courageous women, one of whom was instrumental in bringing the Israelites out of Egypt along with her brothers.

Shifra and Puah
The Torah tells us in Exodus 1:15–22 that there were two Hebrew midwives who defied the decree of Pharaoh to murder every newborn Jewish boy. (We can speculate whether they acted alone, or with other unnamed midwives.) The text is unclear with regards to whether they were Hebrews themselves or non-Jewish midwives who worked in the Israelite camp (rabbinic tradition sides largely with the first interpretation). In any case, large numbers of baby boys were saved through the intervention of these two incredibly brave women, who risked their own lives in order to safely birth the babies, and then lie to Pharaoh about the outcome.

Yocheved
Moses's mother, Yocheved, is not named in the early part of the Exodus narrative; it is not until Exodus 6:20 that we learn her name. We learn early on that she is the daughter of a Levite, and that she is blessed with the skills of planning and forethought. Yocheved hides Moses from the time of his birth, she likely has him circumcised, and then puts him in the Nile protected by a basket made watertight by using pitch to seal the cracks (perhaps a trick learned from a lifetime of making bricks for another use).

She not only places Moses in the reeds at the edge of the river where it must have been common knowledge that the princess and her entourage bathed, but instructs her daughter to position herself in order to see what would become of the baby.

Miriam

Like Yocheved, we do not learn the name of Moses's sister in the early stories of the Book of Exodus. Miriam is named in connection with her role in the crossing of the Sea of Reeds, in Exodus 15:20, when she leads the women in song praising God following their safe passage. The first thing we learn about Miriam is that she is a quick thinker. She not only follows her mother's instructions to keep a close watch on her brother, but she shrewdly offers immediately to find a wet nurse (having her own mother in mind) for the princess, who obviously cannot feed the baby she has just found.

Later on in the story of the Exodus, Miriam's role as a leader of women is highlighted at the Song of the Sea, and rabbinic and modern commentators portray Miriam as a leader whose voice is important to the story and to the Israelites themselves. According to the midrash, Miriam is even responsible for Moses's birth! The story goes that because of Pharaoh's decree, the Jewish men and women stopped engaging in sexual relations, fearing the murder of the newborn boys likely to come from their union. Miriam admonished her parents, telling them that while Pharaoh was killing only the boys, they were doing worse, by preventing girls from being born as well!

The midrash continues by relating how all the husbands and wives reunited, ensuring the birth of countless children, including Moses. The midrash also credits Miriam with ensuring the Israelites' supply of drinking water, which came from a miraculous well that followed the people throughout the wilderness until her death.

Bitya

The Pharaoh's daughter is given the name Bitya (meaning "daughter of God") in the Book of I Chronicles. In addition, the rabbis credit her not only with saving Moses and raising him as her own child, but they recount in the midrash how she converted to Judaism and was rewarded with the name "daughter of God" because of her heroic actions.[1]

Hebrews, Hyksos, and Hapirus

Scholars have debated the historicity of the Torah's account of the Exodus for centuries. During the past several decades, historical and archaeological research have uncovered new information that makes for some interesting theories about the Exodus and the movement of the Hebrew people from Canaan to Egypt and back again.

As mentioned in the previous chapter, archaeological evidence suggests the appearance of a people called the Hapiru (which some scholars conjecture were in fact the early Hebrews) in the region of Egypt and southern Canaan around the 1500s–1300s BCE. In addition, a people called the Hyksos—which other scholars believe to be the early Hebrews—formed a kingdom in the Nile delta after driving the Egyptians further south some time between the seventeenth and fifteenth centuries BCE. The name Hyksos means "rulers from the hill country" and these people did in fact come from the area to the northeast of Egypt—modern-day Israel.

The Hyksos in turn were driven from Egypt in about the fifteenth century. Interestingly, while some scholars think the Hyksos and the Israelites are one and

[1] Vayikra Rabbah 1:3; a translation of these rabbinic stories can be found in Yishai Chasidah, *The Encyclopedia of Biblical Personalities*, Brooklyn, NY: Shaar Press, 1994.

the same, others believe instead that they were in fact the Amalekites with whom the Israelites engaged in battle during their wandering in the wilderness of Sinai. (Some sources also accuse these Hyksos/Amalekites of being the thieves who plundered the tombs of the Pharaohs during this time period.)

The Hyksos may also have brought their families with them during their travels. Such evidence would support either the theory that the Hyksos were the Israelites escaping from Egypt, or that they were perhaps part of the "mixed multitude" described in the Torah—those non-Israelites who left Egypt together with the Jews.

Archaeological evidence supporting the Hyksos-Hapiru-Hebrew connection as well as the Exodus exists in a number of forms. In addition to the Egyptian historical record of military engagement and expulsion, several writings of the period survive, largely in the form of stone monuments and tablets. They mention, among other things, an early Hyksos king named Jacob-El who invokes "Yahweh" in a treaty, an Egyptian "tale of two brothers" similar to the account of Joseph and Potiphar's wife in the Torah, and the defeat of the Hapiru in an epic battle. That many of these artifacts are found throughout Egypt and Canaan attests to the constant movement of these groups throughout the region during this period.

One of the most important discoveries that relates to the time of the Exodus, and mentions "Israel" by name, is the Merneptah stele, or stone monument. This late-thirteenth-century text quotes Merneptah, the king of Egypt, boasting that he has destroyed his enemies in Canaan. He states: "Plundered is Canaan with every evil; carried off is Ashkelon; seized upon is Gezer; Yanoam is made as

that which does not exist; Israel is laid waste, his seed is not." The word "Israel" is written in Egyptian with the nuance of a people rather than a geographical location. The name Merneptah may have a Hebrew counterpart as well, in the "well of waters of Nephtoah" mentioned in Joshua 15:9 and 18:15. If the Israelites were already in Canaan at the time of Merneptah, the dating of the Exodus is much closer to that of the biblical account than previously thought by modern scholars.

Wandering in the Wilderness

The remaining portions of the Torah—the Books of Exodus, Leviticus, Numbers, and Deuteronomy—all detail the wanderings of the Israelites in the Wilderness of Sinai with Moses as their leader. Several themes emerge from these travels that are echoed throughout Jewish history, especially in the writings of the prophetic period.

Israelites Behaving Badly

Throughout the Torah, Moses tries to shepherd the people and lead them in a way consistent with God's expectations of them, especially following the giving of the Torah. However, the people rebel, sin by idolatrous behavior and otherwise, and further indicate their belief that they might have been better off in Egypt, forgetting that the "good old days" were anything but.

These rebellions lead to some of the more notable episodes in the Torah, including the incident of the Golden Calf (Exodus 32), the harrowing report of the spies (Numbers 13–14), and the rebellion of Korach (Numbers 16). For their part, Miriam and Aaron criticize Moses's wife and Miriam (but not Aaron, interestingly) is punished with a weeklong case of leprosy (Numbers 12). Finally, Moses also loses his temper, hits a rock to obtain water when God tells him to speak to it, and forfeits his chance to enter the Promised Land (Numbers 20). What do we learn from these incidents? That God has a lot of patience (although at times, God also plagues the people with illnesses and supernatural consequences), and that the promises of the covenant aren't made void by rebellions—just delayed.

The Torah As a Blueprint for Life
After God gives the Israelites the Torah on Mount Sinai, the people are expected by Moses and God to follow the commandments contained therein. To this day, observant Jews use the Torah as their first resource for understanding what God wants of them and how to fulfill these expectations in every area of life from what to eat and wear to how to treat others.

The Promise of the Land of Israel
In our day and age, it is often difficult to understand why the Torah seems so nonchalant in its treatment of the peoples who are to be conquered in order for the Israelites to settle in the land promised to them by God. We are told to wipe out Amalek, destroy the seven Canaanite nations, and avoid their religious practices—cutting down altars and killing people who refuse to obey these commandments.

It's both difficult to view these passages from a twenty-first-century standard, and it's impossible to ignore the troubling ramifications of texts that encourage us to wipe out some people while being scrupulous in our morals and values as set out elsewhere in the Torah.

As with the paradox of leaders such as Moses who embody such profound greatness and such impetuousness at the same time, it is up to us to recognize that this sacred and yet very human text has a lot to teach us.

CONNECTING TO OUR TRADITION
The period of the Exodus and the actions of Moses as described in the Torah provide many enduring examples of how we as a people are encouraged and expected to connect to God and our tradition.

Talmud Torah (the study of Torah)
Solidifying our relationship with God
Pursuing justice
Communal responsibility

IMPORTANT TERMS
Stele

Names, Places, and Events
Moses
Exodus
The Golden Calf
The Spies
Levites
Amalek
Hapiru
Hyksos
Shifra
Puah
Miriam
Aaron
Bitya
Yocheved
Shifra

DISCUSSION QUESTIONS
- What role did the Israelites play in their own rescue from slavery? While the focus is usually on the miracles wrought by God, or the role of Moses, the people themselves began the process by crying out to God in their misery. What does this say about the Israelites' relationship with God and their covenant with God?
- Several stories in the Torah feature men (and more often, women) who act, but

are not named until many centuries later, in the historical books of the Bible and in rabbinic writings. Some of these individuals are detailed above (Bitya, for example) and others feature prominently elsewhere in the Torah—such as the unnamed man who is stoned for violating Shabbat. Why do you think that the Torah chooses to leave these individuals unnamed? What does it say about *our* role in history—since many of us will remain "unnamed" in the historical annals of our time? If we refuse to accept that we are unimportant, or that God considers us to be unimportant, there must be another way to view this reality with regard to our relationship with God. What might that be?

- How does the relationship between Moses and God change throughout the Torah? How does the Israelites' relationship with God change?
- The Torah has been described as God's love letter to the Jewish people. Do you agree with this assessment? What role do you see the Torah playing in our lives as a community, and in your own life?
- How does a rational, scientific approach to understanding the history of the Torah affect our belief in the covenant between God and the Israelites? How do we balance faith and reason?

ACTIVITIES

Reminder: Feel free to adapt these suggestions to your particular situation. For example, activities that are described here for younger students can be expanded for older students, and those suggested for more advanced classes can be simplified for elementary school groups.

Time Travel (E, S, A)
Invite the students to travel back in time to the giving of the Torah on Mount Sinai. How did we receive the Ten Command-

ments? What was happening in the camp of the Israelites? What was God doing? What was Moses doing? This activity can be acted out in costume, with an art activity (for example, create a rendition of the Ten Commandments as it might have been presented to the community by Moses), or as a writing activity.

For a more sophisticated group, ask your students to read several midrashim (rabbinic teaching stories) about the giving of the Torah, and use those midrashim as the basis for their presentations. This activity can also work well in informal settings with families, for example, a Shavuot family program. (Please see the resource list for this chapter for two suggestions as to where to locate a variety of midrashim in English translation.)

Character Interview (E, S)
Invite a guest to come to the classroom to play the part of one of the characters involved in the Exodus from Egypt, for example, Pharaoh, Moses, Aaron, God, Miriam. Help your students to focus their questions on the actions this character took in order to either help or hinder the Israelites' ability to leave Egypt, as well as his or her motivations.

For example, if the guest is God, ask why God "hardens Pharaoh's heart" when Moses and Aaron are asking God to "let my people go." If the guest is Moses, is he acting solely to cement God's covenant with the Israelites, or for other reasons? After the interview, have the students write letters to the character thanking him or her for coming to visit and saying what they found most interesting about the character's experience.

You're the Author (E, S, A)

In this activity, provide your students with copies of the Ten Commandments as ten strips of paper. Ask the students to put them in the order that they think is the right one—which may or may be the order of the Ten Commandments written in the Torah. Ask the students why they chose the order they did, and to explain in detail their underlying reasons for doing so. For younger groups, after teaching the text of the actual Ten Commandments, ask the students to create their own "ten commandments." This activity could work beautifully as a "classroom contract" for the beginning of the year.

Israelites on Trial: The Sin of the Golden Calf (S, A)

Assign teams to take the sides of the Israelites and God in a courtroom drama or debate the outcome of the incident of the Golden Calf. Witnesses can include Aaron (questions for him should include why he allowed the people to act as he did in Moses's absence), Moses (questions for him should include why he smashed the tablets), and God (questions for God should include why God smote the revelers with a plague).

Each side should prepare for the debate by focusing on the issues of covenant. What does the people's action say about their faith in God and Moses? What do they need to help restore that faith? What could God have done differently?

DID YOU KNOW?

- During the reign of the pharaoh Amenhotep IV in Egypt (approximately 1385 BCE), all but one of the old gods was destroyed and a monotheistic religion revolving around the worship of Aton, the sun god, was established. This monotheism was short-lived, however,

since Amenhotep's successor, Tutankhamen, reinstated the earlier deities.

- During the time that the Torah was recorded, other important texts were also being written down for the first time, including the Epic of Gilgamesh, a Babylonian legend with similarities to the story of Noah and the flood.

TIMELINE

Because of the difficulty of accurate dating during the early biblical period, dates are approximate.

Sometime between the 15th and 13th centuries BCE
> Moses leads the Israelites out of Egypt

1279–1212 BCE
> Reign of Ramses II, known for waging numerous wars as well as his great building enterprises

RESOURCES

Books and Articles

Barnavi, Eli, ed. *Historical Atlas of the Jewish People: From the Time of the Patriarchs to the Present.* New York: Schocken Books, 1992.

Bialik, Ḥaim Naḥman, and Yehoshua Hana Ravnitsky. *The Book of Legends/Sefer Ha-Aggadah: Legends from the Talmud and Midrash.* New York: Schocken Books, 1992.

Chasidah, Yishai. *Encyclopedia of Biblical Personalities.* Brooklyn, NY: Mesorah Publications,1994.

Grun, Bernard. *The Timetables of History: A Horizontal Linkage of People and Events.* New York: Simon & Schuster, 1979.

Pasachoff, Naomi, and Robert J. Littman. *Jewish History in 100 Nutshells.* Northvale, NJ: Jason Aronson, 1995.

The Rabbinical Assembly and The United Synagogue of Conservative Judaism. *Etz Hayim Torah and Commentary.* Philadelphia: Jewish Publication Society, 2001.

Sarna, Jonathan D., and Jonathan B. Krasner. *The History of the Jewish People: A Story of Tradition and Change.* Springfield, NJ: Behrman House, 2006 (see especially pp. 2–5).

Internet
Visit www.behrmanhouse.com/booklinks for links to Web sites that offer additional resources for this chapter.

CHAPTER SIX

JUDGES, KINGS, AND PROPHETS

WHAT'S THE BIG IDEA?
Covenant
Imagine that you are a Jew during the early years following the conquest of the land of Canaan—a Jew living in freedom instead of slavery. What's changed about your relationship with God under these new conditions?

INTRODUCTION
When most people hear the word "judges," they think of black-robed legal experts who hear testimony and decide the outcome of court cases. The judges who led the Israelites immediately following the entrance of the Jewish people into the Promised Land, however, acted instead primarily as spiritual and military leaders.

The Israelites lived within a tribal structure, engaged mostly in farming. They followed the leadership of the judges in their continued battles against their enemies. Having conquered many of these enemies, the Israelites insisted on crowning a human king to rule them, and a transition from the period of the judges to that of a monarchy took place. Under these first kings—Saul, David, and Solomon—a unified Israel was born.

During Solomon's reign a magnificent Temple dedicated to God was constructed, and it became the envy of the surrounding nations and an inspiration to all who saw it. Although the kingdom split after the death of Solomon, the inhabitants of Israel and Judah enjoyed a relative peace. And yet, a problem existed—the Israelites' connection with God was waning.

The prophets came onto the scene as the moral conscience of the people in a time when they had chosen a human king to rule them instead of the heavenly One, particularly when the prophet believed that the current ruler was not providing the moral example necessary to keep this connection alive.

The roles of the prophets were simple: to remind the people, including the rulers, what God requires of them and to tell them in no uncertain terms the fate that awaits those who disobey. Although God's covenant with the people remained unbroken, when the Israelites acted in a manner that threatened to alter or suspend that covenant, the prophets' role was to try to stop it from happening—or at the very least, to warn the sinning populace before it was too late.

BACKGROUND INFORMATION
Israelite vs. Jew: An Explanatory Note
During the biblical period, and in fact until the end of the Second Temple period, the children of Israel were referred to almost exclusively as "Israelites." In the ancient world, the concept of a Jewish Diaspora was virtually nonexistent. People were defined by where they lived. The case of the children of Israel—enslaved in a land not their own, and returning to their homeland hundreds of years later—was a new experience. When the Israelites returned to the Promised Land, they

continued to be called "Israelites," or the children of Israel in biblical parlance.

The term "Jew" was first used late in the Second Temple period, which we will explore further in future chapters. The term "Jew" originated from the term "Judean," meaning someone who lived in the Southern kingdom of Judah. Since that is the term most familiar to modern Jews, it is used interchangeably with "Israelite" throughout this book.

The Judges

Turning the Israelite people from a tribal society into a sovereign nation was a major challenge in the period following the Exodus. This transformation was primarily the work of the judges and the kings.

The role of the judges was multifaceted. Most judges were warriors who led the people in battle against the enemies of the time—primarily the Canaanites and the Philistines. The biblical books of Joshua and Judges describe in detail their exploits and their triumphs. Primarily, the judges functioned as tribal chieftains, who fought different foes plaguing their particular parts of the Land. Judges 3:3 lists these enemies as "the five governors of the Philistines, all the Canaanite, the Sidonite, and the Hivvite that dwell on Mount Lebanon, from the mountain of the plain of Hermon until the approach to Hamath."

Some judges—like the prophet Deborah—did in fact serve as an actual judge, and many of them were extremely righteous individuals (Deborah herself also led the people in battle along with her general, Barak, as described in Judges 4–5). Others—like Samson and Jephthah—fulfilled their warrior function without the same moral integrity, and thus were unable to model righteous behavior for those who looked to them for leadership (Judges 11–16). For example, Jephthah's mission was to defeat the Ammonites, and he vowed to sacrifice the first thing that emerged from his house upon his return if God would deliver the Ammonites into his hand. Sadly, it was Jephthah's only daughter who emerged from the house to greet him when he returned victorious from battle, and he refused to renounce his vow. The Book of Judges ends with these foreboding words: "In those days there was no king in Israel and every man did what was right in his own eyes" (Judges 21:25), lamenting the moral disintegration of Israelite society and foreshadowing changes to come.

The Early Kings: Saul, David, and Solomon

The transition from a tribal society ruled by judges to a monarchy governed by kings took place during the lifetime of Samuel, both judge and prophet, and Saul, who was crowned king—albeit reluctantly—by Samuel, in deference to the wishes of the people.

Samuel was the first judge who functioned more as a national leader than a tribal one, and so the people came to him to insist on the crowning of a king (I Samuel 8). The anointing of a king was seen as the solution to the weakness of tribal society—lack of a centralized governmental authority. To put it plainly, the Israelites wanted to be like everybody else in the ancient world at that time—one nation with one king.

Saul, however, didn't behave like a traditional king. He didn't build a palace, and he spent most of his time engaged in battle rather than ruling the country. Saul fell from favor with God—and from Samuel—following his disastrous handling of the defeat of Agag, king of the Amalekites. Saul was told to slaughter every Amalekite man, woman, child, and animal, but saved the king alive and allowed his troops to loot the Amalekite camp; the chapter (I Samuel 15) ends with the words "Adonai had reconsidered making Saul king over Israel."

Saul's successor, David—already a member of his court and his son Jonathan's best friend—engaged in a protracted rivalry with Saul until David's ultimate defeat of Saul. King David succeeded in defeating the Philistines, capturing Jerusalem and turning it into a national capital, and—arguably most important—unifying the twelve tribes into one nation.

David, however, was not without faults. When David desired a beautiful woman (Bathsheba) he saw bathing on a nearby rooftop, but discovered she was married, he sent her unsuspecting husband (Uriah) to the front lines where he was sure to be killed in battle. The first child of their union—a baby boy—died as a punishment for David's sin (II Samuel 11–12). David was also denied the privilege of building the Temple to God because of his brutality in battle, although those battles won Israel its freedom; that honor would go to David and Bathsheba's second child—Solomon.

Solomon was the last king of a unified Israel. His main accomplishment was the building of the Temple—an awesome structure that stood for four hundred years and marked the final transition of the Israelites as a people wandering in the wilderness to one settled in the land that God had promised to their ancestors. In addition, Solomon fortified many of the border towns, stabilized the structure of twelve regions that paid taxes and

supported the army, and created royal alliances with the neighboring nations through political marriages (I Kings 3:1; I Kings 11:1–2).

Although able to quash rebellions during his own reign, his sons could not resolve their differences. The kingdom was divided when Solomon's son Jeroboam led the northern tribes to secede, and his other son Rehoboam ruled over the remaining southern kingdom. Moreover, the Torah tells us that the seeds of this division were sown during Solomon's own reign due to his participation in idol worship in his later years (I Kings 11).

During the next several hundred years, many kings would come and go—some good, some not so good. And so, a central question remained: If the king ruling the people of Israel was a mortal man and not God, who would keep the king in check and make sure he, too, obeyed the covenant between God and Israel? Who would advise the people when their leaders were morally corrupt? The answer: the prophets.

The Davidic Monarchy and the Messianic Promise

When Solomon put the finishing touches on the Temple, he also put in place the theological underpinnings that have lasted until this day—the firm belief that King David, as God's anointed, began the line of kings that would ultimately culminate in the crowning of the Messiah.

The belief that the Messiah (literally, anointed one) would be descended from him was crystallized during the rabbinic period, which we will study in future chapters. However, the seeds of this belief in the Messiah and the Messianic Era— one of hope and rebirth for the world—

had their start during this time and must not be overlooked. The covenant that God began with Abraham, Isaac, and Jacob was therefore continued via the Davidic dynasty, and traditional Jews believe that it will continue into the future, including the Messianic Era.

The Early Prophets

Prophecy was a common thread running through the fabric of life in most ancient cultures; the Bible itself speaks of the prophet Bilaam, who was commissioned to prophesy on behalf of Balak, the king of Moab (Numbers 22–24). In most of these societies—including Israel—the main job of the prophet was to bring messages from the deity to the king and the common people, and all were expected to take note.

Many different types of prophets existed in ancient Israel. Sometimes, they were seen as members of the upper class of Israelite society, often serving in the king's court. Samuel, for example, anointed Saul as king (I Samuel 9–10) and remained such an integral part of the court and of Saul's entourage that Saul even tried to contact Samuel through a medium after the prophet's death (I Samuel 28).

Sometimes, entire groups of prophets acted as a social class unto themselves, behaving as the king's "yes men" (I Kings 22) in contrast to the "true prophets" of God. Although they expressed their independence by castigating the rulers over infractions of God's law—Nathan rebuked David following his affair with Bathsheba, for example—many of these prophets were still seen as part of the ruling establishment.

The Classical Prophets

The era of "classical prophecy" began when the prophet's main role was no longer that of court adviser, but of God's messenger to the Israelite people, reminding them of their moral and religious obligations to God and to one another. According to the biblical text, prophets such as Elijah employed various means to get their message across, including oratory, foretelling the future, and miracles, such as reviving the dead and other supernatural phenomena.

Often the classical prophets were seen as being pitted against the prophets of the idolaters, of whom Israelites made up a growing percentage, especially in the Northern Kingdom, and against the rulers that condoned idol worship, such as Ahab and Jezebel (I Kings 18). Many legends grew up around the exploits of these classical prophets, and are recorded in rabbinic writings such as the Midrash (rabbinic teaching stories from the second century CE onward).

Many of the prophets, such as Amos, have been referred to as "literary" prophets because their messages were transmitted not only through oratory and miracles, but through written works containing warnings, predictions, and visions. These books— which were ultimately canonized—not only reflected the system of belief that the prophets wished to transmit to the people, especially in the absence of kings who took the covenant with God seriously, but served as an important source of information about life in Israel and Judah during the late First Temple and early Second Temple periods.

The basic message of literary prophets such as Amos, Ezekiel, Isaiah, and Jeremiah was that as the Creator, God serves as the ultimate author of the fate of the world—individuals, countries, and history. The prophets saw history—including the rise and fall of nations, and the difficulties that befell rulers and commoners in the wake of events such as war and famine—as an instrument of God's sovereignty, engineered by God in order to teach people the correct way to behave.

A Judaism that incorporated a belief in the ability of individuals to exercise their free will at the same time as God's will is manifest in the world is the theological legacy of this period. This system of belief is encapsulated in the story of Jonah—one in which the prophet is sent to foretell a particular future, and sees that future change as the sole result of the actions of those who were warned.

The belief that the actions of individuals and nations can influence the will of God was (and is) quite empowering. The prophets sought to capitalize on this theology in order to convince the people to see the events of history—such as the destruction of the Northern Kingdom and the exile of the ten tribes, and the destruction of the Southern Kingdom and the exile to Babylonia—as tragedies that could be overcome with a return to God. Such a theology also served the prophets in another important task: comforting the people once the inevitable disaster struck.

The Later Prophets

Following the conquest of Babylonia by the Persian king Cyrus, the exiled Jews were given permission to return to Zion and rebuild the Temple. Although King Cyrus certainly did so in order to encourage the loyal and grateful Israelites to resettle the western outpost of his vast empire, his motivation was almost entirely beside the point to those who had been waiting for two generations to end their exile.

Not all the exiled Jews left Babylonia, since many of those exiled—largely the leaders, scholars, and wealthy merchant class—had created a vibrant Jewish life in the Diaspora that would thrive for more than one thousand years to come. But some did return, and those who came back were faced with a new reality.

During the intervening years, a large number of their compatriots who had stayed behind had in fact intermarried with the inhabitants of the land. Understandably, they had no interest in adopting the form of Judaism forged in the Diaspora by those who returned to Judea. Guidance for those rebuilding the Temple as well as those whose ancestors had never left the Holy Land was provided by the later prophets.

Ezra and Neḥemiah, two important leaders of the people who returned from Babylonia, sought to bridge the gap between these two populations who now had to coexist in the new conditions. Over the course of several decades they introduced and then standardized many Jewish practices, including the reading of the Torah aloud on Shabbat and on market days—Mondays and Thursdays—a practice that has endured to the present day in traditional synagogues. They also worked to rebuild Judah's economy in order to support its growing population.[1]

According to scholars, the last work in the biblical canon to be composed was the Book of Daniel. The Book of Daniel is very mystical in nature and is written in a combination of Hebrew (the holy tongue) and Aramaic (the language of the common people). Although the rabbinic sages dated Daniel to the period immediately following

---

[1] This information is also covered in the student text, Jonathan D. Sarna and Jonathan B. Krasner, *The History of the Jewish People: A Story of Tradition and Change*, Springfield, NJ: Behrman House, pp. 13–15.

the destruction of the First Temple, similarities between the Book of Daniel and the writings of later mystical communities such as the Dead Sea/Qumran sect have led scholars to date the Book of Daniel to the second century BCE —around the time of the Maccabees.

The Book of Daniel may have been written in order to bring comfort and strength to those Jews being oppressed by the tyrant Antiochus Epiphanes during this period of time. An important focus of the Book of Daniel is the end of days and the coming of the final Redemption, topics of great concern to late Second Temple Jews.

According to Jewish tradition, the final prophet was Malachi, whose words comprise the final book in the Prophets section of the Hebrew Bible, or Tanach. Malachi was the last of the "minor prophets," so named because their writings were short, not because they were thought to be unimportant. However, it is likely that he was in fact not the last prophet to put pen to paper in ancient Israel. Malachi, which means "my messenger" and may not have been the prophet's actual name, probably lived in Israel during the fifth century BCE, immediately preceding the reforms by Ezra and Nehemiah.

Like those who came before him, Malachi affirms God's love for the chosen people, while admonishing the people that God will judge them for their actions. Malachi also foretells that Elijah will be sent to herald the "great and terrible day of the Lord" (Malachi 4:5). This book "closes" the canon of prophecy in the Tanach.

CONNECTING TO OUR TRADITION
The Message of the Prophets
The prophets' message is an enduring one—that's why the public recitation of

their writings constitute a central part of our Shabbat morning worship, why we engrave their words on our synagogue buildings, why their prophecies still resonate with us even today. Below is a selection of texts that encapsulate some of the main messages of the prophets, with themes ripe for exploration:

Social Justice
"Thus said Adonai: Observe what is right and do what is just; for soon My salvation shall come and My deliverance be revealed." (Isaiah 56:1, the prophetic reading, or *haftarah*—meaning "addition"—for fast day afternoons). "He has told you, O man, what is good, and what Adonai requires of you: Only to do justice, love mercy, and to walk humbly with your God" (Micah 6:8; *haftarah* for the portion of Balak). "I hate and loath your festive offerings, and I will not be appeased by your assemblies. . . . Hear this, you who devour the needy, decimating the poor of the land . . . should not the land quake for this, and all its inhabitants will be destroyed?" (Amos 5:21; 8:4, 8).

Praise of God
"Praise Adonai, proclaim God's name, make God's deeds known among the peoples; declare that God's name is exalted. Sing hymns to Adonai, for God has done gloriously; let this be made known in all the world! Oh, shout for joy, you who dwell in Zion! For great in your midst is the Holy One of Israel" (Isaiah 12:4-6; *haftarah* for the eighth day of Passover).

Forgiveness for Sin
"Who is a God like You, forgiving iniquity and remitting transgression; Who has not maintained God's wrath forever against the remnant of God's own people.

. . . God will take us back in love; God will cover up all our iniquities. You will hurl all our sins into the depths of the sea" (Micah 7:18–19; *haftarah* for the Shabbat before Yom Kippur).

Restoration of the Jewish People

"The day is coming when watchmen shall proclaim on the heights of Ephraim: Come, let us go up to Zion, to Adonai our God! . . . They shall return from the enemy's land, and there is hope for your future; declares Adonai: Your children shall return to their country" (Jeremiah 31:6; 16–17; *haftarah* for the second day of Rosh Hashanah). "Be glad with Jerusalem and rejoice in her, all you who love her; exult with her in exultation, all you who mourned for her. . . . for thus said Adonai: Behold, I will extend peace to her like a river and the wealth of nations like a surging stream" (Isaiah 66:10, 12; *haftarah* for Shabbat Rosh Ḥodesh).

IMPORTANT TERMS

Judge
Prophet
Midrash
Tanach

Names, Places, and Events

Judah	Philistines
Israel	Canaanites
Saul	Assyria
David	Babylonia
Solomon	Cyrus
Samuel	Persia
Nathan	Elijah
Samson	Amos
Jephthah	Isaiah
Deborah	Jeremiah
Barak	Micah
Moab	Malachi
Ammonites	Daniel
Amalekites	Philistines

DISCUSSION QUESTIONS

- The judges were faced with the task of leading the people in battle and providing moral leadership as well. Do you think it is possible for the same person to do both of these things well? Can you think of examples among our own modern leaders who have tried to do both of these tasks and succeeded—or failed?

- How does the relationship between the Jewish people and God change once we have our own land and are no longer dependent upon God for miracles? How does the leadership of a human king change our relationship with our God?

- The people of early Israel demanded that a king be anointed to lead them. Do you think that every nation needs one leader? Why or why not?

- The prophets described above lived centuries—even millennia—ago. Although the sages of our tradition teach that prophecy ended in the time of the Second Temple, do we still have a need for prophecy today?

- Which messages of the prophets resonate the most with you? How would you put them into your own words?

- Modern scholars disagree on how many of the prophecies contained in the books of the prophets were actually written by the individuals named on the cover. Some scholars believe that many of the prophecies attributed to them were actually written down by court historians with a particular allegiance to one ruler or school of thought. How does a rational approach to trying to understand these texts in a political and historical context affect our belief in the covenant between God and the Jewish people?

- In a post-Holocaust world, how do we relate to the prophetic message that when we don't act in accordance with God's wishes, terrible things may happen?

ACTIVITIES

The Play's the Thing (S)

Have students read Judges, chapter 4 (the story of Deborah), and invite them to travel back in time to the battle with the Canaanites. Have the students write the story in their own words as a play. Have students play the parts of Deborah, Barak, the general Sisera, and Yael. Costumes add more realism (and fun!) to this activity.

For older students, have a follow-up discussion based on an analysis of Deborah and Barak's poem of glory in Judges chapter 5: why do you think some tribes participated and others opted out? Do you understand their decision? What should the consequences, if any, be for their desertion of this important conflict?

Character Interview (E, S)

Invite someone to come to the classroom to play the part of one of the prophets. Make sure students read the relevant chapters in the Tanach prior to the visit. If your goal is to focus on social justice, invite Amos or Micah to visit. Ask students to focus their questions on such issues as what made the prophet speak out against the established authority and how they felt their connection to God. Make sure to have students write letters to the character thanking him or her for coming to visit, and saying what they found most interesting about the character's experience.

Building the Temple (E, S, A)

With your class, read the account of the building of the Temple by Solomon in I Kings 6–7. Gather materials and have your students build a simple model of the First Temple; this activity can be as basic or as complex as you wish.

As an alternative, have students draw a mural based upon the same descriptions in the Tanach. As a follow-up activity, enjoy a dedication party! This activity would work nicely in an informal setting, such as a family education event, particularly in conjunction with the holiday of Ḥanukkah, which celebrates the rededication of the Temple following the Maccabean revolt.

Debate: Do We Need a King? (S, A)

With your class, read I Samuel 8–10. Assign teams to take the sides of "pro" and "con" with regard to the question of whether the Israelites need any king other than God. Each side should prepare for the debate by focusing on the issues of covenant. (What does the people's choice say about their faith in God? What is Samuel trying to achieve by both promoting and disabusing the people regarding the election of a human king?)

DID YOU KNOW?

- Our sages tell us that the rise of the wicked leader Haman was due in part to King Saul's disobedience in the episode of the Amalekites in I Samuel 15. Tradition[2] tells us that during the period of time that King Agag was kept alive by Saul in disregard for God's instructions to kill all the Amalekites that had been captured, Agag had time to father a child. That child was the ancestor of Haman, who is called "the Agagite" in the Megillah (Esther 3:1).
- Ethiopian Jews trace their origin to the relationship between King Solomon and the Queen of Sheba (I Kings 10:1–13). They believe that when the Queen of Sheba returned to Ethiopia, she was pregnant with their

---

[2] Babylonian Talmud, Megillah 13a.

child, and that that child—King
Menelik—was the father of the
Ethiopian Jewish community.

TIMELINE
Because of the difficulty of accurate
dating during the early biblical period,
dates are approximate.

12th–11th centuries BCE
    The period of Joshua, Judges, and
    the conquest of Canaan
1029–1007 BCE
    Reign of King Saul
1000 BCE
    David anointed as the king of a
    unified Israel[3]
967 BCE
    Death of King David; beginning
    of the rule of Solomon
965 BCE
    Solomon begins building the
    Temple in Jerusalem; it is
    completed several years later.
928 BCE
    Death of Solomon; division of the
    kingdom into Israel (North) and
    Judah (South)
722 BCE
    Fall of the Northern Kingdom to
    Assyria; exile of the "ten lost tribes"[4]
586 BCE
    Fall of the Southern Kingdom to
    Babylonia; exile of the leaders of
    the Judean community
538 BCE
    Cyrus, King of Persia, decrees that
    the Jews may return to Judea
515 BCE
    Dedication of the Second Temple
    in Jerusalem

458 BCE
    Ezra the Scribe organizes a mass
    "*aliyah*" of Jews to Judea and
    becomes their leader followed by
    Nehemiah

RESOURCES
Books and Articles

Barnavi, Eli, ed. *Historical Atlas of the Jewish People: From the Time of the Patriarchs to the Present.* New York: Schocken Books, 1992.

Chasidah, Yishai. *Encyclopedia of Biblical Personalities.* Brooklyn, NY: Mesorah Publications,1994.

Cogan, Lainie Blum, and Judy Weiss. *Teaching Haftarah: Background, Insights and Strategies.* Denver, CO: A.R.E. Publishing, 2002.

Gordon, Cyrus H., and Gary A. Rendsburg. *The Bible and the Ancient Near East.* New York: W. W. Norton, 1997.

Grun, Bernard. *The Timetables of History: A Horizontal Linkage of People and Events.* New York: Simon & Schuster, 1979.

Naim, Asher. *Saving the Lost Tribe: The Rescue and Redemption of the Ethiopian Jews.* New York: Ballantine, 2003.

Pasachoff, Naomi, and Robert J. Littman. *Jewish History in 100 Nutshells.* Northvale, NJ: Jason Aronson, 1995.

---

[3] David was first anointed in secret while Saul still reigned, and then was publicly anointed a second time after Saul's defeat.
[4] The "ten lost tribes" is the common term used for the ten northern tribes exiled by the Assyrians in the eighth century BCE.

The Rabbinical Assembly and The United Synagogue of Conservative Judaism. *Etz Hayim Torah and Commentary.* Philadelphia: Jewish Publication Society, 2001.

Sarna, Jonathan D., and Jonathan B. Krasner. *The History of the Jewish People: A Story of Tradition and Change.* Springfield, NJ: Behrman House, 2006 (see especially pp. 6–15).

Scherman, Nosson, ed. *The Stone Edition Tanach.* Brooklyn, NY: Mesorah Publications, 1996; text and appendices (particularly Appendix A, Timelines 3 and 4—the era of the judges and the Jewish monarchy).

Internet
Visit www.behrmanhouse.com/booklinks for links to Web sites that offer additional resources for this chapter.

CHAPTER SEVEN
EXILE: THE DESTRUCTION OF THE FIRST TEMPLE

WHAT'S THE BIG IDEA?
Diaspora

Since the Exodus from Egypt, the Israelites had lived almost exclusively in the land of Israel, Eretz Yisrael. Two exiles changed all that—first, the exile of the Israelites from the Northern Kingdom in 722 BCE, and then the Babylonian exile a little more than a century later. The Jewish people had to transform itself from a group tied exclusively to a land without which it could not survive, to a group yearning to go back to that land, but finding ways to live and maintain their Judaism while away from their homeland.

BACKGROUND INFORMATION
The Northern Kingdom

In the year 722 BCE, the Assyrians invaded the Northern Kingdom of Israel, capping a series of Assyrian attacks against neighboring regions that spanned more than twenty-five years. Always the weaker of the two kingdoms, Israel was already torn by internal religious wars between idolaters and monotheists, and was ruled by a series of kings who were often either unfaithful to the religion of the Israelites, corrupt, or both. Samaria—despite two years of revolts against the invaders—finally succumbed to Assyrian domination under the leadership of King Sargon in 720 BCE. Sargon's own military records describe the conquest:

"I captured Samaria, [with] 27,290 people dwelling in it. . . . I rebuilt the city of Samaria and made it bigger than it was. People from the land which I conquered I settled in it and directed them in their own particular skill. I placed over it my palace-official as governor and imposed upon them a tax payment as on the citizens of Assyria."[1]

In order to break apart the power structure of Israel, Sargon deported the rulers and community leaders—economic, military, political, and religious—to other parts of his empire and brought in his own citizens in order to rend the social fabric of those who stayed behind. A substantial portion of the civilian population of the ten tribes of Israel was also exiled, thus breaking up the established tribal social structure as well. In all practicality, the Northern Kingdom had ceased to be part of the Israelite nation.

The Southern Kingdom: The Heartland of Judah

Although the Southern Kingdom had its share of corrupt leaders and social difficulties, it had always been the stronger of the two nations after the division of the kingdom following King Solomon's death. Like the North, however, it was susceptible to invasion and attack, and in 701 BCE King Sennacherib of Assyria did in fact

---

[1] Naomi Passachoff and Robert J. Littman, *Jewish History in 100 Nutshells*, Northvale, NJ: Jason Aronson, 1995, p. 29

besiege Jerusalem. Not surprisingly, the Assyrian and Hebrew accounts of these events differ substantially. According to the "Sennacherib Prism," an Assyrian royal record, Hezekiah refused to submit peacefully to an Assyrian conquest, and so Sennacherib laid siege to Jerusalem and imprisoned Hezekiah in his palace "like a bird in a cage," increasing the tribute due to Assyria by the kingdom of Judah. However, two separate accounts in the Hebrew Bible, in 2 Kings 18–19 and 2 Chronicles 32, describe the events far differently.

According to these texts, King Hezekiah—either alone or aided by the prophet Isaiah—prayed to God for assistance, and an angel responded by slaughtering all 185,000 Assyrian soldiers in their own camp. According to the biblical accounts, King Sennacherib then returned to his capital city of Nineveh whereupon he was slain in his own temple by his own sons.

Despite these events, it is clear from subsequent accounts in the Tanach that because the Northern Kingdom was seen by the rulers and the people alike as an entirely separate nation, the Assyrian conquest—while seen as unfortunate—was almost beside the point for the rulers and civilian population of Judah. While the prophets railed against idol worship and unjust behavior, and pointed to the fate of the North as an example of what would happen to those who followed the same path, the people of the South largely ignored this message.

King Josiah's Reforms

Toward the end of the seventh century BCE, the nation of Judah was instead besieged by internal turmoil. King

Manasseh, the son of Hezekiah, had broken with tradition and brought the worship of idols and foreign gods to Judah, going so far as to sanction tribute to Molech, the fire god, and even child sacrifice within the grounds of the Holy Temple. Because he ruled for fifty years, many of those practices became normative for two generations of Judeans. Manasseh's grandson, King Josiah, had an uphill battle as he sought to reform the nation's religious practices and return to a pure monotheism not seen in many decades.

Part of Josiah's plan was to completely cleanse and rededicate the Temple, foreshadowing the events of the Maccabean revolt to come hundreds of years in the future. His renovations began in 628 BCE, and six years later, during the rebuilding project, an amazing discovery was made. According to the biblical account in 2 Kings 22–23 (and echoed in 2 Chronicles 34–35), the High Priest Hilkiah tells the scribe Shaphan that he has found "a Scroll of the Torah in the Temple of Adonai."

Whether this book was the entire Torah—forgotten in the previous generations' abandonment of their ancestral religion—or solely the Book of Deuteronomy is a subject of intense debate among scholars. In addition, the debate includes both traditional voices as well as secular scholarship that contends this book may not have been discovered, but actually written by Hezekiah, Shaphan and/or King Josiah in an attempt to validate the sweeping reforms of his administration. Whatever the case, the public reading of the scroll and the ensuing reformations—the celebration of Passover for the first time in generations, and the insistence that the royal court and those under its control adhere to the *mitzvot* (commandments)—galvanized the people of that generation toward true worship of God.

Unfortunately, the changes brought about by King Josiah were not to last. Prior to his death, the prophet Huldah (2 Kings 22:15–20) foretold that the reading of the Torah had almost the opposite effect from that which had been desired—rather than placating God, God was instead enraged when reminded that the commandments had been forsaken, and God promised retribution against the wicked of the next generation.

The Fall of Jerusalem

In accordance with the prophecy of Huldah and those who came before her, destruction did finally come to the Southern Kingdom at the hands of King Nebuchadnezzar of Babylonia.

The Torah's take on Nebuchadnezzar is that he served as an instrument of God to punish the faithless people of Judah. The Chaldeans, a group of invaders who made Babylon their home, joined with the surrounding nations to destroy the Assyrian Empire in around 620 BCE. By 600 BCE they governed much of the Near East, including Egypt. The only thing standing between the Babylonians and complete control of the region was the Kingdom of Judah.

Nebuchadnezzar, who ruled from 604 to 552 BCE, first marched on Jerusalem in 597 BCE, capturing the city and deporting large numbers of her inhabitants to Babylonia—ten thousand people, according to the biblical account (II Kings

24:14). He exiled King Jehoiakim and installed Zedekiah as a puppet king.

King Zedekiah, trying to play both sides of the board, entered into a secret agreement with the king of Egypt to revolt against Babylon's rule there. His plan backfired when the pharaoh Psammetichus died in 589 and Nebuchadnezzar was able to solidify his hold on the entire region. In the winter of 587 BCE, Nebuchadnezzar once again invaded Jerusalem, and this time he completely devastated the city and its surrounding areas, burning the Temple to the ground (after carrying off the Temple treasures as spoils of war). Like his predecessors, he exiled much of the population—particularly the leaders—to Babylonia. King Zedekiah tried to avoid capture but failed; in the manner of despots before and after, Nebuchadnezzar tortured Zedekiah by forcing him to watch the murder of his sons, blinding him, and dragging him off to captivity in chains.

While the prevailing wisdom is that the exile of the Southern Kingdom was somehow less devastating than that of the North because fewer people were deported, this perception has serious flaws. To give the devastation some perspective, Judah's population fell from 250,000 in the eighth century BCE to 125,000 a century later. After the exile, the total number of Judean inhabitants of the land was a mere 20,000, because the Babylonians did not replace the indigenous population with members of their own society, as the Assyrians had done in the North.

The Book of Lamentations, most likely written during the early years of the exile in Israel, describes the impact of the destruction: "How [can this be]?! Lonely sits the city once full of people! . . . Judah has gone into exile miserable and enslaved; when she settled among the foreign nations, she found no rest; all of her pursuers overtook her in the narrow places" (Lamentations 1:1, 3). The book goes on to describe the fate of the city under siege—starving women forced to eat their own children, the dead and dying lying in the streets, and other horrors of war. With devastation so complete, how did the people of Judah manage to survive?

Life in Exile

In order for the Israelites to survive in exile, away from the Land of Israel promised to them by God, and without a Temple serving as a central place of worship, the Jewish people had to almost completely reimagine itself. That they were successful is a testament to their leadership, their ingenuity, and their covenant with the Almighty. How did they do it?

Leadership in Exile

When the Babylonians deported the leaders along with the people, they unwittingly helped the Jews exiled to Babylonia stay together as a community. In fact, the Babylonian Jewish community became so strong and vibrant that it served as the primary Jewish voice of the Diaspora in religious, political, and educational matters for well over a millennium.

First and foremost, the Jews in exile had their prophets, whose work shifted focus as they ministered to the Israelite community in Babylon. While the primary mission of the prophets in the Land of Israel *before* the Exile had been to try to steer the people back on track toward

justice, mercy, and their relationship with God (to paraphrase Micah), the prophets *during* the Exile had a new mission. Before, the prophets railed against the people, trying to get them to change their ways before the worst happened. In exile, when the worst *had* happened, the mission of the prophets changed to one of bringing comfort to the people and helping to create solidarity in the community. Promising that God's covenant has not been inexorably broken, the prophets told the people that the Exile would end, their enemies would be struck down, and God would bring them back to the Land of their ancestors.

The Jews in exile also had their community and religious leaders. Although the Temple was destroyed and inaccessible to them, their religious leaders— *kohanim* (priests), Levites, and others— helped the community to refashion the manner in which they practiced Judaism. Under their leadership in the Diaspora community of Babylonia, Judaism became *portable*. No Temple? We'll create our own, smaller, houses of worship. No system of animal sacrifices? We'll take the prayer and biblical portions of the sacrificial service—such as the psalms, Bar'chu, and the Sh'ma—and create a worship service that centers around them.

In addition, the exiles to Babylonia in 586 BCE joined an already established Jewish community. As early as 722 BCE, Jews exiled during the Assyrian conquest scattered far and wide throughout the Near East, and it is likely that some of them settled in Babylon. In 597 BCE, when King Nebuchadnezzar deported King Jehoiakim with ten thousand others from Judah to Babylonia, they joined these few Israelites and created an organized community. It was this established community to which the next wave of Jewish exiles came following the defeat of the Southern Kingdom in 586 BCE.

Adaptation—A Formula for Jewish Survival

All the conditions above would not have been enough had the Jews not been willing to adapt to their new surroundings. After all, many other ancient peoples, when conquered, completely assimilated into their new surroundings and cultures and disappeared forever. Not so the Jewish people. Instead, the Jews in exile adapted to their new environment, settling into Babylonian life as another community of foreigners in this vast cosmopolitan empire. This adaptation served the Jewish community well and allowed them to maintain their separate identity in exile. The only other time the Jews had been exiled en masse to one place had been during their sojourn in Egypt hundreds of years before. The difference this time was that instead of being enslaved, most of the Jews used their resources and ingenuity and prospered.

daughters. Most of our information about the Babylonian Jews in the sixth and fifth centuries BCE comes from our own Hebrew Scriptures, particularly the Books of Ezekiel, Jeremiah, Ezra and Nehemiah. While still in Eretz Yisrael, Jeremiah writes a letter to those exiled with King Jehoiakim, stating that God wants them to "build houses and settle; plant gardens and eat their produce. Take wives and beget sons and daughters; take wives for your sons and give your daughters to husbands, and let

them give birth to sons and Multiply there; do not let your numbers diminish. Seek the peace of the city to which I have exiled you and pray for it to Adonai, for through its peace you will have peace" (Jeremiah 29:5–7).

Ezekiel, writing in exile, describes a community that is so comfortable and entrenched that they are in danger of reverting to idol worship, and he accuses them of declaring, "We will be like the nations, like the families of the lands, to worship wood and stone" (Ezekiel 20:32). Nehemiah was himself a member of the king's court, and Jews in Babylonia were wealthy enough to help finance the return to Judah and the rebuilding of the Temple (although many did not themselves return to the Land).

Some adaptations made by the Babylonian Jewish community are still with us today. For example, the names of the Babylonian months were adopted, and Israelites began to use Babylonian names (for example, "Zerubbabel" probably means "seed of Babylon"). There is even scholarly evidence that some biblical books, such as the Books of Kings, were edited to resemble Babylonian royal chronicles of the same period.

These conditions allowed the Jewish community in Babylonia to thrive and grow, and when the opportunity came to return to the Land, they had the luxury of choosing whether or not to answer the call.

The Persian Conquest

By 539 BCE the Babylonian Empire, weakened over the ensuing decades by a series of wars against Egypt and other border nations and by factional struggles among the leadership following Nebuchadnezzar's death in 522 BCE, was ripe for a takeover. The Persian army, under the command of King Cyrus, conquered Babylonia almost without a fight.

Cyrus, who by this time ruled all Western Asia, decided that the best way to consolidate his rule over such a vast amount of territory was to adopt a policy of tolerance toward the conquered peoples all over his empire. In keeping with this policy, Cyrus issued a proclamation in 538 BCE granting the Israelite exiles in Babylonia permission to return to their homeland and rebuild their Temple. Our information about these events comes largely from the biblical books of Haggai, Zechariah, Malachi, Ezra, and Nehemiah.

The text of Cyrus's decree is preserved in the Book of Ezra 1:2–4:

"Thus said Cyrus king of Persia: All the kingdoms of the earth has Adonai, God of heaven, given to me and has commanded me to build for Adonai a Temple in Jerusalem, which is in Judah. Whoever is among you of God's entire people—may his God be with him!—let him go up to Jerusalem which is in Judah and build the Temple of Adonai, God of Israel—Adonai is the God who is in Jerusalem. And all those who remain, in whatever place he dwells, let the inhabitants of that place bestow upon him gifts of silver and gold, of valuables and animals; together with the contribution for the Temple of God which is in Jerusalem."

Following the decree, a caravan of leaders and workers left for the Holy Land. Led by Sheshbazaar (possibly the son of the exiled King Jehoiakim), Zerubbabel (son of Shealtiel, and grandson of Jehoiakim), and Joshua the *Kohen* ("priest"), son of the High Priest Jehozadak, they headed the first wave of several *aliyot* that would return more than fifty thousand people to the Land of Israel over the next century. (The word *aliyah* literally means "to go up"; *aliyot* is the plural form of the word.)

While each successive wave had leadership figures, most of the immigrants came from among the poorer segments of the Babylonian Jewish community. It was these returnees who interacted with the *amei ha'aretz* (literally, "people of the land")—the descendants of the Jews who, being poor and without influence themselves, had remained behind under Babylonian rule in Judah while their brethren were in exile.

Rebuilding the Temple proved to be a difficult task for a number of reasons. The challenges of making *aliyah* to Israel were just as arduous then as they have been for many in modern times. Those wealthy leaders who left Babylonia for Israel with plenty of monetary resources saw those resources dwindle away in a land crippled by conquest and drought, and many found themselves reduced to poverty within a short time.

The leaders were also in conflict with each other. Zerubbabel, who had royal blood, wanted to reestablish the Davidic dynasty and sought political independence from Persia. Joshua, on the other hand, was comfortable living under the relative autonomy and religious freedom granted by the generous Persian rulers.[2]

Perhaps the largest number of difficulties arose between the returnees, who saw

---

[2] Eli Barnavi, ed., *A Historical Atlas of the Jewish People: From the Time of the Patriarchs to the Present*, NY: Schocken Books, 1992, p. 28.

themselves as the true, authentic representatives of Judaism, and both the *amei ha'aretz* and the Samaritans, who saw themselves as the guardians of Israel and the true Jews. This conflict created almost insurmountable tensions. In fact, the term *amei ha'aretz* took on a derogatory gloss during this period, which lasted into the rabbinic age and came to mean "ignoramuses." The leadership team excluded Samaritans from the rebuilding of the city, and the Samaritans in turn fought against its construction.

The Second Temple was in fact completed within a generation and dedicated in 515 BCE. However, the city walls were not reconstructed until Neḥemiah—both an influential court official with the secular government and a religious leader in the Jewish community—was able to oversee its completion.

A renaissance of Jewish religious practice and thought heralded by Ezra and Neḥemiah marked the return of a portion of the Jewish people to its home-land, while the Diaspora communities in Babylonia and elsewhere served as vital Jewish outposts. Judaism had managed, even with the challenges of exile and conquest, to adapt in order to meet the challenges of living in the Diaspora while maintaining an everlasting connection to the Holy Land. This dual character of Jewish life would continue to serve the people well in the short term, and even better in the long term.

CONNECTION TO OUR TRADITION: WORSHIPPING GOD IN THE DIASPORA

While the Second Temple stood in Jerusalem, Jewish communities were developing all over the known world. The model of having centers of worship outside Jerusalem had begun much earlier

than the Babylonian exile. During the time that the First Temple stood, shrines dedicated to the God of the Israelites were also established in the Northern Kingdom.

The religious worship that took place at these shrines consisted of sacrifices and prayers in a replication of the services that took place at the Temple. An echo of this tradition came in the fourth century when Manasseh, a Samaritan opponent of Neḥ emiah, built a rival temple on Mount Gerizim in the North.

After the Babylonian Exile, however, local places of worship in the rest of the Diaspora began to acquire a different cast. Jewish communities in Egypt, Persia, and Mesopotamia swelled with immigrants who came by choice, not only because they had been exiled. These communities created power and leadership structures, built their own houses of worship, developed an internal method of taxation in order to maintain community buildings and services, and developed vibrant cultural achievements, including art, literature, and religious innovations. Many of these Jews also adapted to the surrounding culture, which by the fourth century BCE had become known as Hellenism (or Greek culture). Our next chapter will focus on both the richness of Jewish practice and the challenge of maintaining these traditions within the surrounding Hellenistic culture.

DID YOU KNOW?

- The Jews of Elephantine, Egypt, had a progressive Jewish society in which women could own their own businesses and initiate their own divorces, contrary to Jewish law in the rest of the Diaspora and in Israel. According to the records of the

Persian king Cambyses, who conquered Egypt in 525 BCE, they also had their own temple and observed the Sabbath and celebrated Passover.

- According to scholars, the story contained in the biblical Book of Esther, which forms the basis of our celebration of Purim, may be based on actual events. The Persian king Artaxerxes (Achashverosh in Hebrew) reigned in the fifth century BCE, employed a Jewish scribe in his court, and sought to consolidate his hold over dozens of provinces in a swath of land reaching from Egypt to Afghanistan.

- The first-century BCE king Mithridates VI ordered a general slaughter of "all who were of Italic race," men, women, and children of every age, in the Roman province of Asia which he had just conquered. The killing was to be done at the same time everywhere, namely on the thirtieth day after the date of the royal order. Regarding the possibility of a princess of the doomed people disguising herself, "the future mother of Harun al-Rashid presented herself as an orphan and did not inform the khalif about her family until after the birth of her two sons."[3]

IMPORTANT TERMS

Diaspora
Eretz Yisrael
Aliyah
Am ha'aretz, amei ha'aretz

---

[3] H. L. Ginsburg, *The Five Megilloth and Jonah: A New Translation*, Philadelphia: Jewish Publication Society, 1969, p. 86.

Names, Places, and Events

Assyria	Zedekiah
Babylonia	Lamentations
Samaria	Ezekiel
Samaritans	Ezra
Sargon	Nehemiah
Hezekiah	Jeremiah
Sennacherib	Cyrus
Josiah	Haggai
Manasseh	Zechariah
Chronicles	Malachi
Kings	Ezra
Hilkiah	Zerubbabel
Shaphan	Persia
Huldah	Elephantine
Nebuchadnezzar	

DISCUSSION QUESTIONS

George Santanaya said, "Those who do not learn from history are doomed to repeat it." Do you agree with this quote? How does it relate to the events preceding the exile of the Southern Kingdom? How does the relationship between the Jewish people and God change when not all the Jews live in the Promised Land?

ACTIVITIES

Debate: Should We Return? (S, A)
Assign your students to form two groups: a group that plans to follow Ezra and Nehemiah to resettle in Judah, and a group that plans to remain behind in Babylonia. Have each group develop the arguments for their decision, and then stage a debate.

Arguments could include the following factors: The *aliyah* group can share religious reasons; the chance for poor immigrants to have new opportunities; or the desire to reclaim family lands. Those remaining in Babylonia can share their desire to hold on to family businesses, lands, and wealth acquired during the exile; the quality of religious life in the Diaspora; or the hardships of moving to a land plagued by famine, drought, and conflicts with the Samaritan neighbors.

Esther versus Hadassah (S, A)

Have students read the Book of Esther, specifically to pull out details of Jewish life in the Persian Diaspora. What was it like? What were the religious and cultural challenges of the Jewish community? What opportunities did Jews have? What limitations or difficulties did they experience?

Experiential Text Study: The Book of Lamentations (S, A)

Traditionally, the Book of Lamentations is read on the evening and then again in the morning of Tisha B'Av, the ninth day of the Hebrew month of Av, the date when the destruction of the Temple is thought to have taken place. When read on Tisha B'Av, many communities chant the book out loud in a keening voice and sit on the floor in a darkened room as if in mourning.

Assign students to read different chapters of Lamentations, in pairs or in small groups. Have students imagine what it must have been like to live during the time of the siege of Jerusalem. Ask the groups of students to present either a dramatic reading or a skit based on the chapter that they read. If this activity is being done in the summertime around the time of Tisha B'Av, you may want to ask the rabbi of your congregation to consider allowing the students to participate in worship services for this commemoration.

TIMELINE

Because of the difficulty of accurate dating during the early biblical period, dates are approximate.

722 BCE

Fall of the Northern Kingdom to Assyria; exile of the "ten lost tribes"

701 BCE

Siege of Jerusalem by Assyria; failed

597 BCE

Siege of Jerusalem by Babylonia; resulted in a Babylonian-supervised government in Judea

586 BCE

Fall of the Southern Kingdom to Babylonia; exile of the leaders of the Judean community

538 BCE

Cyrus, King of Persia, decrees that the Jews may return to Judah

515 BCE

Dedication of the Second Temple in Jerusalem

458 BCE

Ezra the Scribe organizes a mass *aliyah* of Jews to Judea and becomes their leader along with Neḥemiah

RESOURCES

Books and Articles

Barnavi, Eli, ed. *Historical Atlas of the Jewish People: From the Time of the Patriarchs to the Present.* New York: Schocken Books, 1992.

Bright, John. *A History of Israel,* 3rd ed. Philadelphia: The Westminster Press, 1981.

Gordon, Cyrus H., and Gary A. Rendsburg. *The Bible and the Ancient Near East.* New York: W. W. Norton, 1997.

Grun, Bernard. *The Timetables of History: A Horizontal Linkage of People and Events.* New York: Simon & Schuster, 1979.

Pasachoff, Naomi, and Robert J. Littman. *Jewish History in 100 Nutshells.* Northvale, NJ: Jason Aronson, 1995.

The Rabbinical Assembly and The United Synagogue of Conservative Judaism. *Etz Hayim Torah and Commentary.* Philadelphia: Jewish Publication Society, 2001.

Sarna, Jonathan D., and Jonathan B. Krasner. *The History of the Jewish People: A Story of Tradition and Change.* Springfield, NJ: Behrman House, 2006 (see especially pp. 16–20).

Scherman, Nosson, ed. *The Stone Edition Tanach.* Brooklyn, NY: Mesorah Publications, 1996.

Internet

Visit www.behrmanhouse.com/booklinks for links to Web sites that offer additional resources for this chapter.

CHAPTER EIGHT
HELLENISM AND HASMONEANS

WHAT'S THE BIG IDEA?
Acculturation and Assimilation

Which word should come first in the title of this chapter: Hellenism or Hasmoneans?[1] This question illustrates the tension between acculturation (the ability to blend or borrow certain aspects of one's own tradition and culture with those of another community) and assim-ilation (becoming entirely absorbed in that alternative culture to the point where one loses one's own). These tensions permeate Jewish life in today's modern world, and they were no less a factor in Israel during the Second Temple period.

BACKGROUND INFORMATION
Israel under the Persian Empire

At its height around 500 BCE, the Persian Empire stretched from modern-day Bulgaria to Afghanistan, controlling all the land in between as well as trade routes and waterways including parts of the Mediterranean, Black and Caspian Seas, the Persian Gulf, and the Gulf of Oman. Within this massive structure stood the tiny outpost of Judah, a quiet province near the edge of the empire. Judah, like all other Persian provinces, was administered by a *satrap*, or governor, who was in charge of collecting taxes and conscripting soldiers for the imperial army. Within this framework, the people of Judah enjoyed a period of relative peace and economic stability marked by religious reform and literary advances (the Book of Chronicles, for example, was probably composed in

approximately the year 400 BCE). Changes loomed, however, as the Persian Empire fell into decline and Judah found itself under the control of the Hellenistic empire headed by Alexander the Great.

The Rise of Hellenism

In 336, after the assassination of Philip of Macedon, his son Alexander III—known as Alexander the Great—assumed leadership of Macedonia (incorporating parts of modern-day Bulgaria, Greece, and Turkey) and began a military campaign against the Persian Empire. Within three short years, Alexander the Great and his army had conquered all of Persia, including the province of Judah.

Alexander differed from many of his predecessors in his approach to ruling conquered peoples. Unlike the former Persian rulers, who believed that the strength of the empire lay in allowing conquered territories to retain their own religions and cultures, Alexander sought to impose his own culture—Hellenism—on the various groups under his control. Although Alexander died in 323 BCE at the age of thirty-three, the influence of this cultural mandate survived him for hundreds of years.

After Alexander's death, his generals—most notably Seleucus and Ptolemy—fought for control of the Greek Empire. Because no one general was strong enough to gain complete control, the empire of Alexander the Great was split into more than a dozen different territories, of which the most

---

[1] Another name for the family of the Maccabees, to be explained later in this chapter.

important were the Seleucid Kingdom in the Near East (including Syria and the territory of Judah), the Ptolemaic Kingdom in Egypt, and the Kingdom of Greece and Macedon. These ruling powers continued Alexander's practice of imposing Hellenism—an all-encompassing Greek culture including elements of language, religion, athletics, philosophy, and other disciplines—on the people under their control.

On the positive side, Hellenism brought with it the opportunity for many cultural advances. The translation of the Bible into Greek—known as the Septuagint (based on the Greek word for "seventy," in homage to the seventy elders the tradition says concurred exactly regarding the trans-lation)—allowed it to be disseminated much more widely in the Diaspora community than before. Centuries later, Philo of Alexandria incorporated the Greek model of philosophy into his writings while advocating Jewish traditional practices and modeling them in his personal life. Economic advances were made as well, including the extension of trade routes throughout the kingdom. Hellenized Jews living in the Greek Diaspora could live a secular lifestyle and still participate in Jewish ritual life by sending money to the Temple in Jerusalem and observing holidays locally. In Judah, however, these opportunities for assimilation and acculturation also became the flash point for a civil war that threatened the very fabric of Judean society.

Social Unrest in Judah

During the course of the third and fourth centuries BCE, the province of Judah bounced back and forth between Seleucid and Ptolemaic control, which wasn't entirely a bad thing. The Ptolemies considered Judah to be "the land of the Jews" and allowed a fair degree of independence in the government and religious affairs of the province, as long as the Judeans paid their taxes. Even the Syrian Greeks began their rule of Judah in a friendly manner, reducing the tax burden and elevating the status of Jewish law. In the year 200 BCE, the Seleucid emperor Antiochus succeeded in achieving complete control of the area. By 188 BCE, the cordial relationship between Syria and Judah had changed, and with Seleucid control came a challenge to the centuries-old dominance of Hebrew language and Jewish religion in the Land of Israel.

A series of conflicts stemming from this challenge began brewing among the leadership and population of Judah. Those who were firmly in the camp of the traditional Jews sought to maintain the culture, language, and religion that had been in place for hundreds of years. They opposed the Jewish Hellenizers who sought to incorporate various aspects of Greek culture, often including some contrary to Jewish law.

For example, Greek sports contests were conducted in the nude and required participants to be uncircumcised. Hellenizers, including Jews, often promoted the supremacy of Greek literature to the exclusion of Jewish sacred texts, and changes in worship to include reverence of Greek gods. They also chose Greek names, dressed in the Greek manner, and spoke in Greek—both in Judah and in the growing Diaspora.

The conflict was deepened by the fact that it was most often split among socio-economic lines. The Jewish leadership, including many of the priests, was firmly in the camp of the Hellenizers and encouraged pagan observances, a fact borne out by the text of the book of I Maccabees. Much of the populace, however, opposed this type of Hellenism and attempted to maintain traditional Jewish practices, even in increasingly adverse conditions. In fact, a close reading of I and II Maccabees—historical books from the biblical period—seem to prove that this civil unrest *preceded* the struggles between the Seleucid Greek authorities and the Judean populace.

The Maccabean Revolt

The growing civil unrest between the Hellenistic Jews and the traditionalists was highlighted by the fact that many of the Hellenists seemed to side with the Greek political authorities. The situation reached a boiling point in the year 167 BCE. The Greek ruler Antiochus IV—enraged by a challenge to his authority posed by the deposed High Priest Jason (removed from power by Antiochus and replaced by a puppet named Meneleus)—sought to reestablish control and to punish the Jewish populace for siding with Jason against Antiochus's authority. The emperor passed decrees forbidding the practice of the Jewish religion, including observing the Sabbath, practicing circumcision, studying Torah, and observing the dietary laws.

Adding insult to injury, the priests in Jerusalem, loyal to the Greeks, looked the other way as the decrees came down. As a final blow, Antiochus sent his soldiers to the town of Modi'in (between modern-day Tel Aviv and Jerusalem) in order to force the Jews there to sacrifice pigs. When faced with this order, a local priest named Mattathias not only refused, but also killed both the Jew who agreed to perform the sacrifice and the king's commissioner who had given the order. According to I Maccabees 2:27, Mattathias then ran through the town, shouting at the top of his lungs, "Let everyone who has a fervor for the Law and stands for the Covenant come out and follow me!"

Mattathias was joined by his sons and an increasingly large number of traditional Jews known as Hasidim, or the "devout." During the next three years, under the leadership of Mattathias's son Judah, this band became known as the Maccabees (an obscure name, sometimes connected with the Hebrew *makevet,* meaning "hammer"). They fought valiantly against the Greeks. Employing methods of guerrilla warfare, mustering in the caves of the Judean hills and winning the support of much of the populace, they won many decisive victories and regained control of Jerusalem.

The death of Antiochus in 164 BCE gave Judah the opening he needed to mount an attack against the Greek army in Jerusalem. In December of that year, Judah Maccabee and his troops conquered the city of Jerusalem, destroyed the pagan altars built by Antiochus, and purified and rededicated the Temple, which had been desecrated by the Seleucid ruler and his troops earlier in the campaign. The holiday of Hanukkah, which literally means "dedication," commemorates this victory.

The Sovereign State of Judah

Peace lasted for only two years, until 162 BCE, when Demetrius I of Macedon attacked Jerusalem. The Judean army, still under the direction of Judah Maccabee, continued to fight and to attempt to negotiate peace treaties as well. Upon his death in 160 BCE, Judah's brothers Simon and Jonathan took up the cause. It wasn't until 141 BCE that the Judean army finally succeeded in crushing its enemies, ushering in a period of sovereignty. The Hasmoneans, the official family name of the Maccabees, functioned as the military, political, and religious leaders of Judah until 63 BCE, when the Roman general Pompey conquered Jerusalem, killing twelve thousand people in the process.

Even during this period of sovereignty, however, civil unrest continued. Although the Hasmoneans had won the war, conflict still raged between traditionalists and Hellenizers. In addition, two groups of Jewish religious authorities—the Pharisees (primarily populist leaders who sought new interpretations of the tradition) and the Sadducees (largely priests who sought to retain control of the interpretation and enforcement of Jewish law based on a literal reading of the Torah)—began to wrangle over how Judaism should be practiced in this new age.

The Pharisees fell from favor with the Hasmonean leadership, who were also fighting among themselves for control. Furthermore, although most believed that having a sovereign state was a good thing and that Roman rule should be avoided, many factions arose among those who opposed Roman rule based on nationalistic or messianic reasons, and those who opposed it on religious grounds. Numerous religious sects formed with adherents who were ascetic separatists, such as the Qumran community (the group thought to have written or at least preserved the Dead Sea Scrolls) and the Essenes. All in all, this extreme lack of unity was a formula for disaster that came to a head in 63 BCE when the Romans finally took control, putting an end to an independent Jewish state for the next two thousand years.

CONNECTING TO OUR TRADITION: HISTORY AND THE HANUKKAH STORY

The explanation above is primarily an historical one, looking at the political, social, and military reasons why the Hasmoneans succeeded and then failed. Such an explanation, however, doesn't fully take into consideration what many believe is the real reason for the Jewish victory over the great and powerful Greek army—that God was on their side.

Several traditional texts deal with the reasons for victory, as well as the "miracle of the oil"—a rabbinic explanation for both the length of the holiday and the design of the ḥanukkiah, or Hanukkah menorah.

The Talmud devotes only a few sentences to this explanation, which may indicate either that it was a late interpretation for the duration of the holiday, or that it was so ingrained already that the rabbis of the Talmud didn't need to explain it at great length. The text reads:

When the Greeks entered the Temple, they defiled all the oil that was there; when the Hasmonean dynasty prevailed and defeated them, they looked and found only one jar of oil carrying the seal of the High Priest, containing enough oil for only one day. A miracle occurred, and they were able to use the oil to light the menorah for eight days. The following year they established these days as a festival, with Hallel [prayers] and thanksgiving (Tractate Shabbat 21b).

Later prayers inserted in the Grace after Meals as well as the Amidah prayer for Hanukkah thank God for "the miracles, the deliverance, the mighty acts, and the triumphant victories which God wrought for our fathers in ancient days." The miracle is described primarily as the delivery of "the many into the hands of the few" and focuses on God's deliverance of Israel and the rededication of the Temple as a sanctification of God's name and the impetus for the eight-day festival.

Both uncanonical works, I and II Maccabees describe the conflict between the traditionalists and the Hellenizers as well as that with Antiochus and his troops. I Maccabees, chapter 4, gives a detailed account of the triumph of the Maccabean army over the Greeks, as well as a description of the rededication of the Temple (based in part on Solomon's original dedication of the First Temple as recorded in I Kings, chapter 8), and the mandate that the festival is to be celebrated every year for eight days. Both books seem to suggest that the reason for the festival is a dedication of the Temple, as well as a celebration of the military victory. The information in these books, moreover, seems to agree with that in the religious texts mentioned above.

One final, very intriguing possibility is that Ḥanukkah is eight days long because the holidays of Sukkot (a seven-day harvest festival) and Shemini Atzeret (literally, the "eighth day of assembly," a final holy day celebrated immediately after the completion of Sukkot) were "skipped" in 164 BCE due to the intense fighting in the fall. II Maccabees, chapter 10, relates:

They celebrated it for eight days with gladness like Sukkot and recalled how a little while before, during Sukkot, they had been wandering in the mountains and caverns like wild animals. So carrying *lulavim* [palm branches waved on Sukkot] . . . they offered hymns of praise [perhaps the Hallel prayer] to God who had brought to pass the purification of God's own place (II Maccabees 10:6–7).

DID YOU KNOW?

- The Books of the Maccabees, the main historical source for the period discussed above, are not included in the Tanach, or Hebrew Bible. They are part of a collection of literature called the Apocrypha, or "hidden" books. Written mostly in Greek rather than Hebrew, the Books of the Maccabees, as well as other apocryphal literature such as the Books of Judith and Tobit, were incorporated into the Vulgate (Latin Bible) and are found today in the Catholic Bible.

- Judah's only queen to rule independently of any man was Salome Alexandra (Shlom-tzion in Hebrew, meaning "Peace of Zion," a fitting name). Reigning from 76 to 67 BCE, following the death of her husband Alexander Yannai, Queen Salome ushered in a period of peace and prosperity. A supporter of the Pharisees (the new populist religious leaders) and of public education (her brother Shimon ben Shetach instituted a system of free public schools), Queen Salome helped Judah become a thriving international metropolis unmarred by military strife. Her death marked the end of this period of tranquility, and the ensuing civil war between her sons only helped the Romans to gain control of the region.

IMPORTANT TERMS

Hellenism
I and II Maccabees
Apocrypha
Ḥanukkah
Ḥanukkiah
Satrap
Book of Chronicles

Names, Places, and Events

Persia	Judah Maccabee
Seleucids	Demetrius I
Ptolemies	Pharisees
Philip of Macedon	Sadducees
Alexander the Great	Qumran
Antiochus	Dead Sea Scrolls
Maccabees	Essenes
Jason	Hasmoneans
Meneleus	Salome Alexandra
Mattathias	Pompey

DISCUSSION QUESTIONS

- What's more important—to blend in with the surrounding culture or to maintain your own traditions that are different from everyone else's? Is it possible to do both equally well? Why or why not?
- It seems that in ancient Israel, it was much more difficult to keep foreign powers out when the Israelites themselves disagreed about government and religion. Why do you think this is? How do you see this dynamic in modern-day Israel?
- Many Jews living in the Diaspora during the time of the Maccabees still maintained their connections to Judah and to the Temple by contributing money and visiting occasionally for festivals while living a Greek lifestyle in other surrounding countries such as Greece and Egypt. How important is it for you and your family to maintain a connection to the modern State of Israel while living in a secular country across the world? What are the ways in which you can maintain that connection?

ACTIVITIES

Debate: Who's Right? (S)

Assign students to two groups: those who sympathize with the Hellenizers, want to see Greek culture reign supreme, and are happy to be ruled by the Syrian Greeks, and those who sympathize with the Hasmoneans, want Jewish religious law to reign supreme, and want to kick the Syrian Greeks out of Judah. Have them focus on the question of which way Judah would be better off. (Advanced: Have students use the texts found in I and II Maccabees to bolster their arguments.)

History Repeating Itself (S, A)

Assign students to compare the texts in I and II Maccabees concerning the rededication of the Temple during the time of the Hasmoneans with the original account in I Kings 8 about the dedication of the First Temple by King Solomon. How are they similar? How are they different?

As a follow-up activity, have students stage a play in several acts focusing on the rededication of the Temple in the Ḥanukkah story. Different groups can script their rededication according to the primary texts, for example, one group focuses on the Sukkot connection and one on the miracle of the oil.

Character Interview (E, S)

Invite Antiochus to come to your classroom. Have students prepare questions ahead of time, focusing both on Antiochus's strategy with regard to suppressing Jewish culture and his loss in the battle. (One of the goals of this activity is to help students better understand the mind-set of anti-Semitic rulers who want to squash Jewish culture and tradition. Antiochus is one of many in a long line leading up to modern times.)

Alternatively, invite Judah Maccabee or Mattathias to your classroom. Students' questions should focus on their motivation for standing up as they did to preserve Jewish independence and culture, with the goal of reaffirming students' positive Jewish identity.

You're the Author (E, S, A)

Assign students to write an original prayer, poem, or song for Ḥanukkah, focusing on the aspects of the holiday most meaningful to them.

Follow-up activity: Students can present their original work at a family program, assembly, or display for the holiday.

TIMELINE

332 BCE

Alexander the Great conquers all
of Persia

323 BCE

Alexander dies

250 BCE

King Ptolemy II orders the Greek
translation of the Bible, known as
the Septuagint

175 BCE

Antiochus IV becomes king

169 BCE

Antiochus IV invades Jerusalem

167 BCE

Beginning of the Maccabean
revolt

164 BCE

Death of Antiochus; Judah
Maccabee and his army defeat the
Greeks and rededicate the Temple

141 BCE

Hasmoneans gain complete control
of a sovereign Judah

76 BCE

Death of King Alexander Yannai;
his widow, Salome Alexandra,
rules Judea

67 BCE

Death of Salome Alexandra;
beginning of a civil war between
her sons Hyrcanus II and
Aristobulus II for control

63 BCE

Pompey conquers Jerusalem

RESOURCES
Books and Articles

Barnavi, Eli, ed. *Historical Atlas of the Jewish People: From the Time of the Patriarchs to the Present.* New York: Schocken Books, 1992.

Gilbert, Martin. *The Routledge Atlas of Jewish History,* 6th ed. London: Routledge, 1995.

Grun, Bernard. *The Timetables of History: A Horizontal Linkage of People and Events.* New York: Simon & Schuster, 1979.

Pasachoff, Naomi, and Robert J. Littman. *Jewish History in 100 Nutshells.* Northvale, NJ: Jason Aronson, 1995.

Sarna, Jonathan D., and Jonathan B. Krasner. *The History of the Jewish People: A Story of Tradition and Change.* Springfield, NJ: Behrman House, 2006 (see especially pp. 16–27).

Internet

Visit www.behrmanhouse.com/booklinks for links to Web sites that offer additional resources for this chapter.

Rabbinic Period

CHAPTER NINE

END OF AN ERA: THE LAST YEARS OF THE SECOND TEMPLE PERIOD

WHAT'S THE BIG IDEA?

Choosing one "big idea" for this time period is difficult, because it is such a transitional century in our people's history—perhaps the most critical until the present in determining how Judaism was ultimately shaped.

The big ideas for this period are:

Diaspora and Building Community

At the end of the Second Temple period, a large portion of the Jewish population was exiled from the Holy Land, with no real possibility of returning. Jews spread far and wide, and ultimately joined or created communities in the Diaspora in order to maintain their identity, traditions, and way of life.

Jewish Culture and Thought

The century before the destruction of the Second Temple was one in which Jewish thinkers and religious leaders sought to incorporate some of the more palatable aspects of Hellenistic learning and philosophy, and to make Judaism more viable in a modern age. Several autonomous Jewish groups developed during this period, challenging the authority of the Temple priests and centuries-old practices. Issues raised by these groups changed Judaism forever, helping it to become adaptable in the face of adversity, and thus viable in the Diaspora.

BACKGROUND INFORMATION
The Roman Period

As mentioned in the previous chapter, Judah's independence as a sovereign nation came to an end in 63 BCE when the Roman general Pompey, as part of a larger regional expansion, conquered Jerusalem and killed twelve thousand people in the taking of the city. Pompey appointed a member of the Hasmonean royal family, Hyrcanus II, as High Priest (but not as king) and cemented Roman domination over the region. During the next two-and-a-half decades, things went from bad to worse as the Temple treasury was raided by the Roman general Crassus, and Hyrcanus II was defeated by the Hasmonean king Antigonus. Finally, in 37 BCE, the Romans recaptured Jerusalem and beheaded Antigonus, and the Roman Senate proclaimed Herod the Great king of Judah.

Herod

Herod, a Galilean leader with some Jewish ancestry whose father, Antipater, had been a Roman governor and closely allied with Julius Caesar, was an inspired builder, a cultural giant, a brilliant politician, and cruel beyond belief. Herod insinuated himself with the Hasmonean family by marrying Mariamne, the granddaughter of Hyrcanus II (who was himself involved in a power struggle with Antigonus II) in order to lay claim to the Hasmonean throne. His building programs were monumental, surpassing even those of King Solomon, and included palaces, aqueducts built with new technology, new cities, and a restoration and expansion of the Temple in Jerusalem. Culturally, Herod surrounded himself with scholars, musicians, poets, and athletes, yet maintained his observance of Jewish religious practices.

Herod's political finesse was evident through the juggling of these different roles, his firm alliance with Rome (switching allegiances from leader to leader as was politically expedient), and his disparaging of the role of the High Priest (thus minimizing the power of that office).

Herod had a dark side, however. Although it was common for many rulers in the ancient world to kill the relatives most likely to plot against them and challenge their authority, Herod surpassed even the most vicious. Upon gaining the throne, he murdered the children of Caesar, Mark Antony, and Cleopatra so that none could grow up to challenge his reign and claim the throne. He then killed forty-five members of the Sanhedrin who had supported the Hasmoneans against him, his brother-in-law Aristobulus (also a Hasmonean), his wife's grandfather and former king Hyrcanus II, his mother-in-law Alexandra, his wife Mariamne, and even his own sons. Two years after Herod's death of natural causes in 4 BCE, Judea had become firmly established as a Roman province.

The Pharisees and the Sadducees

At the same time that Judea was undergoing political upheaval, its religious life was also in flux. Although many different Jewish groups coexisted at that time (similar to our own), two distinct sects stand out: the Sadducees and the Pharisees.

The Sadducees, who held the roles of the priests and guardians of the Temple in Jerusalem, were named as a group after Zadok, the High Priest at the time of King David. In general, the Sadducees were wealthy men of power and influence who not only controlled the Temple and its sacrifices, but the Sanhedrin (religious court) as well. As biblical literalists, the Sadducees sought to enforce the rules and regulations of the Torah as they were written, without much additional interpretation. As the ruling body of the Temple, they viewed themselves as closest to God, whose spirit resided within the Temple's walls.

Although the Sadducees had been around as a group for hundreds of years, the Pharisees were newcomers to the religious scene in the second century BCE. Most likely, the Pharisees took their name from the Hebrew word *parash*, which means "separated" (either from the Sadducees, or those who were deemed impure, or both). The Pharisees saw themselves as the spiritual descendants of those who had kept the Jewish community in the Diaspora flourishing by adapting the Torah to their changing reality, which included an inability to worship at the Temple in Jerusalem. They therefore approved of and facilitated a creative interpretation of the law to suit the times.

Another major motivating factor for the Pharisees was independence—both individual and communal. Thus, they helped to establish independent synagogues in various communities throughout Judea from at least the second century BCE, similar to those built throughout the Diaspora following the Babylonian exile. The Pharisees also placed a greater emphasis on literacy, which became increasingly widespread. Not surprisingly, these Pharisaic innovations put them at great odds with the ruling class of Sadducees. With the building of local synagogues, the Temple in Jerusalem was no longer the only place to pray, and the Sadducees feared a loss of stature as their services in overseeing sacrifices dwindled. With an increased emphasis on literacy, people could read the Torah for themselves (or with a local teacher), and the Sadducees feared a loss of power as their arbitration skills were needed less and less.

With the Pharisaic concept that God was everywhere, people no longer had to go to the Temple to access God's presence, and the Sadducees found themselves losing authority as individuals began coming to the Temple only for the Torah-mandated pilgrimage festivals, and less and less on other occasions. Thus, the Pharisees became viewed as populists, with the interests of the people at heart, while the Sadducees became increasingly viewed as elitists, with their own interests and those of the ruling class at heart. The strife caused by this religious rift became more and more pronounced as time went on.

The Jewish War
Along with the ongoing religious conflict among the Pharisees, Sadducees, and other groups too numerous to mention, was an ongoing political and military conflict that would prove to be disastrous to the Jews.

During the first century CE, the Romans had continued their quest for complete control of Judea and its population. Through a system of procurators, or governors, the Romans gained control not only of Judea in the south, but Galilee in the north as well. The Roman procurators harassed the people, collected exorbitant amounts of taxes—their incentive to do so was that they got to keep a percentage of the "take" as their salary—and even began looting the Temple for personal gain. In

fact, the revolt that resulted ultimately in the destruction of the Temple and the exile from Judea began with such an event.

In 66 CE, the Roman procurator Florus stole money from the Temple treasury. Incensed at this final "straw that the broke the camel's back," the Jews of Jerusalem rioted, and Florus responded by sending troops who looted the marketplace. A number of armed Jews were able to gain control of the Temple mount, and cut it off from the Roman garrison. During the next several months, hostilities continued not only between the Jews and the Romans, but between the Jewish moderates, who hoped to work with the emperor Agrippa II in restoring peace, and the Jewish extremists, who sought to get the Romans out of Judea once and for all.

Although there were several smaller groups of extremists, the most powerful were known as the Zealots. The Zealots agreed with much of the philosophy popular with the Pharisees. In addition, their focus on independence and freedom meant that they believed in God as their only master, and thus were ideologically opposed to Roman rule. They also found support among much of the general populace, who were fed up with what they viewed as the Sadducees' pandering to the Roman rulers and their focus on money and power instead of God, whose Temple they were running.

Full-scale revolt broke out in 66 CE, and within two years the Romans, under the leadership of Nero's great general, Vespasian, conquered the entire Galilee with the help of sixty thousand experienced Roman troops. It's also possible that Vespasian was helped in this matter by the general and historian Josephus, who may have turned traitor and handed over his garrison to the Romans in exchange for clemency.

After Vespasian was crowned emperor in 69 CE, his son Titus took over his command and led his troops to the conquering of Jerusalem in 70 CE. With four entire Roman legions under his command, Titus had little trouble sealing off the walled city from food, water, and outside reinforcements. With Jewish factions inside the city fighting each other and famine killing many of the rest (survivors subsisted on grass and straw), the city finally fell on the ninth day of Av (late July). The Romans burned the Temple to the ground and massacred thousands. It would be almost nineteen hundred years before Jerusalem was fully in Jewish hands again.

Masada

While the Romans were vanquishing Jerusalem, a small band of extremist Zealots managed to escape from the city and take refuge in the fortress on top of Masada, several miles to the south of Jerusalem. King Herod had fortified Masada during his reign a century earlier, and the Romans had placed a garrison there after Judea became a Roman province. The Zealots captured the fortress and began a three-year holdout against the Romans following the fall of Jerusalem. Between 72 and 73 CE, the Romans turned their attention to defeating the last stronghold of the Jewish war. Flavius Silva, the Roman governor, brought the 10th Legion along with thousands of Jewish prisoners of war to build the ramp (which still exists), siege wall, and towers that would enable the Romans to take Masada.

After sealing off the fortress to prevent supplies from getting up the mountains, similar to the strategy that the Romans used against Jerusalem, the Romans began their final assault in 73 CE by attacking the fortress with battering rams and catapults. Finally, they set the fortress on fire and stormed in wearing full armor, expecting a battle. According to Josephus's account in *The Jewish War*,

"they saw no enemy, but a terrible solitude on every side, and fire and perfect silence within the place, so they were at a loss to make out what had happened; and at last they raised a shout ... and two women heard this noise and came out of their underground cavern, and informed the Romans of what had been done . . . . "

According to Josephus, everyone save these two women had committed mass suicide under the direction of the Zealot leader, Eleazar ben Yair. And so, when the Roman troops stormed the fortress, they found the bodies of families lying together in the burnt-out palace of Masada. The final holdout against the Romans came sixty years later, at Betar. With the support of the famous scholar and leader Rabbi Akiva, a man named Simon bar Kosiba, whom Akiva and many others believed to be the Messiah, began a three-year rebellion against the Romans that lasted from 132 to135 CE.

Known as Bar Kochba (son of a star), this military leader led a revolt against the anti-Jewish policies of the Roman emperor Hadrian, which included the building of a pagan city on the ruins of the Second Temple in Jerusalem. The rebellion began in Judea and spread throughout the Diaspora. Although Bar Kochba experienced some early victories and indeed gained control of Jerusalem at one point, the Romans responded with decisive force.

Marching with twelve legions, the Romans squashed the rebellion in Judea so thoroughly that it is said that the Jordan River ran with the blood of the thousands slain in the massacre. The Roman historian Dio Cassius puts the number at over half a million. Bar Kochba was one of those slain, and tradition holds that the date of the massacre at Betar was the ninth of Av, the same as that of the destruction of both the First and Second Temples. Rabbi Akiva and his supporters were arrested and tortured; the accounts of that torture survive today in the martyrology section of the Yom Kippur liturgy. The Romans changed the name of Judea to Syria-Palestina, and the name of Jerusalem to Aelia Capitolina.

CONNECTING TO OUR TRADITION
Hillel and Shammai, Rabbi Yohanan and the Academy at Yavneh

Rabbinic tradition traces its inception back to forward-thinking scholars who lived around the time of the destruction of the Temple. The debates of the great rabbinic thinkers Hillel and Shammai and their students, for example, preserve the tradition of argument, discussion, and consensus that inform the development of Jewish law, or *halachah*. During the siege of Jerusalem, the great scholar Yohanan ben Zakkai sought to ensure the future of this type of Jewish study despite the impending destruction of the Temple and exile from Judea. According to various accounts in the Talmud, Yohanan ben Zakkai engineered his escape from within the walls of the besieged city by pretending to be dead: he had his students place him in a coffin with foul-smelling items, making the case to the Roman guard that they needed to take him outside the city walls for burial.

Once outside the walls of the city, ben Zakkai met up with the Roman general Vespasian. Ben Zakkai predicted that Vespasian would become emperor, and—according to the Talmud's account—word reached Vespasian at just that moment that the emperor had died and that he, Vespasian, was to report to Rome to be crowned emperor in his place. At that point, Vespasian gave ben Zakkai the proverbial "one wish," and ben Zakkai asked for the garrison town

of Yavneh (only a few miles away from Jerusalem) "and its sages," thereby ensuring the continuation of Torah study at the academy there, to which Vespasian acquiesced.

Over the next hundred years, the sages of Yavneh and their students in the Land of Israel oversaw several critical innovations. The primary achievement was the adaptation of Jewish rituals so that they were no longer dependent upon the existence of a Temple, giving Judaism the ability to thrive in the Diaspora. Another was the systematic development and codification of *halachah* (Jewish law) in the Mishnah—which we will explore in the next chapter—giving it a series of explanations and practical applications. These developments helped to coalesce the various sects and factions of Jewish survivors into one group, something that was impossible when they were fighting during the decades before and during the destruction of Jerusalem. This unification of these various groups enabled people to see "the rabbis" as the "go-to group" for interpretation of Jewish law and practice, a totally new innovation. These achievements, created in one of the most stressful times in Jewish history, have helped Judaism survive and thrive until the present day.

DID YOU KNOW?

The Tanach, or Jewish Bible, was "closed" at Yavneh. Discussions of the books of the Bible included deciding which were "in" (those that we have today in the Five Books of Moses, the Prophets, and the Writings) and those that were "out" (which we call the "Apocrypha" or hidden works, including the Books of Maccabees).

After this period, all Jewish bibles since—in whatever translation they may appear—have the same number of biblical books, in the same order. The Dead Sea Scrolls, discovered in 1947 by a teenage shepherd, contain portions of every biblical book except the Book of Esther.

IMPORTANT TERMS

Pharisees
Sadducees
Sanhedrin
Procurator
Garrison
Legion
Zealots

Sicarii
Mishnah
Pirkei Avot/Ethics
  of the Fathers
Talmud
Tanach
Apocrypha

Names, Places, and Events

Pompey
Hyrcanus II
Antigonus I
Antigonus II
Herod
Mariamne
Caesar
Mark Antony
Cleopatra
Aristobulus
Alexandra
Zadok
Florus
Nero

Vespasian
Titus
Flavius Silva
Josephus
Hillel
Shammai
Yohanan ben Zakkai
Eleazar ben Yair
Masada
Rabbi Akiva
Bar Kochba/
  Simon bar Kosiba
Hadrian
Dio Cassius

DISCUSSION QUESTIONS

In 68 CE and in 132 CE, many Jews revolted against their Roman conquerors while others believed that fighting the Romans was a mistake. In both instances, the revolts lasted for a few years and then were squashed by the mighty Roman army, resulting in widespread persecution and loss of life. Do you think that the Jews should have revolted? Why or why not? Can you think of modern-day examples of people revolting against a conquering army to ensure that their own way of life survives?

ACTIVITIES

You Are the Detective (S, A)

Assign students to read Josephus's account of what happened on Masada. Ask them: What do you think happened? Was it right for the Jews to commit suicide rather than be subjected to slavery by the Romans? What do you think was

Josephus's goal in telling the story the way he did? Did he succeed in this goal?

Cabinet Advisers: Rabbi Yohanan and the Emperor (S)

Have students become Rabbi Yohanan's advisers as he gets ready for his meeting with the emperor. Discuss: What are you going to ask for? (The Temple to be spared? An academy for Jewish learning at Yavneh? A position in the Roman Court?) Have students come up with good arguments for each to advise Rabbi Yohanan.

TIMELINE

63 BCE
    Pompey conquers Jerusalem
37–4 BCE
    Reign of King Herod
70 CE
    Destruction of the Temple
73 CE
    Masada
135 CE
    Betar

RESOURCES
Books and Articles

Barnavi, Eli, ed. *Historical Atlas of the Jewish People: From the Time of the Patriarchs to the Present.* New York: Schocken Books, 1992.

Gilbert, Martin. *The Routledge Atlas of Jewish History,* 6th ed. London: Routledge, 1995.

Vermes, Geza. *The Complete Dead Sea Scrolls in English.* London: Penguin, 2004.

Williams, G. A., trans. *The Jewish War by Flavius Josephus.* New York: Dorset Press, 1985.

Internet

Visit www.behrmanhouse.com/booklinks for links to Web sites that offer additional resources for this chapter.

CHAPTER TEN
THE RABBINIC PERIOD

WHAT'S THE BIG IDEA?
Covenant
The truth is that all our "big ideas"—Diaspora, acculturation, assimilation, building community, Jewish culture and thought, and covenant—are pertinent to a discussion of this watershed period in Jewish history. However, by looking at the rabbinic period from the "inside"—from the mind-set of the rabbis themselves—it is clear that *their* main concern was the Jewish people's covenant with God. To answer the question "What does God want from us?" the rabbis who lived in the years immediately following the destruction of the Temple crafted an ingenious system of Jewish law and literature. Transcending time and place and becoming almost universal, this system was truly a great achievement for their day and ours.

BACKGROUND INFORMATION
The crowning achievements of the rabbis had their roots in the period of the Second Temple. A brief review of the previous chapter yields many building blocks needed to understand the rest of the rabbinic period. Once the Temple was destroyed and the Sadducees had ceased to function as the primary leaders of the Jewish people in their homeland, the Pharisees stepped into the breach. The Pharisees did two things: they took over the leadership so that the people had authority figures to look up to, and they unified (with increasing success) the vast majority of the remaining Jewish splinter groups. At some point during the late Second Temple period, individuals who taught and maintained the practice of Jewish law and system of Jewish thought became

known as "rabbis." The word "rabbi" means "my teacher," and teaching was, and continues to be, the primary function of most rabbis.

Teaching in the rabbinic sense, however, is more than simply delivering a lecture. When the classical rabbis taught, their mission was to engage their students—often other rabbis—in active discussions of the finer points of Jewish law, philosophy, customs, and history. As the great rabbinic "sparring team" of Hillel and Shammai proved, not only could the rabbis agree to disagree, they could still manage to craft laws that applied to everyone, at least in principle.

This type of dialectic—deciding what Jewish law and practice should be by learning and debate—was championed by Rabbi Yoḥanan ben Zakkai and the scholars at Yavneh, the academy founded on the outskirts of Jerusalem in 70 CE. The rabbis and scholars who continued the work of those at Yavneh created a formidable library of Jewish legal, spiritual, practical, and anecdotal material that is still studied and applied all over the world today. The two primary works of literature that comprise the core of this library are the Mishnah and the Talmud.

The Oral Law
It is not without irony that we refer to a library containing dozens, if not hundreds, of large bound volumes as "oral" rather than "written" law. This distinction stems from the rabbis' desire to make plain the difference between the Torah's status as Written Law and the rabbis' explanations as Oral Law. Before it

was written down, the Oral Law was in fact disseminated orally, through ongoing discussion among and between the rabbis of each generation. As such, it was also open to change and interpretation, although those interpretations are still seen by traditional Jews as having originated at the same time as the giving of the written Torah to Moses.

The Oral Law was written down in about the sixth century CE by rabbis and scholars who feared that as the Jewish population became even more dispersed throughout the world, often to areas lacking rabbinic leadership, the practice of Jewish law would become increasingly difficult to follow. They believed that a written record of the rabbis' discussions of how to observe the laws found in the Torah would ensure Judaism's survival even in remote communities. Thus, we still refer to the Mishnah and Talmud as the Oral Law, even though they are written works.

The Mishnah
The Mishnah, which has the dual meaning of "teaching" and "repetition," is divided into six "orders" that contain a systematic codification of the laws found in the Torah, along with anecdotal material describing Jewish practice. Like the Torah, the Mishnah is written in Hebrew, and was compiled in the Land of Israel. Edited in its final form in about 200 CE by Rabbi Yehudah Ha-Nasi ("the prince"), a descendant of the famous rabbi Hillel, the purpose of the Mishnah was twofold. First, the Mishnah sought to compile a clear record of the laws of the Torah so that they could be understood and followed by generations of Jews living without the benefit of a priesthood and a standing Temple in Jerusalem. Second, Rabbi Yehudah Ha-Nasi wished to preserve the arguments of the rabbis, including minority opinions, so that the methodology by which the Torah's laws

were explicated would be available to later generations. Although the Mishnah sought primarily to further the study and practice of Jewish law, Yehudah Ha-Nasi understood that dry lists of Torah laws, while important, might not be the best way to encourage people to connect with God. Therefore, the Mishnah includes anecdotal material, stories, references to other texts within the Torah, and other passages to help the reader personalize the material.

For example, one of the Mishnah's sections is called *Pirkei Avot,* or "Chapters of the Fathers" (sometimes translated as "Ethics of the Fathers"). This famous compilation of sayings by the rabbis on matters of everyday living is still relevant today. Containing such gems as Shammai's instruction to "make your Torah [study] a set priority; say little and do much and receive every person with a pleasant face," *Pirkei Avot* continues to be one of the most widely studied sections of rabbinic literature.

The Talmud
While the Mishnah did much to bring the understanding of the Torah to both scholars and the common people, the nature of the Mishnah as Oral Law meant that discussions about what it said continued for centuries after it was closed in 200 CE. These rabbinic discussions flourished in two main communities: Eretz Yisrael and Babylonia. When people today refer to the Talmud, they usually mean the Babylonian Talmud (sometimes referred to as the *Bavli*), which was completed about 500 CE in Babylonia, mainly at the prestigious rabbinic academies of Sura and Pumbeditha. The word Talmud literally means teaching. Its discussions follow a fairly consistent format: a law from the Mishnah is cited, followed by rabbinic deliberations on its meaning.

The sections following the Mishnah are called collectively the Gemara (literally, "completion" in Hebrew and "to learn" in Aramaic, the language of most of the Talmudic text), although the words Talmud and Gemara are often used interchangeably. The Talmud is written in a combination of Hebrew and Aramaic, the language of the Jewish people of the Near East at the time of its compilation. Rabbis whose views are cited in the Mishnah are known as *tannaim* (Hebrew for "teachers"), whereas the rabbis quoted in the Gemara are called *amoraim* (literally, "speakers"). Although living centuries apart, these teachers are often quoted side by side on a page of Talmud.

A page of Talmud can contain arguments, stories, and legal material that can be seemingly unrelated to the discussion at hand save for the "train of thought" of the rabbi being quoted. Many of the rabbinic teaching stories in the Talmud are referred to as "midrash" (explanation), and collections of midrashim (pl.) exist in separate books as well. In addition to extensive legal discussions (in Hebrew, *halachah,* or "way"), the rabbis incorporated into the Talmud guidance on ethical matters, medical advice, historical information, and folklore, which together are known as *aggadah* (literally "tale," a variation of the more familiar word "haggadah").

Although the Babylonian Talmud is considered to be the most authoritative version, an earlier edition of the Talmud was compiled in the Israel during the fifth century CE. Referred to as the Jerusalem Talmud or *Yerushalmi* (also called the Palestinian Talmud), this edition was finalized in approximately 425 CE in Tiberias.

Suffering from the triple stigmas of originating in Eretz Yisrael (which was viewed by much of world Jewry as a backwater in the fifth century), and coming almost a century before the more influential *Bavli*, and being less well edited (and thus more difficult to navigate), most Talmudic scholars have focused on the *Bavli* rather than on the *Yerushalmi*. More recently, however, some have begun to study this little-known work, which provides a window into the lives of Jews in the Land of Israel at the end of the Roman period.

Today, virtually all editions of the Talmud follow the format of the authoritative printed edition, first issued in Venice in the 1520s. The first page of a section of Talmud shows the Mishnah centered in the upper half of the middle column, followed by the Gemara. Surrounding the primary text are a wide variety of traditional commentaries, proving that even though the Talmud was closed in the sixth century, the door has remained open to further insights and interpretation ever since.

CONNECTING TO OUR TRADITION

Although our tradition places much emphasis on doing *mitzvot,* Torah study is seen to be just as critical. One of the passages recited by traditional Jews at the beginning of morning worship states:

"There are deeds from which one eats the fruit in this world and receives the principle in the next world, and they are: honoring one's father and mother, performing acts of loving-kindness, coming to the house of study on time in the morning and the evening, welcoming guests, visiting the sick, attending the bride . . . But the study of Torah is equal to them all" (Adapted from Tractate Shabbat 127a).

DID YOU KNOW?

It takes 2,711 days to read the entire Talmud at a rate of a page a day. All over the world, *daf yomi* (daily page) groups study one page of Talmud a day—in person, over the phone, and even on the Internet! Every seven-and-one-half years, those who have completed the cycle celebrate a *siyyum* (ceremony of completion). The first such celebration of the twenty-first century took place on Tuesday, March 1, 2005. Hundreds of thousands of people all over the world participated, filling arenas such as Madison Square Garden in New York City to capacity.

IMPORTANT TERMS

Mishnah	*Halachah*
Pirkei Avot	*Aggadah*
Talmud	*Amoraim*
Pharisees	*Tannaim*
Siyyum	*Bavli*
Gemara	*Yerushalmi*
	Daf yomi

Names, Places, and Events

Hillel	Tiberias
Shammai	Babylonia
Yoḥanan ben Zakkai	Sura
Yavneh	Pumbeditha

DISCUSSION QUESTION

Originally a spoken record of conversations (and hence termed the "Oral Law"), rabbinic literature was eventually written down in order to save it and make it accessible to people throughout the world. How does writing something down preserve *and* change it?

ACTIVITIES

Siyyum (E, S, A)

Upon completing a course of study (a book of Torah, ten centuries of Jewish history), have your class plan a *siyyum* party. Research what components go into a traditional *siyyum* (they include a public reading of the last piece of text, prayers, and a festive meal). Invite others—parents and siblings, the entire school or congregation—and have a party to celebrate your accomplishment!

Oral versus Written Law (E, S, A)

Decide on a topic relevant to your class that needs further clarification and legislation, such as rules for homework or class conduct. Divide the class into two groups. In one group, have the students discuss the issues and come to conclusions *without writing down* any of their discussions. In the other group, have them provide a written record. Invite representatives of the groups to share with the class. What's similar in the presentations? What's different? Which leaves more room for debate?

TIMELINE

c. 50 BCE –30 CE
  Shammai active
c. 10 BCE –10 CE
  Hillel active
70 CE
  Destruction of the Temple and creation of the Academy in Yavneh
200 CE
  Redaction of the Mishnah by Rabbi Yehudah Ha-Nasi
425 CE
  Redaction of the Jerusalem Talmud
500 CE
  Redaction of the Babylonian Talmud

RESOURCES
Books and Articles

Pasachoff, Naomi, and Robert J. Littman. *Jewish History in 100 Nutshells.* Northvale, NJ: Jason Aronson, 1995.

Sarna, Jonathan D., and Jonathan B. Krasner. *The History of the Jewish People: A Story of Tradition and Change.* Springfield, NJ: Behrman House, 2006.

Internet

Visit www.behrmanhouse.com/booklinks for links to Web sites that offer additional resources for this chapter.

CHAPTER ELEVEN
THE GREATER JEWISH DIASPORA

WHAT'S THE BIG IDEA?
Diaspora

Aside from a small community still living in the Land of Israel, by the end of the rabbinic period most Jews were spread throughout the world. A primary goal of Diaspora Jewry was maintaining their identity and sense of community wherever they settled. However, Diaspora Jewish communities didn't exist in a bubble— they existed within a variety of established surrounding gentile cultures. Over time, Jewish families incorporated local customs and cultural aspects that didn't interfere with their ability to practice Judaism, and often contributed to the surrounding culture as well. Therefore, when we speak of "Jewish culture," we really need to think in terms of *many* Jewish cultures.

BACKGROUND INFORMATION

The Jewish Diaspora actually began in the eighth century BCE when the Assyrians conquered the Northern Kingdom and the ten "lost" tribes were exiled throughout the Near East. By the time of the Babylonian Exile in the year 586 BCE, Jewish communities were already established in Babylon and Egypt. For centuries under the Persians, the Greeks, and the Romans, Jews had the opportunity to move and settle throughout the region. In fact, the Romans recognized Judaism as one of the official religions of the Roman Empire.

The Assyrian, Babylonian, Persian, Greek, and Roman Empires covered vast swaths of land that would (on today's globe) span dozens of countries on three continents. Many difficulties often accompanied the Jews' exile throughout these enormous territories, such as the relocation to new places without the comforts of home, family, and possessions, and the necessity of leaving behind businesses and land.

However, a number of advantages became clear as well. First, the residents of many Jewish communities managed to stay in contact with one another, providing Jewish travelers with the ability to find lodging, synagogues, and business opportunities. Second, the network of rabbis made it possible for Jews in one community to send legal questions to rabbis in another, so as to better observe the mitzvot and follow in God's footsteps even while in exile. Although Jewish tradition taught that a period of exile—or *galut* in Hebrew—was punishment for sins against God and fellow human beings, Jews sought to practice their religion as best they could while awaiting the Messianic Age that would bring them back to the Holy Land.

Jews of the modern age are fortunate to have historical evidence of events that occurred during the Middle Ages, which helps us to better understand the challenges facing Diaspora Jews of the period. For example, records of rabbinic questions and answers, or responsa literature (in Hebrew, *sh'eilot u't'shuvot*), provide insight into the issues that were of utmost importance to these far-flung Jewish communities. Written records from these communities also provide critical information necessary to understanding the day-to-day life of Diaspora Jews. For example, an interesting text from the Council of Elvira (fourth-century Spain) warned Christians not to have Jewish priests (kohanim) bless their crops—a good indication that the practice was happening, and that the Jewish and gentile communities were integrated from a very early time.

A Word about the Jewish Community of Eretz Yisrael

While no one would think to refer to the Jews of the Land of Israel as though they lived in the Diaspora, in fact their community had much in common with Jewish communities dispersed throughout the world. For one thing, other nations and empires ruled the Land of Israel, as they ruled over Jewish communities outside the Land.

Although the Jews were denied self-rule in their own land, small groups of Jews always continued to live in Eretz Yisrael during the era between the end of the Second Temple period and the establishment of the State of Israel in 1948. During the rabbinic period, the Jewish community's leader in Israel was called the patriarch, a religious and political leader descended from the family of Hillel. The last patriarch died in 425 CE, and the Romans abolished the office in 429 CE. As mentioned in the previous chapter, rabbis at academies in Eretz Yisrael completed their own version of the Talmud, and Israel remained an important part of Jewish consciousness.

Jewish culture in Israel developed and changed according to the empires that ruled it. So, for example, under Roman rule, Jews held their meals in the Roman fashion, reclining on couches whenever possible and referring to their dessert course as the "afikoman." Vestiges of these practices remain in our own Passover seder, which was scripted largely during the rabbinic period by rabbis living in Eretz Yisrael under Roman rule. In the Middle Ages when the Ottomans ruled the Land of Israel, Jewish buildings reflected Arabic architectural styles, and so on.

Babylonia

Jews had been living in the Babylonian Empire for hundreds of years prior to the destruction of the Second Temple in 70 CE. Author Solomon Grayzel estimates that the Jewish community numbered one million in 70 CE, and two million by the fifth century.[1] The community was so well established that many rabbinic texts reflect the view that Babylonia—with its wonderful culture, its rabbinic academies at Sura and Pumbeditha, and the lush orchards and gardens of the Fertile Crescent—was the true *Eretz Yisrael*, in essence if not in actuality.

Babylonian Jews were a welcome minority community in most of the empire. The Jewish community's leader, called the exilarch, was ushered into office with the pomp and circumstance befitting a monarch. Many rabbinic texts attest to the close relationship between the rabbinic elite and the empire's gentile rulers and wealthy laity. Jews in Babylonia earned their living by raising cattle, operating vineyards, engaging in commerce, performing manual labor, and farming (especially notable, since in other areas Jews were prohibited from owning land). A vibrant Jewish community remained in modern-day Iraq until 1949, when conditions became so poor that most moved to the new State of Israel.

---

[1] Solomon Grayzel, *A History of the Jews*, Signet, 1968, pp. 212ff.

North Africa

By the first century CE, over a million Jews were living in the metropolitan area of Alexandria, Egypt. Conquered by the same empires that overran Eretz Yisrael, Egypt boasted a large Jewish community for most of the late biblical period and for centuries afterward. Under the Greeks, Jewish scholars and elders undertook the task of translating the Bible into Greek. This translation was known as the Septuagint, from the word meaning "seventy" and referring to the seventy elders who by tradition came up with the exact same translation, even though each was separated from his counterparts.

In the political arena, Jews in Egypt waged their own revolt against the Romans in the year 115, but it was quickly quashed. Nevertheless, the community in Egypt and other parts of North Africa continued to flourish for centuries. In the Middle Ages, Jews fled from Christian Spain to North Africa because the Muslim rulers were seen to be more tolerant of Jews than their Catholic counterparts in Europe.

The Cairo *Geniza*

Today, we owe much of our knowledge of the Jewish communities of Egypt and the rest of North Africa to the discovery in the late nineteenth century of the Cairo *geniza*. The word *geniza* means "hiding place" (Hebrew) or "storehouse" (Persian), and the Cairo *geniza* was a large repository of documents stashed away in a synagogue of Fostat (Old Cairo) in Egypt. Traditionally, sacred Hebrew documents that are damaged or no longer needed have been buried in cemeteries or deposited in enclosed chambers such as the Cairo *geniza*. We know more about Egyptian Jewish society at this time than we do about any other Jewish community of the Middle Ages, thanks to the discovery by

the Conservative rabbi and scholar Solomon Schechter. Actually, the original discoveries were made by two Christian travelers who had gone to Egypt in 1896 and were sold ancient Jewish documents by a broker who told them that there were more to be had, for a price. Intrigued, they brought their findings to Solomon Schechter, who was at the time a professor of rabbinics and Hebrew literature at Cambridge University in England. Recognizing the documents as part of the Hebrew Book of Ben Sira, an ancient work that had survived until that time only in Greek translation, Schechter immediately traveled back to Egypt and began exploring the *geniza*. He brought about 100,000 documents back with him to Cambridge University in England, and more were later distributed among libraries and collections in Europe, North America, and the Middle East.

Although Jewish law dictates that sacred texts in Hebrew should be buried once damaged or no longer needed, documents far from sacred were found as well. Medieval shopping lists, divorce and marriage documents, business contracts, poetry, literature, and letters were found in the *geniza*—one amazing find was written and signed by Moses Maimonides himself. These treasures have revolutionized scholarly understanding of the region. Not only have we learned about Egyptian Jewish life, but about the lives of those from other countries bordering the Mediterranean Sea and along the trade route to India, from which some of the documents originated.

Europe

As mentioned above, Judaism was recognized as an official minority religion of the Roman Empire. As such, Jews were generally free to move about and settle within the confines of the empire, which stretched at its height from England, France and Spain in the west to Mesopotamia in the east, and all along the Mediterranean coastline. Jewish communities became established in the areas of modern-day France, Spain, Germany, Italy, Greece and elsewhere, with Jewish travelers and traders moving throughout the empire.

A Jewish settlement was established in Rome as early as the first century BCE, and the population increased when Roman generals, such as Pompey in 63 BCE, brought Judean captives back to Rome after conquering portions of the Holy Land. These same Jews, when freed from slavery, often went to southern Italy and Sicily, and many became merchants and agents of commerce because of their proximity to the sea-based trade routes. Historian Cecil Roth believes that during the Middle Ages, Jews played a preponderant part in Italian commerce and became the most serious rivals to the Catholic Italians involved in similar business ventures. Back in Rome, the Jewish population took part in the political and cultural life of the city; when Nero was emperor, the most noted actor in Rome was a Jew, and a Jew named Cecelius was one of the city's most outspoken literary critics.

As the Romans advanced west into the areas that are today France, Belgium, and Germany, Jews from Rome came to sell provisions to the soldiers and to establish settlements. These Jewish peddlers helped lay the commercial foundations of the new towns, even as the Roman soldiers were laying the physical foundations. Established as early as the first century CE, many of these towns became cities that remained vibrant throughout the Middle

Ages and some—such as Paris, Lyons, Cologne, and Mainz—had Jewish communities that flourished well into the modern period. In fact, a majority of Jews living in the western part of the world today have their roots in this region, known by Jews as Ashkenaz.

Perhaps the earliest Jewish settlements in Europe were those of the Iberian Peninsula. Jewish communities in Spain and Portugal claim roots going as far back as King Solomon. While unlikely, this assertion is far from impossible, because kings of the biblical period used the same trade routes as the Romans that their foreign trading partners did. And, as evidenced by the text from the Council of Elvira mentioned above, Jews were certainly well integrated and on friendly terms with their gentile neighbors by the fourth century CE, if not before.

The fact that Jews were integrated into local commerce is also evident from a text from another council, the Fourth Council of Toledo, in 633 CE. In it, the Visigothic kings (Germanic monarchs who converted to Catholicism in the late sixth century and conquered Spain soon after) decreed that Jews should be prohibited from purchasing Christian slaves and that they should be forced to let any Christian slaves they already owned go free. This declaration is notable not only for the inherent tone of anti-Semitism implied, but because it demonstrates that the Jews of Toledo were wealthy enough to own slaves, and most probably owned land, since they required slaves to help work it.

Other Diaspora Communities
By the time the Muslims came to dominate the Near East in the seventh century CE, Jews had established communities throughout the Arabian

peninsula, as well as eastward all along the trade routes to places such as India, Afghanistan, China, the Carpathian Mountains (near modern-day Hungary), and other locations throughout the world. Depending on where they settled, Jews could count on a variety of receptions at different times, ranging from extremely welcoming to bitterly hostile. Because of the Jews' ability to move between the Christian and Muslim worlds, they were generally able to pick up stakes and relocate when the situation became dangerous. As mentioned above, the widespread nature of the Jewish Diaspora ensured—and continues to ensure—that (as the popular camp song by Noah Budin goes) "Wherever you go, there's always someone Jewish."

CONNECTING TO OUR TRADITION

One of the most interesting and varied aspects of Jewish culture is its food. Differences between various Jewish communities' cuisines astound the average culinary student. One chief objective transcended any communal differences in taste, however: the priority of keeping kosher. The basic tenets of *kashrut* (keeping kosher)—avoiding shellfish and pork, and refraining from mixing meat and dairy products—meant that Jewish food was similar to and yet different from the food of their neighbors.

In Arab lands, keeping kosher was easy, since Muslim dietary restrictions have much in common with Jewish dietary laws. In Christian and other gentile regions, it was a little more complicated. Nevertheless, Jewish communities in Italy, Spain, India, and Asia have found ways to cook ethnic foods similar to those of their neighbors, using local ingredients while not compromising *kashrut*.

DID YOU KNOW?

Contrary to myth, women were active participants in synagogues throughout the world during the rabbinic period and early Middle Ages. The writings of Paul, the Christian apostle, confirm that women were present at sermons and study sessions delivered at synagogues throughout the Near East, and approached him to ask questions with no restrictions because of their gender.

No evidence of separate seating for women in synagogues exists until approximately the ninth century CE. Many Talmudic texts mention women's synagogue attendance, and the female Torah scholar Beruriah is praised for her erudition (sometimes at the expense of less insightful male counterparts). Finally, the historian Bernadette Brooten has done extensive research on inscriptions found in synagogues and on tombstones throughout the Jewish Diaspora, and she has found many that refer to women as patrons, donors, leaders, and (in Greek) "Mother of the Synagogue."

IMPORTANT TERMS
Galut/Exile
Diaspora
Kashrut
Responsa literature/*she'eilot u'teshuvot*
Patriarch
Exilarch
Septuagint
Geniza

Names, Places, and Events
Ashkenaz
Council of Elvira
Solomon Schechter

DISCUSSION QUESTIONS
- Do you think that living outside the Land of Israel means that you are in the Diaspora (that is, *choosing* to live elsewhere), or in exile (that is, being

somehow *forced* to live elsewhere)?
Explain your reasoning.
- Do you think it is easier or harder today to maintain Jewish identity while living in a surrounding gentile culture? Why?
- Have you ever visited a far-off Jewish community? What similarities did you find between the other community and your own? What differences did you experience?

ACTIVITIES
Around the World (E, S)
Assign small groups of students to research the Jewish communities in a variety of locations. Help them find out about the community's clothing, food, synagogues, schooling and other customs. Have each group make a booth or poster featuring their Jewish community with items and information from that country. Have a fair and invite the rest of the school to learn about Jewish communities around the world.

You Are What You Eat (E, S, A)
Assign students to research the general cuisine as well as the Jewish foods of a particular region of the world. (See the bibliography at the end of this chapter for cookbook suggestions.) Depending on the age group involved, students can participate in shopping for, cooking, and serving an authentic meal from an area where Jews settled, in a manner that incorporates the tenets of *kashrut* (taking into consideration the level of observance in your particular synagogue or school). Find out if the synagogue kitchen is available, and have your students make Shabbat dinner for their families.

I've Got a Question (E, S, A)
In order to understand the dynamics of responsa literature, have students pose a halachic question, for example, having to do with an ethical dilemma or a point of Jewish law concerning a ritual practice, to one or more area rabbis. Have students write the question down, and send a letter to the individuals selected. (As the teacher, you will need to scout out clergy willing to answer the students' questions on their particular academic level, and to send a letter back to complete the activity.) When the students receive the letter, have them read and discuss the answer to their question. Were they surprised by the answer? If a point of ritual practice, will it be easy or difficult to incorporate the steps mandated?

Complete the discussion by having the students describe what it would have been like to wait for months for a reply, and then have to figure out how to do what the rabbi instructed. An optional follow-up activity could be going on an "ask-a-rabbi" Internet site and posing the same question. Debriefing questions could include the following: Was the question answered immediately? What was different about the response of the "cyber-rabbi"? Did it feel different having to wait for a written response than getting it quickly? If you had a religious question, how would you choose to go about finding an answer?

TIMELINE
25 CE
> Possible date of the founding of the synagogue in Cairo which was home to the Cairo *geniza*

70 CE
> Destruction of the Temple; beginning of the greater Diaspora/Exile

1st–4th centuries CE
> Early Christianity

c. 300 CE
> Council of Elvira, Spain (regulating relations between Jews and Christians)

429 CE
Romans abolish the office of the
nasi (patriarch) of the Jewish
community of Eretz Yisrael
October 5, 871 CE
Earliest dated document of the Cairo
geniza (a Hebrew marriage contract)

RESOURCES
Books and Articles

Barnavi, Eli, ed. *Historical Atlas of the Jewish People: From the Time of the Patriarchs to the Present.* New York: Schocken Books, 1992.

Gilbert, Martin. *The Routledge Atlas of Jewish History,* 6th ed. London: Routledge, 1995.

Grossman, Susan, and Rivka Haut, eds. *Daughters of the King: Women and the Synagogue.* Philadelphia: Jewish Publication Society, 1992.

Marcus, Jacob Rader. *The Jew in the Medieval World, A Source Book: 315–1791.* Cincinnati, OH: Hebrew Union College Press, 1990.

Marks, Gil. *The World of Jewish Cooking: Traditional Recipes from Alsace to Yemen.* New York: Simon & Schuster, 1999.

Pasachoff, Naomi, and Robert J. Littman. *Jewish History in 100 Nutshells.* Northvale, NJ: Jason Aronson, 1995.

Roden, Claudia. *The Book of Jewish Food: An Odyssey from Samarkand to New York.* New York: Alfred A. Knopf, 1996.

Roth, Cecil. *The Jews in the Renaissance.* Philadelphia: Jewish Publication, 1959.

Sarna, Jonathan D., and Jonathan B. Krasner. *The History of the Jewish People: A Story of Tradition and Change.* Springfield, NJ: Behrman House, 2006.

Internet
Visit www.behrmanhouse.com/booklinks for links to Web sites that offer additional resources for this chapter.

Medieval Period

CHAPTER TWELVE
JEWS IN THE MUSLIM WORLD

WHAT'S THE BIG IDEA?
Diaspora

As mentioned in the previous chapter, the Jewish Diaspora began in the eighth century BCE, and Jews had lived in the Arabian Peninsula for centuries by the time Muhammad was born about the year 571 CE. They had developed strong communities, were well integrated into the life and culture of the region, and generally enjoyed an atmosphere of tolerance with their neighbors. With the wave of Islam that swept the region in the seventh century, the whole idea of what it was to live as a Jew in the Arab world changed, creating new conditions for the Jews of the area, and a very different Diaspora experience.

BACKGROUND INFORMATION
The Beginning of Islam

Muhammad, the founder of Islam, was born in the city of Mecca. Located near the center of modern-day Saudi Arabia, Mecca was a bustling metropolis positioned not far from the eastern shore of the Red Sea, along the trade routes between Yemen, Egypt, Syria, and Persia. During his lifetime, Muhammad had the opportunity to travel with caravans throughout Arabia and into Syria, where he encountered (and was presumably influenced by) Syrian monks, as well as Jewish and Christian merchants. These individuals, and many others whom Muhammad met, spread the message of monotheism, the belief that one God created the heavens and the earth, revealed a moral code of conduct to human beings, and promised to punish those who disobey God's will while rewarding those who honor it. This message found a home among many preachers in the heart of pagan Arabia, and the most successful was Muhammad.

Muhammad differed from other preachers of the time by claiming that God (Allah), through the angel Gabriel, had revealed the truest form of the message of monotheism to him alone, and that God spoke in the language of the people—Arabic. Muhammad named the new religion "Islam," which means "submission [to the will of God]," and which shares the same Semitic root for the Hebrew word "shalom," or peace.

Muhammad achieved his first successes with family members who were captivated by his sincerity. Others, however, were put off by his complete disavowal of Arab paganism and his insistence that those who did not believe in Allah and follow his rules would be eternally punished. As a result of the widespread rejection levied at him by his neighbors, Muhammad left his hometown and went to Yathrib, or Medina, an oasis about 250 miles north of Mecca. (Muhammad's emigration, or *hijra*, is seen as an important turning point in Muslim tradition and theology.) The community of Medina had been settled by Jewish farmers centuries before; Medina, in fact, comes from the Semitic root word meaning "district." (The modern State of Israel is referred to as *medinat Yisrael*.) The Jews of Medina comprised the majority of the population, and were organized into tribes, similarly to the pagan Arabs among whom they lived. Both Muslim and Jewish sources note that the presence of an established Jewish community may have provided the familiarity necessary for the pagans of the town to accept monotheism when Muhammad introduced it to them. In fact, by the year 622 many of the formerly pagan town elders had already converted to Islam. They invited Muhammad to become the town's chief magistrate or *hakam* (elder). In this position he would be expected to settle disputes between the various tribes living in Medina, becoming the community's spiritual as well as administrative leader. While in this position, Muhammad began to share that his visions came directly from Allah, and he began with the help of his followers to collect these revelations into a book, called the Koran.

By now, Muhammad was known simply as the Prophet, and he spread the word that conversion to Islam and submission to Allah superseded all other bonds and alliances. This situation set up an obvious conflict with the Jewish community. The observant Jewish scholars and leaders were opposed to Muhammad's growing influence; it is also possible that Muhammad's leadership highlighted a conflict already present *within* the Jewish community, between the more cosmopolitan Jews who backed Muhammad, and the religious Jews who opposed him.

Whatever the situation within the Jewish community, by the year 624 Muhammad had amassed an armed force of believers and had developed a plan to spread Islam throughout the region. Muhammad's force first attacked Mecca, and then opposition groups in Medina. After assassinating two pagan poets who had written satirical verses mocking him, Muhammad achieved the unconditional surrender of the weakest of the Jewish tribes in Medina. A second Jewish tribe left Medina rather than surrender. They were massacred two years

later when the Muslims overran their new home, the nearby Jewish town of Khaybar. After announcing that he had received a vision from Allah commanding that he do so, Muhammad's army attacked the third Jewish tribe, beheading hundreds of men in the marketplace, throwing their bodies into open trenches, and enslaving the women and children. Thus began a pattern repeated over and over during the next ten years of Muhammad's life as well as the following decades: non-Muslims were given the chance to convert to Islam; if they agreed, all was well, and if they refused, they were murdered, enslaved, or exiled.

For some, however, another option existed. Officially, Islam considered non-Muslim monotheists, or "People of the Book," to be of a higher status than pagans, and referred to them as *dhimmis* (protégés, or protected people). As Islam spread throughout Arabia, the Jews and Christians of Yemen and other communities began to pay tribute to their new rulers. This tribute was called the *jizya*, or "compensation," and it was paid in the form of produce and other goods. The practice of accepting this compensation was given sanction in the verses of the Koran that encouraged Muslims to fight against *dhimmis* "until they pay the *jizya* out of hand, and have been humbled." Accordingly, some Muslim communities chose to tolerate Jews and Christians as long as they paid their taxes and lived in a manner befitting their lower status. This situation was reinforced a few decades later by the Pact of Umar.

The Pact of Umar
By the middle of the seventh century, most of the Middle East was under Muslim rule, with Islam operating both as a religion and as a political entity. The new leaders, however, found themselves

in a bind: they were a very small minority ruling a very large majority of different faiths. Although some communities developed their own ways of enforcing the *jizya* and the land tax (*kharaj*) on their *dhimmi* communities, a uniform system didn't exist until the Pact of Umar.

When the Christian rulers of Jerusalem surrendered to the Muslims around the year 634, the new caliph (Islamic leader), Umar ben al-Khattab, wrote a document outlining the expectations that the Muslim rulers had for the conquered inhabitants of the city. The Pact of Umar was a writ of protection extended by the Muslim rulers to the minority non-Muslim monotheistic community, which included Jews, Christians, and, later, Zoroastrians. The Pact of Umar promised safety for these individuals and their belongings and the right to worship as they chose in exchange for payment of the *jizya* and the *kharaj,* and the promise that they would conduct themselves in a manner befitting a subordinate population.

For example, they were not permitted to build new houses of worship or repair old ones. They had to wear clothing distinguished by a special badge or belt. They couldn't ride horses, raise their voices loudly in prayer, proselytize, or inflict physical harm on any Muslim. Later restrictions appended to the pact included the prohibition against building houses higher than those of the Muslims, adopting Arabic names, reading the Koran, or selling fermented beverages, an activity prohibited under Muslim religious law. With more changes made over the years, the Pact of Umar was enforced in some fashion up until the nineteenth century. On the whole, Jews living under Muslim domination adapted to these rules fairly well, which is fortunate since by the eighth

century, 90 percent of the world's Jews resided in Arab lands. Having lived as a subject people for hundreds of years already, they were familiar with the concept of being considered permanent outsiders.

In the Muslim world, moreover, the Jewish community had leaders to intercede for them with the Muslim rulers, such as the *geonim* (heads of the Talmudic academies) and the exilarch, the political leader of the Jewish community who was treated much like a prince. The Pact of Umar was enforced strictly under some rulers and lightly under others, so that a Jewish populace who could roll with the changes was more likely to be tolerated by the host community than those who could not adapt.

In keeping with this set of circumstances, many Jews continued to live much as they had before, paying their taxes, not drawing too much attention to themselves, and enjoying a full Jewish life within the confines of their own community. (One major change, however, was that due to the increasing burden of the land tax, many Jews left their agrarian lifestyle and began migrating to the urban centers, so that over time, the majority of Jews in the Muslim world were involved in commerce, similar to their brethren in Europe.)

The Umayyad and Abassidian Empires

In 661, the first Muslim caliph who was not a direct descendant of Muhammad took over leadership of the Muslim world. The caliph Mu'awiya began the Umayyad dynasty and transformed the Arab world into a primarily secular state rather than a religious one. Although the official religion continued to be Islam, the Umayyads were very tolerant of the *dhimmis* living in their midst, and enforced the Pact of Umar lightly. Jews moved freely throughout the region; in fact, the caliph believed that Jews would be faithful allies and he purposely encouraged them to settle in the more far-flung regions of the empire such as North Africa. He also transferred his capital to Syria.

In 750, a violent uprising led to a shift in power, with the Abbasids replacing the Umayyads as the rulers of the Muslim world. The new rulers moved the capital from Syria to Baghdad, already the home of a prominent Jewish community. Baghdad quickly became not only the political and military capital of the empire, but the cultural seat as well. Jews participated to such an extent in this new culture that by the ninth century, a new development had taken place in the realm of Jewish language. Arabic written in Hebrew characters, or "Judeo-Arabic," became the predominant language among the Jews of the region and remained so until the modern age. Arabic became not only the spoken language of the Jewish population, but the language in which cultural and even religious treatises were written.

Combined with the shift from farming to urban living, this cultural renaissance also brought with it practical applications. Because the Jews now knew Arabic, they were able to succeed more easily in commercial and financial enterprises. A new class of Arab Jewish merchants called Rhadanites traveled the world and brought news of Jewish happenings in Europe and the Muslim world from one part of the globe to the other. Jews were uniquely suited to travel between these two spheres because they—unlike Muslims and Christians—were permitted passage into parts of the world where those of "enemy religions" were not allowed to travel. Multilingual Jews participated in affairs of state as well; a Jewish interpreter known only as Isaac was a member of the delegation sent by Caliph Harun al-Rashid, an eighth-century

Muslim leader, to none other than the emperor Charlemagne.

Jews in Muslim Palestine
During the centuries that Jews lived in Eretz Yisrael under foreign rule, some of the best years were arguably those of the early Muslim period.

By the year 641, all of Palestine was under Muslim rule. Following the Arab conquest of Jerusalem by Caliph Umar ben al-Khattab (originator of the Pact of Umar), Jews began to move in larger numbers back to the region. During the Byzantine period (roughly the fourth and fifth centuries CE) the Jews and Christians of the Holy Land had been frequently at odds with one another. The Muslim conquest improved the Jews' quality of life because the new rulers were fairly tolerant of both Jews and Christians. The Umayyads formally allowed Jews to take up residence in Jerusalem once again, something that had been forbidden to them under the Byzantines. The Talmudic scholars in Tiberias officially moved their academy to Jerusalem, attracting more rabbis and their families to settle within the city walls. Pilgrimages to the city were once again allowed, and increased in popularity, so much so that during Sukkot, Jews from all over the Middle East converged on Jerusalem as in Temple times, helping the city to regain its status as the religious capital of the Jewish people. Tiberias also retained a large portion of its population along with its rabbinic influence. The scholars who produced the authorized Masoretic text (the word *masorah* means "tradition" in Hebrew; the Masoretic text is the standard version of the Hebrew Bible) hailed from there, and communities of Jews in the Galilee and throughout the Land of Israel reinvigorated the region. This renaissance lasted until the eleventh century, when several tragedies struck the community in a short span of time. Famine, epidemics, two earthquakes, Bedouin attacks, and finally the Crusades resulted in an almost (but not complete) erosion of the Jewish community of the Holy Land for the next two centuries or so.

CONNECTING TO OUR TRADITION

Throughout history, Jews both were influenced by the cultures in which they lived and influenced those cultures in return. Under the Umayyads and the Abbasids, Islam began to absorb ideas found in Greek culture, thought, and science. Jews living in these lands were in turn affected by the new Islamic culture, to the point where the works of many Jewish thinkers, philosophers, and religious scholars were influenced by these new ideas and methods. Some of the great scholars we will meet in chapters 14 and 15, such as Saadia Gaon, Yehudah Ha-Levi, and Moses Maimonides—to name a few—incorporated these ideas into their own works. Their books in turn have influenced generations of Jews until the present day.

DID YOU KNOW?
The Golden Age of North Africa

We will explore the more well-known Golden Age of Spain in chapter 15, but did you know that North Africa also experienced a golden age in the ninth through eleventh centuries? The Jewish community of Tunisia was ruled by its own *nasi* (prince) and enjoyed economic affluence. The region's celebrated center of learning was so well respected that religious scholars in Spain adopted the Talmudic decisions of its local rabbis. Other learned Jewish scholars wrote influential treatises on medicine, philosophy, and poetry.

IMPORTANT TERMS

Dhimmi	*Kharaj*
Koran	Pact of Umar
Jizya	*Hakam*

Names, Places, and Events

Muhammad	Medina
Hijra	Yemen
Mecca	

DISCUSSION QUESTION

Judaism and Islam share many similarities both in the major tenets of their belief, as well as in particular rituals and laws. For example, Jews and Muslims have dietary restrictions that include a prohibition against eating pork and shellfish. Both religions have multiple set prayer services each day, and both require their adherents to face in a particular direction for prayer (Mecca for Muslims and Jerusalem for Jews). Why do you think, then, that there has always been so much animosity between Jews and Muslims, persisting into the present day? If you were a world leader, how would you encourage Jewish and Muslim communities to explore their similarities rather than their differences?

ACTIVITIES
Biography (E, S)

Assign each student to research an important Jewish figure from the time period, dress up as the character, and address the class. Examples might include Saadia Gaon, the ninth-century Jewish philosopher, or Benjamin of Tudela, who wrote a diary of his travels throughout the Jewish world in the twelfth century.

History Quest (E, S)

World history at the time of the Muslim conquest was a fascinating mix of old and new, rural and urban, class warfare and military warfare (sort of like today). Have students look at what life was like in the Arab world between 650 and 1500 CE, either by reading encyclopedia articles, watching a video, or looking on the Internet. Imagine what life might have been like for the majority of world Jewry living in these areas of the world at that time. Optional follow-up activities might include a creative writing assignment such as a journal entry or a bulletin board display highlighting the different areas of the world in which Jews lived under Muslim rule.

Is That Legal? (E, S, A)

Assign students to read the text of the Pact of Umar, paying particular attention to the types of rules that were enacted in order to govern Jews and Christians under Muslim domination. What trends do you notice in these laws? How might they have been enforced? What advantages might there have been for Jews who had to adhere to these laws? What disadvantages might they have had to deal with on a personal, religious, and business level? Optional follow-up activity: First research laws that still exist in some parts of the world today that place members of minority communities in a subordinate position. Then find out whether any efforts to eradicate these injustices have been successful, for example, in South Africa.

TIMELINE (all dates are CE)

c. 571
  Birth of Muhammad
c. 610
  Muhammad receives his first revelation
622
  Muhammad's pilgrimage to Mecca
630
  Mecca surrenders to Muhammad
632
  Death of Muhammad
661–750
  Umayyad Caliphate
711
  Muslims conquer Spain
750–1258
  Abbasid Caliphate

942
  Death of Saadia Gaon
1085
  Christians recapture Toledo
1096
  First Crusade
1204
  Death of Maimonides
1492
  Expulsion of Jews and Muslims from Spain

RESOURCES
Books and Articles

Barnavi, Eli, ed. *Historical Atlas of the Jewish People: From the Time of the Patriarchs to the Present.* New York: Schocken Books, 1992.

Gilbert, Martin. *The Routledge Atlas of Jewish History,* 6th ed. London: Routledge, 1995.

Marcus, Jacob Rader. *The Jew in the Medieval World, A Source Book: 315–1791.* Cincinnati, OH: Hebrew Union College Press, 1990.

Pasachoff, Naomi, and Robert J. Littman. *Jewish History in 100 Nutshells.* Northvale, NJ: Jason Aronson, 1995.

Sarna, Jonathan D., and Jonathan B. Krasner. *The History of the Jewish People: A Story of Tradition and Change.* Springfield, NJ: Behrman House, 2006 (see especially chapter 6).

Stillman, Norman A. *The Jews of Arab Lands: A History and Source Book.* Philadelphia: Jewish Publication Society, 1979.

Internet

Visit www.behrmanhouse.com/booklinks for links to Web sites that offer additional resources for this chapter.

CHAPTER THIRTEEN
JEWISH-GENTILE RELATIONS IN MEDIEVAL CHRISTIAN EUROPE

WHAT'S THE BIG IDEA?
Covenant

Jews have traditionally understood the events that befell them to be the will of God, part of God's overarching plan for Jewish history in particular and human history in general. Intrinsic to this view has been the idea that the Jews are God's chosen people, singled out for a special covenant that promised them Eretz Yisrael and prosperity for their people.

This conviction was tested over and over again during the Middle Ages throughout Jewish and gentile communities in Christian Europe, as the Christian rulers—both secular and religious—sought to define the status of Jews under their control, as well as the accepted bounds of relations between the two groups.

Christendom

Today, we view Europe in terms of its geopolitical borders, separated into countries and regions. In the Middle Ages, the one thing that unified Europe was its religion—Christianity. Beginning with the conversion of the emperor Constantine to Christianity in the fourth century, the region of Europe and, until the Muslim conquest, some parts of the Near East were enfolded into a geographic entity called Christendom.

In a world where one's allegiance was often to a local duke or lord rather than even a king or queen, the one thing that connected the largest number of people

over a vast swath of land was Christianity. Consequently, most Christians viewed their primary allegiance as belonging to the religious leadership—both human (priests and bishops) and divine (God and Jesus).

BACKGROUND INFORMATION

The main problem for the Jews was that in a worldview of Christendom, the Jews could have no membership. Thus, in Europe the Jews were truly seen as outsiders because they did not attend church, venerate the bishop, or celebrate the Christian holy days and festivals with everyone else. The fact that the Jews also disavowed Jesus as the Messiah often encouraged local Christians and religious leaders to suspect them at best, and demonize them, literally and figuratively, at worst.

Because Jews were seen as religious outsiders, they were treated that way socially as well. Jews were often denied residency rights within Christian neighborhoods, prohibited from owning land, and denied membership in the professional guilds.

These restrictions pushed Jews out of most professions other than trading in goods and money lending, which was forbidden to Christians by Church law but reluctantly allowed for Jews due to economic necessity. These factors all combined to determine the course of Jewish life and Jewish-Christian interaction in Europe for almost two thousand years.

Ashkenaz

According to Kenneth R. Stow in his book *Alienated Minority,* the earliest references to Jews in Ashkenaz (Germany's Rhineland and its surrounding region) deal with Jewish merchants and their involvement in both the production and trade of goods in the eighth and ninth centuries. By the year 888, a church council in the town of Mainz had already set forth rules prohibiting Christians from getting too close to Jews and their "negative influence." While it is likely that Jews had lived both in Christian villages and in small independent settlements in the Rhineland since the 800s, they were not invited to dwell in the larger towns until the eleventh century.

On September 13, 1084, Bishop Rudiger, the religious and secular leader of the town of Speyer, wrote a legal charter giving residency rights to a group of Jews for the stated purpose of adding "to the city's reputation" (most likely referring to its economic health). The invitation was tendered specifically to the Jews of the neighboring city of Mainz who sought refuge after a fire destroyed the Jewish quarter. Bishop Rudiger's generosity is evident not only in the tone of his charter, which gives the Jews residential, commercial, and burial rights, but also in an accompanying "Hebrew Report," written by the Jews themselves thanking the bishop for his help.

Six years later, Emperor Henry IV confirmed and extended these benefits, and similar charters shifted the responsibility for ensuring the Jews' well-being from local bishops to the Crown. In

1236, Emperor Frederick II declared that all the Jews of Germany under his control were to be considered *servi camerae nostrae*, or "servants of our treasury," and thus "belonged" to the emperor similarly to the manner in which serfs "belonged" to feudal lords. Over the next several hundred years, such protection would be both a blessing and a curse to Jewish communities throughout Europe.

The Crusades

In 1086, Pope Urban II gathered a military expedition for the purpose of traveling to the Holy Land in order to recapture Christian holy sites from the Muslim rulers there. The first of three Crusades was carried out by a ragtag mob of individuals fired up by sermons given by a monk named Peter the Hermit, who encouraged a violent overthrow of the Muslims for the glory of God. While crossing large areas of Europe, however, the Crusaders decided that their mandate must extend to the "infidels" right at home—the Jews.

The reaction of local leaders to the Crusaders' violence against the European Jewish communities they encountered varied from a concerted effort to aid the Jews under their protection, to silence, to helping the Crusaders in their rampages.

Bishop John of Speyer, true to the word of his predecessor, Rudiger, protected Jews from the marauding mobs and saved the majority of the Jews in his town. When some of the burghers attempted to round up the Jewish inhabitants of the town and hold them in the synagogue (where they intended to help the Crusaders burn them alive), Bishop John came to the Jews' rescue. He gathered his own force and captured the burghers, even cutting off the hands of the violent leaders, and sheltered the Jews in his own home.

The Jews of other communities, however, weren't so lucky. Both Latin and Hebrew records—called Crusader Chronicles—detail the annihilation of the nearby Jewish communities of Worms, Mainz, and others. Group suicides (perhaps inspired by those committed by the Jews during the time of the Masada uprising a thousand years earlier) were not uncommon, and forced conversions of the survivors were frequent.

Blood Libels, "Ritual Murders," and "Host Desecration"

The fragility of Europe's Jewish communities continued throughout the Crusades and into the following centuries. Due to the gentile population's suspicion of the Jews, often encouraged by local Church leaders if not by secular authorities, Jews were vulnerable to attacks and slander that led to violence against them. One of the most vicious and long-lasting methods of slandering the Jews was the blood libel.

The term "blood libel" here refers to a case in which a Jew or group of Jews was accused of murdering a Christian (often a child) in order to use his or her blood for secret Jewish rituals, such as the baking of matzah for Passover. The fact that such charges are utterly preposterous (matzah is made up of only water and flour, and the consumption of blood—not to mention murder—is forbidden to Jews) is immaterial.

In fact, similar charges have been brought in the *twenty-first century* in the Muslim world in which Jews have been accused of killing children and using their blood to

bake *hamantaschen* for Purim.[1] Such stories were accepted as fact in the medieval world, particularly among the illiterate peasantry that was often dependent upon unscrupulous local leaders for their information.

Another slander against Jews was termed "host desecration," in which Jews were accused of torturing the host (the wafer used in the Catholic ceremony of communion, which the faithful believe is transformed into the actual body of Christ as it is consecrated, and therefore would be capable of feeling pain). This accusation went straight to the mythology of Jews not only refusing to accept Jesus's role as the Messiah, but their need to kill Christ "again." (Christians were told for hundreds of years, based on writings in the New Testament, that the Jews killed Jesus, a tenet of Catholic faith repudiated by the Church only in the 1960s.)

Both host desecration and blood libel were given credence by a population that truly viewed the Jews as the enemies of Christ and Christians, and this notion was responsible for much of the violence against the Jewish community of Europe for centuries.

One of the most infamous blood libel episodes took place in Norwich, England, in 1144, immediately prior to the Second Crusade. A monk named Thomas wrote an account of the blood libel soon after, which gives us a glimpse into the tension between the Jewish and Christian communities of the time. William, described as a "sweet child," was said to have been murdered by two local Jews on the holiday of Good Friday (two days before Easter, on which Christians believe

---

[1]As recently as 2002, such libel charges appeared in the Saudi Arabian newspaper *Al-Riyadh*.

that Jesus was crucified) while the faithful were praying in Church.

According to Brother Thomas's account, the two Jews tied up the body of the boy and were transporting it in a sack tied to their horse's neck, when a faithful Christian named Aelward discovered them in the woods. The Jews fled with the body, which they then hung from a tree, and which was discovered several days later showing "evidence" of torture. Although the sheriff of Norfolk protected the Jews accused of the murder and torture, this story was related as truth for hundreds of years.

Expulsions

Not surprisingly, local leaders and monarchs alike soon began to question whether it was worthwhile to continue protecting Jews if it meant that they would lose favor with the overwhelming majority of their Christian subjects. The need to placate the Christian locals was often at odds with the need to ensure the economic health that the Jews brought to these same communities.

Jews in medieval Europe fulfilled a very important financial function: they were legally permitted to lend money at interest (this practice was forbidden to Christians), and thus much of the banking and finance of the continent depended on Jewish survival and economic fitness. Jews were an integral part of the economic life of medieval Europe's cities and towns, and contributed large sums to their tax base —a fact that Bishop Rudiger of Speyer recognized in 1084.

However, beginning as early as the eleventh century, Jews began facing expulsion from an increasingly larger number of individual communities and, later, entire countries. One reason is that although the Jews as a group provided financial health and growth to communities, people were suspect of Jews as "moneylenders" or "usurers." Lending money at interest was literally seen at the least as un-Christian, forbidden as it was to members of the Catholic faith, and more usually by most as theft. Categorizing usury in this manner played directly into the mind-set of poor Christians who were already inclined to suspect Jews as child-killers as seen in the blood libel episodes mentioned above. Therefore, beginning as early as the twelfth century, an increasing number of secular and religious leaders made the decision that allowing "infidel" Jews to reside in their communities just wasn't worthwhile due to their suspect nature and compromised status.

As a result, communities of Jews in Germany found themselves in dire straits during the Crusades and in the decades and centuries following. Once they were no longer welcome, expelled Jews traveled all over the continent. Jews thrown out of Hungary (between 1349 and 1360), Austria (in 1421), and Lithuania (1495) joined established Jewish communities in Eastern Europe.

The Jews of England were expelled in 1290, and they went in large numbers to France and Holland. The Jews of central France were expelled in 1306, and from there they emigrated to Spain and Provence. When the Provençal Jewish community was expelled in 1394, many traveled east to northern Italy, and settled in communities that would receive another large influx of coreligionists during the Spanish Inquisition (a subject that we will treat in chapter 15). These expulsions changed the face of Europe for the Jews, limiting the number of Jews who remained in Western Europe but encouraging a new, burgeoning Jewish community that flourished in Eastern Europe until the eve of the Holocaust.

Christians and Jews

While historians often view the Crusades as the turning point for Jewish-Christian relations in Europe, the fact is that economics and rivalries had as much to do with the shift that occurred around the twelfth century. As mentioned above, Jews were often invited into towns in order to become part of the economic life. By doing so, they often introduced competition to the local (Christian) merchants that had not been there before.

While the local leaders may have been forward-thinking enough to view such competition as healthy, the people themselves didn't necessarily have the same views, especially when such competition—from Jews, no less—affected their livelihood.

In this climate, church art began to depict Jews as blind (to Jesus's role as the Messiah) and antiquated (the "Old Testament" vs. the "New Testament," which contained the truth). Competition in the business sector began to take on religious overtones, in which Christians accused their Jewish rivals of being enemies of Christ. Such rivalries often erupted into violence, when not tempered by the influence of rulers sworn to protect and defend the Jews under their jurisdiction.

While the information above seems to suggest that life was terrible for Jews living in Christendom, the fact is that for Jews able to operate "under the radar," so to speak, life was lived in a full and happy manner. Areas in which local leaders such as the bishops of Speyer ruled were wonderful havens for Jews, who enjoyed their own jurisdiction over disputes, freedom from heavy taxes, and the ability to make a profit from the sale—for example—of nonkosher meat and nonkosher wine to their Christian neighbors. Jews and Christians even influenced one another's method of scriptural study, a subject we will explore in the next chapter.

CONNECTING TO OUR TRADITION

Although "Ashkenaz" has come to mean the community of Jews originating in the area of Germany's Rhineland, the term is first used very early in the Bible, in Genesis, chapter 10. In this text, Ashkenaz is a person who is mentioned in the genealogy of Noah's descendants, and is thought to be the ancestor of certain peoples in Assyria and nearby Turkey.

Rabbinic literature mentions the term "Ashkenazi" as referring to the Jews of northern and Central Europe, which seems to imply that individuals and families of Jews were residing in Germany well before their first mention in secular texts.

DID YOU KNOW?

Women's Participation in the Medieval Synagogue: The Christian notion that contact between the sexes led to sin may have influenced Jewish sources during the medieval period as well, perhaps leading to increased stringencies in Jewish law that prohibited women from engaging in many *mitzvot* that were integral to men's Jewish life. That's why it's even more fascinating that several female prayer leaders (mainly in Germany) are noted in the literature of the period.

For example, a woman named Urania, the daughter of a Rabbi Abraham, is praised for her work as the cantor of the women in a synagogue in Worms, near Speyer. The wife of celebrated legal commentator Rabbi Eleazar (Ha-Roke'ach), Dulcie of Worms, recited prayers for the women of the synagogue and is commended for "stand[ing] every Yom Kippur to sing." Other women, called *fizogerin* (foresayers, or prayer leaders), penned *techinos*—prayers and liturgical poems written specifically for women—and translated prayers from Hebrew to Yiddish for the women in the synagogue gallery.

Interestingly, the existence of such writings seems to indicate that a large enough number of Jewish women were literate, in order to warrant writing publications that they could read. Rebecca Tiktiner of Prague, Sarah bas Tovim, and others—both named and unnamed—held these leadership positions for years in European communities and provided information and spiritual richness to the Jewish women of their time.

IMPORTANT TERMS
Christendom
Blood libel
Servi camerae nostrae
Host desecration
Crusader
Chronicles
Usury
Money lending
Infidel
Communion
Fizogerin
Ritual murder

Names, Places, and Events
Ashkenaz
Rhineland
Bishop Rudiger of Speyer
Emperor Frederick II
Pope Urban II
Peter the Hermit
The Crusades
William of Norwich

DISCUSSION QUESTIONS
- In the Middle Ages, it was often difficult for a European Jew to practice Judaism while earning a livelihood and protecting his or her family from possible violence at the same time. Why do you think so many Jews stayed in Western Europe rather than move somewhere safer?
- Given these conditions, why do you think so few Jews converted to Christianity voluntarily?
- Why do you think that so much discrimination existed in the medieval period? Why do you think discrimination exists today? What can you learn from the Middle Ages and the poor treatment of people different from the ruling class that can be applied to ensure fair treat-ment for all people in the modern age?

ACTIVITIES
History Quest (E, S)
European history during the Middle Ages was a time of great transition in terms of economics, culture, religion, and other major factors. Have students research what life was like in a typical European town during the Middle Ages and compare that with what they have learned about Jewish life during the same period.

Optional follow-up activities might include a creative writing assignment—

a journal entry or a bulletin board display—highlighting different aspects of medieval culture, such as food, dress, and literature.

Crusader Chronicle (S, A)
Assign students to read one or more of the Crusader Chronicles available in English (see examples in the Resources section by Robert Chazen and Jacob Marcus). What reaction did the Jews have to the devas-tation brought about by the Crusades? In the case of mass suicides and other desperate acts of violence, do you agree with the choices made by the Jews? Why or why not?

Art Talk (E, S, A)
Many representations exist of Ecclesia (the Church, represented as a noble woman, upright, holding a cross) and of Synagoga (the Jews, represented as a downtrodden woman, holding a broken set of tablets and blindfolded). Find a few different examples of this type of Church art, and invite students to study and discuss the differences between them.

Why do you think that the Church chose to represent Christians and Jews in this way? (Women and not men, with differences in posture and different "props.") Where might you see such artwork? (Churches throughout Europe.) What might people think about Jews when they viewed such art, especially in the Middle Ages? Discuss the role that art played in churches and synagogues in the Middle Ages, when literacy wasn't necessarily widespread.

TIMELINE (all dates are CE)
888
    First Jews recorded as living in the Rhineland
1084
    Charter of Bishop Rudiger to the Jews of Speyer
1095–1096
    First Crusade
1144
    Blood Libel of William of Norwich
1145
    Second Crusade
1189
    Third Crusade
13th–15th centuries
    Expulsion of the Jews of Western Europe

RESOURCES
Books and Articles
Barnavi, Eli, ed. *Historical Atlas of the Jewish People: From the Time of the Patriarchs to the Present.* New York: Schocken Books, 1992.

Chazan, Robert. *Church, State, and Jew in the Middle Ages.* West Orange, NJ: Behrman House, 1980.

Gilbert, Martin. *The Routledge Atlas of Jewish History,* 6th ed. London: Routledge, 1995.

Grossman, Susan, and Rivka Haut, eds. *Daughters of the King: Women and the Synagogue.* Philadelphia: Jewish Publication Society, 1992.

Marcus, Jacob Rader. *The Jew in the Medieval World, A Source Book: 315–1791.* Cincinnati, OH: Hebrew Union College Press, 1990.

Pasachoff, Naomi, and Robert J. Littman. *Jewish History in 100 Nutshells.* Northvale, NJ: Jason Aronson, 1995.

Sarna, Jonathan D., and Jonathan B. Krasner. *The History of the Jewish People: A Story of Tradition and Change.* Springfield, NJ: Behrman House, 2006 (see especially chapters 7 and 8).

Stow, Kenneth R. *Alienated Minority: The Jews of Medieval Latin Europe.* Cambridge, MA: Harvard University Press, 1992.

Internet
Visit www.behrmanhouse.com/booklinks for links to Web sites that offer additional resources for this chapter.

CHAPTER FOURTEEN

CODES AND COMMENTATORS: JEWISH LEARNING IN THE MIDDLE AGES

WHAT'S THE BIG IDEA?
Jewish Culture and Thought

Although the Middle Ages in Europe are frequently described as the "Dark Ages," this categorization is inaccurate, especially in the area of religious studies. Jewish thought and learning expanded during this period with original and innovative thinkers who brought new and creative ideas to the field of biblical and Talmudic learning, along with an increasing ability to disseminate new interpretations of sacred literature.

BACKGROUND INFORMATION
Jewish Studies as the Target: Visualizing the World of Codes and Commentaries[1]

Imagine for a moment that you are facing a target with a small circle in the center, ringed by a number of concentric circles. We are going to use this visualization in order to understand how codes and commentaries build upon the words of the Torah.

In the center of the target is the Torah. In the first ring surrounding the Torah are the Prophets and the Writings; together, these three collections make up the Tanach, the complete Jewish Bible. In the widening rings surrounding the Tanach are, in order, the Mishnah, the Talmud, and the

---

[1] Credit for this concept belongs to Rabbi Jordan Friedman and educator Patricia Lackner of Congregation Emanuel in Denver, CO.

Midrash. These collections are the focus of chapter 10 of this book.

Because the essential purpose of Torah interpretation is to understand what God wants of the Jewish community and to put those expectations into practice, the entire enterprise of text study and extrapolation has continued and changed for generations. And so, during the Middle Ages, amid changing circumstances and a growing sophistication among rabbis and lay leaders alike, scholars continued writing commentaries on biblical and rabbinic texts for the edification of their respective communities.

What is fascinating is that during the Medieval period, a number of true geniuses arose in the field of rabbinic scholarship, and their writings were so illuminating that they have become the standard benchmark for understanding Torah and rabbinic text from that point until the present day.

In a similar vein as our target above, these writings began to surround the central texts of a page of Talmud. Today, traditional printed volumes of Talmud (see chapter 10 for more information about the Talmud) include a number of standard commentaries, organized in the same order no matter which edition one studies. We will examine just a few of these luminaries and their writings in order to highlight the scholarly achievements of the medieval period and to understand their impact on Jews from the Middle Ages through modern times.

Codes and Commentaries:
Some Definitions

Torah and Talmud, discussed in previous chapters, are *sources* of law rather than *codes* of law. A code of law, such as the United States Tax Code, takes a source of law and makes it understandable to those who are required to practice that law. In the Middle Ages, as we will see below, it fell to a few brilliant scholars to wade through the sheer volume of legal sources in the Torah and Talmud in order to distill and write codes, or organizational groupings, of law as might be understood and practiced.

Commentaries differ from codes in a significant manner. While *codes*—as established above—take source law and organize it so that it can be practiced, *commentaries* take that same source law and offer explanations and interpretations for the source material, without necessarily taking it out of its context, for example, the Torah, and dropping it into a separate law code.

The purpose of commentary can be the same as that of a code (that is, to understand a law in order to practice it), but often it is simply to understand what the source meant even if the context is not legal (for example, the many narratives in the Book of Genesis that have no legal material inherent in the text, but are still holy and worthy of interpretation for the reader).

The proliferation of both codes and commentaries in the Middle Ages, specifically with the goal of making difficult material accessible to lay people and rabbis alike, changed the landscape for religious Jews worldwide. As we will see through the examples of several extraordinary scholars and their work, the passion associated with Jewish learning broadened to include new processes of interpretation and understanding, bringing the Torah and other religious texts to larger numbers of students in the past, the present, and—presumably—the future.

Rabbenu Gershom of Mainz

A brilliant scholar and legal authority, Rabbenu (literally, "our rabbi") Gershom ben Judah (960–1028 CE) was such a respected scholar that he was also known as *Me'or Ha-Golah* ("Light of the Exile"). A rising star in Ashkenaz (Central Europe) at the time that the rabbinic academies of Babylonia were ceasing to function, Rabbenu Gershom's clear and comprehensive religious rulings were embraced by much of the rabbinic and lay communities. By accepting the rulings of a local rabbi, the dependence on Sephardic and Babylonian religious authorities continued to erode, to the point where Ashkenazic Jews ceased to follow their interpretations.

Among Rabbenu Gershom's more famous decrees were the prohibition against polygamy for Ashkenazic Jews (which also marked a significant split from the Jewish communities of Spain and North Africa, where the practice was still permitted), and the decree that a woman's consent was required for both marriage and divorce.

Rabbenu Gershom also made it a sin to open and read other people's mail (thereby insuring confidentiality in business transactions, the paperwork for which was almost always transported by third-party couriers and thus vulnerable to tampering). He also forbade Jews to embarrass others forced to convert to Christianity at a time when, sadly, such events were all too frequent. In addition to these innovations, Rabbenu Gershom's other claim to fame was that a few decades after his death, his academy produced an even more well-known luminary, the great scholar Rashi.

Rashi

Rabbi Shlomo Yitzhaki, the acronym of which spells "Rashi," the name by which he came to be known, was born in Troyes, France, and lived from about 1040 until 1105. A bustling commercial center and home to a large Jewish community, Troyes had been an important city in the kingdom of Emperor Charlemagne in the early ninth century. The son of a jeweler and himself a vintner, Rashi was a gifted Torah and Talmud student who spent time at the academy founded by Rabbenu Gershom and studied with the late rabbi's most brilliant students.

Back in France, and at the relatively young age of twenty-five, Rashi founded his own academy in Troyes and embarked on a life-long process of writing commentaries for the entire Bible and most of the Talmud. Rashi's commentaries are so integral to the study of Torah that they are considered the key to understanding the text by virtually all rabbinic authorities to the present day. This recognition of Rashi's greatness stems from several innovations that were designed to make Jewish text accessible to even non-scholars, both then and now.

First, Rashi sought to craft his explanations using the simplest terms and the fewest number of words possible. In a type of Jeopardy game, students of Rashi are taught to read a verse and then ask, "What's bothering Rashi?" Because he most often comments on discrepancies in the text, difficulties in grammar and spelling, or gaps of information inherent in the text, asking this question first helps guide the student in discovering these issues for himself or herself. The traditional Jewish edition of a "Student Bible," called *Mikra'ot Gedolot* (literally, "great readings"), includes Rashi's explanations wrapped around the biblical text in order to facilitate attention to both text and commentary.

In addition to his own explanations, Rashi also includes the commentaries of others, particularly the authors of various midrashic texts (rabbinic teaching stories), in order to give an allegorical explanation to various biblical texts. For example, in asking why God chose to clothe Adam and Eve with fig leaves (and not some other kind of leaf) after their sin of eating the fruit from the Tree of Knowledge, Rashi explains that this is because the fig was the fruit that they ate!

Furthering the discussion, Rashi asks, "Why was the name of the tree not publicized?" (A logical question, since the text never tells us specifically the type of fruit.) He continues, "For the Holy Blessed One does not desire to perturb any creature. [And therefore did not state explicitly the species of the tree by which they sinned] so that [people] should not humiliate it, and say, 'This is the one through which the world was stricken.' [This is found in] *Midrash Rabbah Tanhuma*." This homily is a beautiful teaching, because the student can extrapolate that if God doesn't want trees humiliated because of their history, how much more so does God not want people humiliated because of their past deeds either.

In addition to his Torah explanations and his penchant for preserving the works of others, Rashi's writings also illuminate the meaning of many medieval French words and phrases. In fact, both Jewish and Christian scholars rely on Rashi's commentaries as a window into an earlier version of the modern French language.

Rashi's personal life was as interesting as his scholarly works. In addition to his role as a community rabbi, Rashi supported himself and his family through the manufacture and sale of wine. After coming in from the fields, Rashi toiled late into the night answering Jewish legal questions from colleagues and lay people alike. In one such letter, Rashi "apologizes for the briefness of his response, since he and his family had been busy harvesting the grapes."[2]

Rashi had no sons, but he had three daughters—Yocheved, Miriam, and Rachel—whom he taught and who were instrumental in helping him to answer legal correspondence when he was ill. Evidence exists that they wore *tefillin* (phylacteries) like Rashi (and other observant men) with the approval of their father. All three married rabbis, and Rashi's grandsons were noted scholars and commentators whose works also grace the pages of the Talmud and form collections on their own. In addition, his granddaughters were reputed authorities on the dietary laws.[3]

Rashi died in the spring of 1105; world Jewry recently commemorated the nine hundredth anniversary of his death. As luck would have it, the Jewish world would have to wait only another thirty years for perhaps the only luminary to equal Rashi's greatness: Moses Maimonides, or the Rambam.

Maimonides
Rabbi Moses ben Maimon, known by the acronym "the Rambam," was born in Cordoba, Spain, on March 30, 1135, the day before Passover. According to tradition, Maimonides could trace his lineage all the way back to Rabbi Yehudah

Ha-Nasi , the compiler of the Mishnah, and some say to King David. (For more detail about the Mishnah, please see chapter 9.) His father was a Torah scholar in his own right, serving as a *dayan* (judge) on the *beit din* (Jewish law court) of the community of Cordoba, and he also wrote extensively on mathematics and astronomy. Maimon educated his son Moses in these fields of knowledge, and encouraged him to pursue the study of philosophy as well.

When Maimonides was thirteen years old, his family was forced to flee from Spain due to persecutions by the Almohades—fundamentalist Muslim conquerors of the area who sought to eliminate the minority Jewish community in the lands under their control. While some Jews became insincere converts to Islam in order to avoid expulsion, the Maimon family chose exile. They traveled throughout southern Spain, to Morocco, and to the Holy Land, before ultimately settling in Fostat, Egypt.

Soon after their arrival in this suburb of Cairo, the elder Maimon passed away, and responsibility for the family's livelihood fell on Moses's brother David, a jewel merchant. Sadly, on a trip home from India where he had gone to purchase gems and precious stones for his business, David's ship was lost at sea in the Indian Ocean and he was presumed drowned. The responsibility for the family's survival then became Moses's.

Because Maimonides believed that according to Jewish law it was not permissible to earn a livelihood from the study of Torah, he began to practice medicine while continuing to teach Torah for free. His scholarship was of such great renown that at the relatively young age of

[2] Naomi Pasachoff and Robert J. Littman. *Jewish History in 100 Nutshells* , Northvale, NJ: Jason Aronson, 1995, p. 142.
[3] Sondra Henry and Emily Taitz, *Written Out of History: Our Jewish Foremothers*, Sunnyside, NY: Biblio Press, 1988, p. 88.

forty-one, the community of Cairo appointed him their chief rabbi.

Maimonides (the Greek for "son of Maimon") became such a towering figure in the Jewish world that of him it is said, "From Moses [the Prophet] to Moses [Maimonides] there arose none like Moses." This laudatory statement is based on Maimonides' ability to excel in various areas of Jewish thought and to make his works accessible to others. From philosophy to medicine to Jewish law, Maimonides wrote and taught prolifically, all the while acting as a physician for the Egyptian royal household, as a rabbi to his community, and as an activist and advocate for oppressed Jews locally and thousands of miles away.

The Rambam made several important contributions to the body of literature comprising Jewish law and commentaries. His three most influential works in this field were his commentary to the Mishnah, his *Sefer Ha-Mitzvot* (Book of Commandments) and most important, the *Mishneh Torah*. His commentary on the Mishnah was the earliest of the three works, and is written so lucidly that it is also referred to as *Sefer Ha-Ma'or* (Book of Light).

Maimonides himself notes at the conclusion of the work, "I was working on this Commentary under the most arduous conditions . . . as we were driven from place to place . . . while traveling by land or crossing the stormy sea." In the book, Rambam explains each Mishnah, gleaning from the works of the Talmud, other authors, and from his own extensive knowledge base.

The commentary offers something new as well: in cases when many different legal opinions exist, Maimonides offers a final, definitive ruling for future generations to follow.

This methodology served Maimonides well as he embarked on his next project: a commentary on the 613 *mitzvot*. Appropriately entitled *Sefer Ha-Mitzvot* (Book of the Commandments), the text serves both as a stand-alone volume explicating the Torah's positive and negative precepts and as an introduction to his monumental achievement: the *Mishneh Torah,* Maimonides' summary of the entire Talmud.

In fact, at least one such commentary already existed at the time Maimonides began his edition. It had been written some years earlier by Rabbi Isaac Alfasi (known as the "Rif," an acronym of his name), a Sephardic rabbi who lived from 1013 to 1103 in North Africa and Spain. The Rif had undertaken the monumental task of distilling the entire Talmud to the essential arguments presented in each section, and citing the law when it was not apparent from the text.

Although a breakthrough achievement, the Rif's work followed the sections of the Talmud as they were written, and not in a topical fashion that would have made it easier to look things up. Because of this organizational difficulty, the Rif's commentary wasn't as "user-friendly" as those who tried to use it to learn the proper way to observe Jewish law might have hoped. Thus, the task fell upon the Rambam reorganize this material, in order to make it accessible to his generation and those who followed.

In the introduction to the *Mishneh Torah,* Maimonides' law code, Rambam explains the need for such a collection:

"At this time, the sufferings of our people have increased. The pressing need of the moment supersedes every other consideration. The wisdom of the wise has vanished, and the wisdom of our learned men is concealed. Hence, the commentaries, compilations of laws and Responsa of the Geonim [leaders of the Talmudic academies], which they thought were easy to understand, have in our times become difficult to understand, and there are only a few individuals who are able to comprehend them properly . . .

"For this reason, I, Moshe ben Maimon, the Sephardi, have . . . decided to compile the results derived from them as to what is prohibited and what is permitted, what is clean and what is unclean, and all the other laws of the Torah, all in clear language and concise style, so that the entire oral Torah will be systematically arranged for all . . . Therefore, I called this work *Mishneh Torah* (Summary of the Law), for a man should first read the Written Torah and then read this code and he will know from it the entire Oral Law without the need of reading any other book between them."

Written in concise, lucid language and organized according to topic, the Mishneh Torah was all Maimonides could have hoped to accomplish. However, due to his focus on cutting out all extraneous material and concentrating on statements of pure law, the Rambam did have his detractors. Because Maimonides didn't "footnote," leaving out his sources, naysayers (particularly in the Ashkenazic rabbinic community) accused him of making up his rulings rather than arriving at them from a comprehensive study of the traditional texts. Some Ashkenazic communities even went so far as to burn copies of the *Mishneh Torah* and to

excommunicate those who admitted to reading his philosophical works. In fact, it took several hundred years for Maimonides' works to be accepted as authoritative outside of the Sephardic world. Within it, however, Maimonides was hailed as a luminary without compare. His reputation was further bolstered by three additional collections of work: his philosophical treatises, his responsa literature, and his letters to Jewish communities under siege.

Maimonides began to study philosophy at a young age, under the tutelage of his father. While in the Ashkenazic world the study of secular subjects was sometimes frowned upon, no such prohibition existed in Spain and North Africa. In communities where nonfundamentalist Muslims and Jews mixed, advances in literature and philosophy were often topics of conversation and mutual admiration. Maimonides understood that common people, while not as well versed as rabbis and scholars, also sought the answers to the great existential questions: What is the nature of God? What is the meaning of life? Is there Divine Justice? What does Judaism have to say about these issues?

In his philosophical opus, *Moreh Nevuchim* (*The Guide of the Perplexed*), the Rambam explained Judaism's take on these issues and more. In many countries under Islamic influence, such as Egypt, Greek philosophy had become a hot topic and was widely studied by Jews and Muslims alike. Greek philosophers, particularly Aristotle, raised questions that could be troubling to observant Jews. For example, how can one reconcile God's ethereal character with the often anthropomorphic descriptions of God in the Torah? In his work, Maimonides sought to provide Jewish answers to these dilemmas, while continuing to rely on rational thought, which was the foundation of Greek philosophy. Originally written in Judeo-Arabic, his book was an immediate success, spawning three Hebrew translations within a decade. Its study continues into modern times.

The Epistle to Yemen
Because Maimonides was known far and wide as a Torah scholar without par, people wrote to him frequently, asking for Jewish legal rulings on a variety of issues. From marriage and divorce to virtually all areas of Jewish life, thousands of letters arrived by messenger claiming the Rambam's attention. While all were important to the individuals and communities who sought his advice, a few were so profound that Maimonides' responses constitute an important body of literature in and of itself. One such issue was that of forced conversions to Islam.

The fanatical Almohades, whose arrival in Spain caused Maimonides' own family to flee, had by the middle of the twelfth century taken over much of the Muslim world. Minority communities such as Jews were given the choice to convert to Islam, flee, or submit to death. Given these odds, many Jews converted en masse to Islam (foreshadowing the situation that would afflict the Jews of Spain under the Catholic Inquisition a few centuries later) and then wondered about their chances of being accepted into Heaven by God once they passed from this world.

In 1168, a Yemenite rabbi by the name of Jacob al-Fayumi wrote to the Rambam with the following dilemma. Not only had a fanatical Muslim cleric become the ruler of the community, decreeing that all Jews must convert to Islam or suffer the conse-quences, but in fact one of the Jews *had*

converted to Islam and had begun preaching the supremacy of Islam. At the same time, a false Messiah had appeared in the same community, first raising and then dashing the hopes of the Yemenite Jews. Rabbi al-Fayumi addressed his concerns to Maimonides, seeking his advice, and Maimonides replied to the rabbi as the representative of all Yemenite Jews in one of the Rambam's most famous letters: the Epistle to Yemen.

In his letter, Maimonides shares his belief that the root of all anti-Semitism is jealousy of the Jews for being God's chosen people, and by extension a hatred of God. Unable to battle God directly, anti-Semites take on the Jews, whom they seek to dominate and persecute. He then goes on to assure the community that, in fact, Judaism is the true religion, and its laws were given to the Jewish people directly by God. He exhorts the people to study Torah, and thereby come to an understanding that persecutions will end and that the words of the prophets will come to pass, with Jews regaining their former glory in the world.

Maimonides shares historical episodes of other false messiahs, so that the people will know how to recognize another if he comes to their community. Finally, Maimonides ends with a request to send a copy of his epistle to every single community, both rural and urban, so that it may strengthen their faith and cause them to stand firm. Read it communally and individually. In so doing, you will be one of those "that turn the many to righteousness" (Daniel 12:3).[4]

---

[4] Norman A. Stillman, *The Jews of Arab Lands: A History and Source Book*, Philadelphia: Jewish Publication Society, 1979, p. 246.

Following the dissemination of the letter, which was written largely in Arabic so that the people themselves could read it without depending on their rabbis to translate it from Hebrew, Maimonides himself sought intervention from the Caliph of Egypt, Saladin, whom he served as his personal physician. With Saladin's help, the persecution of the Yemenite Jews came to an end, and Maimonides was seen as a hero for his words of Torah and his activism on their behalf.

CONNECTING TO OUR TRADITION

While this chapter highlights three extraordinary rabbis in particular, Jewish scholarship really has no end. Others too numerous to mention in a chapter as short as this continued to elucidate the Torah, Talmud, and Jewish philosophy all over the globe throughout the Middle Ages and continuing forward into our own time. The Sh'ma prayer exhorts us to meditate on the words of the Torah day and night, teaching it to our children and by extension, our students who are considered to be as our children.

The Talmudic scholar Ben Bag Bag said of the Torah, "Turn it and turn it again, for everything is in it" (*Pirkei Avot* 5:25). Even scholars of the caliber of Rabbenu Gershom, Rashi, and the Rambam did just that, and opened up Jewish study to the masses, making it accessible to those who had only a little time to study in the evenings after work, and might not have a rabbi around to translate. With Rabbenu Gershom's emphasis on the practical, Rashi's concentration on clear explication of the words of the Torah, and the Rambam's ability to explain Jewish law and philosophy so beautifully that the common person could understand and practice Judaism, Jewish scholarship rose

to a new level that we still enjoy in the modern age.

DID YOU KNOW?

- Perhaps the reason that Jews (and other intellectuals) suddenly had more free time to study in the eleventh century was that two new inventions changed the lives of everyone in Europe. In 1050, the invention of horseshoes allowed horses hooked up to steel-rimmed plows (invented earlier in the century) to plow fields much more efficiently than oxen, the traditional work animals used until then. With the power produced by the horse hitched to the newer ploughs, a peasant could plow his (or his landlord's) land more efficiently, resulting in much higher food production in a shorter amount of time, and the advent of "leisure time."[5]

- One of the first printed Hebrew books, a copy of Rashi's commentary to the Bible, was published in Italy in 1469. Although the first printing press was created by Johannes Gutenberg in Germany in 1455 (and the first book off that press was a Bible), German Jews weren't allowed to join the guilds, and so it wasn't until those German Jewish printers moved to Italy that Hebrew books came to be published.[6]

- During the second half of the eighth century, a rabbi named Anan ben David, a powerful Babylonian Jew, began a revolution of sorts in the religious world. He began a strong movement opposing the leadership of the *geonim* (academy leaders) on the basis that the Talmudic interpretation of the Torah was incorrect, and

---

[5] Maggie Anton, *Rashi's Daughters*, Glendale, CA: Banot Press, 2005, p. 1.

[6] Naomi Pasachoff and Robert J. Littman, *Jewish History in 100 Nutshells*, Northvale, NJ: Jason Aronson, 1995, p. 156.

advocated a return to a strict reading of the biblical text without rabbinic interpretation.

By the following century, the group was called Karaites (from same root as "written work," referring to the Torah) and they had succeeded in producing some true scholars who challenged the "Rabbanites," or rabbinic Jews.

Although the Karaites believed in keeping the fundamentals of Jewish law and belief relatively unchanged, a schism emerged between the two groups on both religious and political grounds. With the new movement absorbing other sects, such as the Sadducees (of whom a remnant had survived in exile), and gaining ground, they began to proselytize among the Rabbanites. The conflict led to the rabbinic community declaring the Karaites to be heretics and forbidding their followers to marry Karaites or have any business or religious dealings with them.

Despite the acrimony, a Karaite community flourished and spread throughout Babylonia, Egypt, Turkey, and Eretz Yisrael by the twelfth century, with groups living as far north and west as Lithuania by the early 1900s. Although considered to be Jewish by most authorities (even those who relegated them to heretical status) for most of this time, by the eighteenth century Karaites ceased to be part of the larger Jewish community.

This change was mostly due to the absorption of the Jewish population of Lithuania into Russia, and the designation of non-Jewish status on the Karaites by Empress Catherine II, who treated them as a separate group and removed the "Jew tax" from them. A small Karaite community of a few thousand families still exists in Eretz Yisrael, where members tend to marry only other Karaites. Their practice continues to exclude holidays not mentioned in the Bible (such as Ḥanukkah), to include only biblical texts as prayers in the worship service, and to eat only the meat of animals mentioned in the Torah.[7]

IMPORTANT TERMS

Codes	Rabbanites
Commentaries	Sephardic
Mikra'ot Gedolot	Ashkenazic
Mishneh Torah	Almohades
Sefer Ha-Mitzvot	Talmud
Epistle to Yemen	Mishnah
The Guide of the Perplexed	Midrash
Karaites	

Names, Places, and Events
Rabbenu Gershom
Rashi
Maimonides/the Rambam

DISCUSSION QUESTIONS
- The differences between Reform and Orthodox Jews today could be compared to those between the Rabbanites and Karaites of a thousand years ago. Yet, Karaites are not considered to be Jews because their practice differs so greatly from that of rabbinic Jews. Why do you think that is? Do you think that all Jews, whether Reform, Orthodox, Conservative, Reconstructionist, or anything else are equally authentic Jews? Why or why not? How have these divisions affected relations between Jewish groups and communities? How can they be bridged to create more harmony among the Jewish people?

---

[7] Ibid., pp. 115–116.

- How do you think the codes and commentaries written by the scholars of the medieval period allowed Judaism to remain vibrant and helped it survive to the present day?

ACTIVITIES

Mitzvah Quest (S, A)

Today, many *mitzvot* (commandments) are seen as normative and universal despite their absence from the Torah. Often, this disparity exists because rabbinic Judaism took an idea from the Bible and gave it practical application. One of these *mitzvot* is the commandment to light Shabbat candles.

Assign students to read the passage in the Torah that deals with the prohibition against lighting a fire on Shabbat (Exodus 35:3). Then have them look up the practice of lighting candles in the English translation of a traditional law code, such as Maimonides' *Mishneh Torah* or the *Kitzur Shulḥan Aruch* (a very abbreviated version of Maimonides' law code, translated into English and arranged by topic). Ask the students to brainstorm: How do you think the rabbis got from the biblical text to the practice today? As a follow-up to the student discussions, have students ask their own congregational rabbi his or her answer to the dilemma.

Fiction as Midrash (S, A)

In recent years, many wonderful works of fiction, called "modern midrash" by some, have been published by modern English-language authors. These works seek to add a new level of interpretation to biblical and Talmudic texts by making fictionalized accounts of the lives of the main characters accessible to the modern reader.

As a long-term assignment, have students read independently one of the books on the list that follows. In class, have students compare and contrast the fictionalized account with the biblical or Talmudic text. Ask the students to fact-check, looking up details that don't appear in the traditional texts to see if they are in fact plausible. Ask the students to describe what they have learned about what life might have been like for the women and men who constitute the pantheon of our biblical and rabbinic heroes and heroines.

Some suggestions for reading follow (arranged alphabetically by title); you or your colleagues may have others:

Queenmaker: A Novel of King David's Queen by India Edghill (New York: Picador USA, 1999, 2003).

Rashi's Daughters, Book 1: Joheved by Maggie Anton. (Glendale, CA: Banot Press, 2005).

The Red Tent by Anita Diamant (New York: Picador USA, 1997).

Sarah: A Novel (Canaan Trilogy) by Marek Halter (New York: Crown Publishers, 2004).

Zipporah, Wife of Moses: A Novel by Marek Halter (New York: Crown Publishers, 2005).

Principles of Faith (E, S, A)

One of Moses Maimonides' most enduring texts is his "Thirteen Principles of Faith" on which the popular Friday evening hymn Yigdal is based. In pairs, ask students to read the principles of faith on the following page. Ask your students: Are there others that should be added? Should some of these be omitted? Might they be better stated in a different order? Why do you think

Maimonides chose these thirteen principles? Have students write their own "principles of faith" and share them with the class.

Maimonides' Thirteen Principles of Faith:

1. The existence of God
2. God's unity
3. God's spirituality and incorporeality (lack of a physical body)
4. God's eternity
5. God alone should be the object of worship
6. Revelation through God's prophets
7. The preeminence of Moses among the prophets
8. God's law given on Mount Sinai
9. The immutability of the Torah as God's Law
10. God's foreknowledge of human actions
11. Retribution of evil
12. The coming of the Jewish Messiah
13. The resurrection of the dead

TIMELINE (all dates are CE)

8th century

Anan ben David forms Ananism, the precursor of Karaism

Charlemagne crowned emperor of the Holy Roman Empire

c.1000

Rabbenu Gershom outlaws polygamy for Ashkenazic Jews

1040

Rashi born in Troyes, France

1105

Rashi dies

1135

Moses Maimonides born in Cordova, Spain

1166

Maimonides arrives in Egypt

1168

Maimonides completes his commentary on the Mishnah, containing the "Thirteen Principles of Faith"

1172

Maimonides sends his "Epistle to Yemen"

1178

Maimonides completes the *Mishneh Torah*

1190

Maimonides completes the *Guide of the Perplexed*

1204

Maimonides dies in Cairo

RESOURCES
Books and Articles

Anton, Maggie. *Rashi's Daughters: Book One—Joheved.* Glendale,CA: Banot Press, 2005.

Barnavi, Eli, ed. *Historical Atlas of the Jewish People: From the Time of the Patriarchs to the Present.* New York: Schocken Books, 1992.

Gilbert, Martin. *The Routledge Atlas of Jewish History,* 6th ed. London: Routledge, 1995.

Herczeg, Yisrael Isser Zvi. *The Torah: With Rashi's Commentary Translated, Annotated and Elucidated,* The Sapirstein Edition. Brooklyn, NY: Mesorah Publications, 1997.

Holtz, Barry W., ed. *Back to the Sources: Reading the Classical Jewish Texts.* New York: Summit Books, 1984.

Marcus, Jacob Rader. *The Jew in the Medieval World, A Source Book: 315–1791.* Cincinnati, OH: Hebrew Union College Press, 1990.

Pasachoff, Naomi, and Robert J. Littman. *Jewish History in 100 Nutshells.* Northvale, NJ: Jason Aronson, 1995.

Sarna, Jonathan D., and Jonathan B. Krasner. *The History of the Jewish People: A Story of Tradition and Change.* Springfield, NJ: Behrman House, 2006 (see especially chapter 7).

Stillman, Norman A. *The Jews of Arab Lands: A History and Source Book.* Philadelphia: Jewish Publication Society, 1979.

Stow, Kenneth R. *Alienated Minority: The Jews of Medieval Latin Europe.* Cambridge, MA: Harvard University Press, 1992.

Internet
Visit www.behrmanhouse.com/booklinks for links to Web sites that offer additional resources for this chapter.

CHAPTER FIFTEEN
JEWISH LIFE IN SPAIN

WHAT'S THE BIG IDEA?
Jewish Culture and Thought

For hundreds of years, the Jewish community in Spain was among the most cultured, literate, and cosmopolitan in the world. In an era when cooperation between different religious groups was unthinkable in most parts of the globe, Jews, along with their Muslim, Christian, and pagan neighbors, cooperated in multiple areas of business and scholarship to their—and the world's—great benefit. As this era of cooperation and tolerance in Spain came to an end with the advent of forced conversions and expulsion, the Sephardic refugees brought the knowledge gained over the previous centuries with them to their new communities in Europe, the Ottoman Empire, and the New World.

BACKGROUND INFORMATION
Overview: The Golden Age of Spain and Its Decline

One of the names that has stuck to the medieval period—usually unfairly—is that of the Dark Ages, which implies a time when life was grim and people were at best illiterate and at worst barbarian. In Spain, this characterization couldn't be further from the truth.

Jews had lived in Spain since at least the third century CE (and possibly before), at which point they turn up in the writings of the fledgling Catholic Church. At the Council of Elvira, held around the year 300 near Granada in southern Spain, Christians are admonished "not to suffer the fruits, which they receive from God

with the giving of thanks, to be blessed by the Jews." From this text, we can clearly see that Jews were not only integrated into the community along with their Christian (and, most likely, pagan) neighbors, but that these neighbors believed that their blessings held power and were desirable for a good harvest.[1]

From these beginnings, Jews continued to live (although less happily) under the subsequent Visigothic rulers. Germanic conquerors of Spain in the late sixth century, the Visigoths converted to Christianity and often persecuted the Jews under their control, at times engaging in a policy of forced conversion, until the Muslim conquest in the early eighth century.

The Muslim general Tarik ibn Ziyad, successful in his conversion of the North African pagans to Islam, entered Spain from the south and defeated the Visigoths in the year 711. The policy of the Muslim conquerors was to allow Jews living in the conquered territories to fortify the towns under their control. In Spain, this new leadership role, combined with the departure of the Visigoths (including many landowners who abandoned their holdings), made for a hospitable environment not only for the Jews who had continued to live in Spain (some in secret) but for those who returned from

---

[1] Jacob Rader Marcus, ed., *The Jew in the Medieval World, A Source Book: 315–1791* (Cincinnati, OH: Hebrew Union College Press, 1990), p. 101. Marcus notes, "Some farmers evidently valued the blessing of the Jews more than that of their own Christian priests."

exile elsewhere in Europe. The Golden Age of Spain had begun.

The Muslim victors referred to the land they had conquered as *al-Andalus*, the Arabic derivative of the Spanish *Andalusia*, which refers in general to the part of the Iberian Peninsula under Muslim rule from 711 until 1492. Like Egyptian rule thousands of years before, early Muslim rule was divided into dynasties. The Umayyad dynasty was founded in the year 755 by Abd al-Rahman. The Umayyads were tolerant toward Jews, and they encouraged the participation by Arabs and Jews in the sciences, literature, and trade. In the year 929, a descendant of this ruler, Prince Abd al-Rahman III, established an independent caliphate in Spain, and during his reign the Jewish community began to flourish even more.

In the capital city of Cordoba, these rulers were so hospitable that Jews came from all over the world to engage in commerce and Jewish learning there as well as in much of the Iberian peninsula then under Muslim control. During this period the academies of Babylonia were in decline, and new centers of learning in Europe, including Spain, filled that void for the world's Jewish scholars.

Jewish intellectuals also came to learn the disciplines of medicine, geography and cartography from Arab scientists and mathematicians living in this open and cosmopolitan area. This wonderful state of affairs continued into the eleventh and twelfth centuries, and for hundreds of years Spain was on the cutting edge of all types of learning for Jews and Arabs alike.

By the eleventh century, the Umayyad dynasty began to decline and Muslim Spain was divided into smaller principalities. With this decentralization, Jews moved throughout Spain, and became in many places part of the ruling class.

Founding academies of Talmudic learning, functioning as tax farmers[2] and as landlords for Arab landowners, and pursuing all manner of intellectual interests including philosophy, medicine, and poetry, Jews had risen to the pinnacle of life in medieval Spain. However, this decentralization also made it more difficult for the Muslim rulers to defend Spain against both Christian invaders and rival Muslim factions, such as the Almoravids and the Almohads. The Almoravids, a fundamentalist and intolerant Muslim sect from North Africa, invaded southern Spain in 1094. Sixty-eight years later, they were followed by the Almohads, a fanatical Berber sect from the mountains of Morocco who by the year 1172 had conquered most of Islamic Spain. Unlike the more tolerant Umayyads, the Almohads forced all Jews and Christians under their control to convert to Islam, or else face exile or execution. As a result, many Jews fled over the border to northern Spain, much of which had begun to fall under the control of the Christian conquerors moving south.

Paradise Lost: The Reconquista and the Jewish Community

By the twelfth century, Christian armies were moving through Europe to reconquer areas lost to the Muslims over the previous four hundred years. The *Reconquista,* or Christian reconquest of Spain and the Middle East, took another four hundred years, and the fortunes of Spain's Jews began to decline—at first slowly, and then sharply.

---

[2] Tax farmers collected taxes on behalf of the government; if they collected more than what was due, they were permitted to keep the rest. Such a position was given to government officials and other privileged individuals throughout the Middle Ages and was considered to be a perk.

For a time, things were still good for the Jews of Spain. The Christian rulers tolerated the Jewish community, mostly because of its economic and political value. As part of the ruling class, and the emerging middle class, Jews fulfilled an important function in society, paying taxes and sometimes filling administrative roles in local government. The Jews, as a class, were considered to "belong" to the king and were often given special charters granting them protected status, prohibiting Christians from persecuting them, permitting them freedom of movement, allowing them their own law courts, and the like. The Jewish community in Spain also had a remarkable degree of both integration into the general community and independence within it. Creating their own enclaves, called *aljamas*, the Jews collected their own taxes, ran their own law courts, and in general operated in an independent manner as long as the ruler tolerated this status quo.

However, by the thirteenth century a stronger anti-Jewish feeling arose among many in Spain, and for the first time this sentiment was matched by the religious and political leadership. The Golden Age had come to an end.

Diplomats, Poets, Philosophers, and Rabbis: Luminaries of the Golden Age

Primarily during the ninth, tenth, eleventh, and twelfth centuries, many influential individuals rose to prominence, giving the Jewish community of Spain the cultural and religious prominence that led to the designation of this period as the Golden Age. Characterized by their deep learning, openness to a multitude of ideas—both Jewish and secular, and prominence on the international scene, several of these men helped to shape the Golden Age. Their ideas and written works remain influential

even today. In the previous chapter we discussed the life and career of Moses Maimonides, perhaps the most famous of the luminaries to originate in medieval Spain. However, there are many others, and a few are highlighted here.

Hasdai ibn Shaprut (905–975)
Hasdai ibn Shaprut bears a remarkable resemblance to the great Moses Maimonides, who lived two hundred years later. Court physician and adviser to Abd al-Rahman III and his successor, al-Hakam II, Hasdai was called upon not only for his medical knowledge but as a diplomat often trusted with sensitive political negotiations. The Jewish community bestowed upon him the title *nasi,* or prince, as befitted his role as the leading Jewish courtier in the land. Ibn Shaprut, after hearing about the existence of a Jewish kingdom in Khazaria (in the Caucasus Mountains; see chapter 17 for more information), sent emissaries to the king of the Khazars and initiated correspondence with the Khazar king Joseph in Hebrew. Iberian Jews were fascinated with Khazaria, the only independent Jewish kingdom in the world at the time, and Sephardic diplomats were in a position to find out more about them and report back to their coreligionists.

Ibn Shaprut was also a patron of the arts and sciences and employed a personal secretary, Menahem ben Saruq, who was himself a poet, linguist, and the author of the first Hebrew dictionary.[3] Ibn Shaprut also influenced other poets, including Dunash ibn Labrat, a North African who pioneered the composition of Hebrew poetry using Arabic meter, which became the standard for medieval Spanish poetry.

---

[3] Norman A. Stillman, *Jews of Arab Lands*, Philadelphia: Jewish Publication Society, 1979, p. 55.

Under his leadership, the Jewish community of Spain finally made a clean break from the authority of the Babylonian academies, establishing a yeshiva in Cordoba and gaining prominence as an independent entity.

Shmuel Ha-Nagid (993–1056)
With the decentralization of Spain into smaller principalities in the eleventh century, the Jewish community became fragmented as well. The rulers of these various smaller kingdoms were referred to as the "Party Kings,"[4] designated thus because of their different allegiances, such as Berber, Slav, and so forth but also a useful moniker because of the wonderful cultural atmosphere they propagated. Under these rulers, Andalusian civilization flourished and Jews participated fully in both its culture and in Spanish political life, and Shmuel (Samuel) Ha-Nagid (the leader, or prince) was a wonderful representative.

A soldier and politician, a master poet and Talmudic scholar, Shmuel Ha-Nagid's influence reverberated through the upper crust of Jewish society and filtered through to Jews worldwide as well as to Arabic poets and scholars. Ha-Nagid was appointed as the vizier of Badis, the Berber ruler of Granada in 1038. As the commander of Granada's military, his army defeated Seville's army over the course of a series of campaigns spanning eighteen years. In an era when both Jews and Arabs in Spain prided themselves on their purity of language and expression, Ha-Nagid's poetry outshone that of most of his generation. Weaving secular themes such as war and wine with praise of Torah and expressions borrowed from Scripture, his poems still resonate today,

with titles such as "The Poet's Boast," "In the Ruined Citadel," and "Wine." Of course beautiful poetry loses something in translation, but here are two fine examples:

"Take Heart"
In times of sorrow, take heart, even
Though you stand at death's door: the
Candle flares up before it dies, and
Wounded lions roar.[5]

"The Jasmine"
Look at the jasmine, whose branches,
Leaves, and stems are green as chrysolite,
Whose flowers are white as rock crystal,
Whose tendrils are red as carnelian—
Like a white-faced youth
Whose hands are shedding the blood of
Innocent men.[6]

Yehudah Ha-Levi (c. 1070–1141)
Even today, the words of Yehudah Ha-Levi resonate for Zionists everywhere the world over. A physician, poet, essayist, philosopher, and historian, Yehudah Ha-Levi (Judah the Levite) lived during a period when the fortunes of Spain's Jews were changing dramatically year by year. During Ha-Levi's teenage years, the fanatical Almoravids were invading southern Spain, while Christian armies sought to conquer northern Spain, in proximity to Ha-Levi's hometown of Tudela. Although as a young man Ha-Levi followed the popular sentiment that Jews were completely at home in Spain, evidence of a shift in thought can be seen in his later writings.

---

[4] Ibid.

[5] T. Carmi, ed. and trans., *The Penguin Book of Hebrew Verse*, NY: Penguin Books, 1981, p. 296. This wonderful volume contains many hundreds of examples of Hebrew poetry with English translations.
[6] Ibid.

In Ha-Levi's important work, *The Kuzari*, the author uses fiction as a method to share his philosophical approach to Judaism. In the story, a Muslim, a Christian, and a Jew present arguments extolling each religion to the pagan king of the Khazars. After hearing them, the king eventually converts to Judaism. Ha-Levi thus uses the story as a vehicle to explain the benefits of each, while extolling the values of Judaism above all. In his work, Ha-Levi introduces the idea that the Jews do God's work on earth by bringing humanity and enlightenment to all. However, the most advantageous place to do God's work, according to Ha-Levi, is in the Land of Israel.

Ha-Levi's poetry collection entitled *Songs of Zion* praises the Holy Land and its beauty, often utilizing verses from Scripture, and expressing the conviction that only in Eretz Yisrael can the Jews truly be at home, free from persecution. In what is perhaps his most famous poem, "My Heart Is in the East," Ha-Levi writes:

"My heart is in the East and I am at the Edge of the West. Then how can I taste What I eat, how can I enjoy it? How Can I fulfill my vows[7] and pledges While Zion is in the domain of Edom,[8] And I am in the bonds of Arabia? It Would be easy for me to leave behind All the good things of Spain; it would Be glorious to see the dust of the Ruined Shrine."[9]

Eventually, in keeping with his own Zionist convictions, Ha-Levi left Spain, bound for Eretz Yisrael. Most sources state that by 1141 he had made it at least to Egypt, and some say all the way to

Israel before dying either en route, or once he arrived there. A famous story has Ha-Levi arriving in Jerusalem and kneeling to kiss its stones, only to be trampled to death by a passing horseman. In any case, by the time Ha-Levi made good on his vows and undertook his journey, life for Andalusian Jewry had changed forever.

Nahmanides (c. 1194–1270)
By the thirteenth century, Jews made up approximately 3 percent of the total population of Spain.[10] Although Andalusian Jews continued to be represented in financial and political positions of influence all over the land, a conflict was brewing among the highest echelon of leaders. The rulers—the dukes and kings who governed the various principalities in Spain—saw the advantage of having talented Jews in their employ.

The Catholic clergy, however, believed that elevating Jews to high positions in which they came in contact with Christians was deleterious to the morality of their flock. With increased influence of the clergy over the Christian populace, their anti-Semitism became contagious. By the middle of the thirteenth century, both the clergy and the rulers had become more openly hostile toward Andalusian Jewry.

The leader of the Spanish Jewish community at the time was Rabbi Moses ben Nahman, or Nahmanides, also known as the Ramban (the acronym of his name). Nahmanides headed a yeshiva in Gerona, in northeast Spain. Like other luminaries before him, Nahmanides was a philosopher and physician in addition to being a scholar and community leader. His commentaries on the Torah and Talmud are still considered fundamental to an

---

[7] Ha-Levi had by this time made a vow to leave Spain for Eretz Yisrael.
[8] *Edom*, which means "Rome" in Hebrew, is a traditional Jewish name for Christian lands.
[9] T. Carmi, ed. and trans., *The Penguin Book of Hebrew Verse*, NY: Penguin Books, 1981, p. 347.

[10] Naomi Pasachoff and Robert J. Littman, *Jewish History in 100 Nutshells*, Northvale, NJ: Jason Aronson, 1995, p. 134.

understanding of the sacred text, as are his writings on Jewish law and on Jewish mysticism, or kabbalah (from the Hebrew word meaning "tradition"). In this position, it was only natural that when the Church sought learned Jews to debate Christian clergy in theological matters, they sought out a strong leader such as Nahmanides.

In 1263, following several decades in which Jews (and Muslims) were encouraged to convert to Christianity, the Church began a policy of instituting forced sermons, in which Jews were required to listen to hours-long messages extolling the values of Christianity and demeaning those of Judaism. Soon after, the Catholic Church called for a debate in which Nahmanides would defend Judaism against the arguments of the Church, represented by a Jewish convert to Catholicism named Pablo Christiani (Paul the Christian) and backed by none other than King James I of Aragon.

For four days in July of that year, the debate raged on in the Spanish port city of Barcelona. Nahmanides was at a disadvantage, having been warned not to say anything negative about the Church, although King James I had assured him complete freedom of speech. In spite of these impediments, after a few days, Nahmanides seemed to be winning the debate. At this point, accounts differ. The Christian sources say that the debate ended because Nahmanides ran away from the city, while Jewish sources say that he stayed in Barcelona, was allowed to respond to a sermon by the king in his synagogue, and received a monetary sum for his participation in the debate. Whatever the true outcome of the disputation, Nahmanides did in fact leave Spain for the Land of Israel, where he

arrived in 1267 and spent the final three years of his life.

The Jews of Spain, having begun their downward spiral, continued failing fast. Pablo Christiani, by most accounts the loser of the debate, convinced Pope Clement IV to censor and burn Jewish books—including the Talmud and Maimonides' *Mishneh Torah* law code—because he perceived them to say negative things about Jesus.[11] In fact, Christiani took his case all the way to Paris, persuading King Louis IX to institute the Jewish badge,[12] a measure that monarchs all over Europe began to emulate.

By the fourteenth century, anti-Semitism was widespread throughout Spain and France, where the Inquisition had been established a century earlier. Letters written by King Peter IV of Aragon called for a halt to the violence inflicted by the Christian populace against the Jews in the wake of the devastating bubonic plague, which killed one-third of Europe's people between 1348 and 1349, and for which the Jews generally were blamed.[13] And then, in 1391, outright disaster struck the Jews of Spain.

A Century of Decline: From 1391 to 1492

In 1391, the archbishop of Spain died and his right-hand man began to advocate an *increase* in violence against Jews. On June 4, 1391, the Christian populace of Seville, near the southern tip of Spain, rioted, murdering Jewish men, burning down the Jewish quarter, and selling many of the women and children into slavery. As the violence spread to other cities throughout Spain, the authorities were silent, which

---

[11] Ibid., pp. 135–136.
[12] Robert Chazan, *Church, State and Jew in the Middle Ages*, New York: Behrman House, 1980, p. 261. For a portion of the text containing both the Christian and Jewish reports of the Disputation, see pp. 265–276.
[13] Ibid., pp. 128–131.

served to encourage the mobs. As Jews by the thousands sought to avoid death by converting to Christianity, others chose martyrdom rather than conversion, and those who could flee the country did so. By September, up to 100,000 Jews had converted to Christianity and as many as 50,000 Jews had been murdered.[14]

Laws restricting all aspects of Jewish life followed the riots. Echoing the persecution of Jews throughout the ages from the time of the Maccabees, Jews were banned from holding public office, studying Talmud, increasing the size of their synagogues, or withholding inheritances from children who converted to Catholicism. Forced sermons continued, and Jews were prohibited from marrying Christians (and vice versa).

Once King Ferdinand and Queen Isabella married, uniting their territories to comprise almost all of the Iberian Peninsula, the situation only worsened. Jewish communities that had been independent entities for centuries lost the right to manage their own affairs, including the right to have their own law courts, collect their own taxes, and more. Some Jews were forcibly removed from their homes and transferred to ghettoes, and others were forced to wear clothing and badges identifying them as Jews.[15] The institution of the Inquisition in Spain created a climate of secrecy and fear that, along with further discriminatory laws and restrictions, resulted ultimately in the expulsion of the Jews from Spain in 1492.

The Converso Question: Forced Conversions, Marranos, and Limpieza de Sangre
Imagine 100,000 Jews converting to Catholicism within a period of three months. This situation faced Church officials throughout Spain in 1391: What to do with all the new converts?

Once an individual converted to Christianity, he or she was not only responsible to observe all of the ritual laws and sacraments of Catholicism (the breaking of which could compromise one's ability to enter Heaven), but fell under the jurisdiction of the Inquisition (see below). This observance necessitated religious education for all converts, which most did not receive, having converted quickly and under duress. However, any baptism—done under pain of death or not—was still binding, regardless of whether the postulant knew anything about how to observe his or her new religion.

Compounding this problem were the laws of *limpeza de sangre,* or "purity of blood." Once a Jew was baptized, theoretically anyway, he or she was once again eligible to live in any town, work in any job, or marry any person of his or her choosing. Church officials and ordinary Christians alike became suspicious of *nuevos Christianos* (new Christians) and so sought out ways to identify them and bar them from holding public office or joining guilds; these endeavors set up competition between new and old Christians that the latter sought to eliminate. (Modern economic ideas regarding the value of competition in the marketplace had not yet been accepted; a person who set up a competing business interest—especially if that person had been a Jew—was viewed as stealing from others rather than increasing the value of their work or product.) At the same time as barriers were put in place to prohibit new

[14] Naomi Pasachoff and Robert J. Littman, *Jewish History in 100 Nutshells*, Northvale, NJ: Jason Aronson, 1995, pp. 145–146.
[15] Ibid.

Christians from advancing in business or society, new derogatory labels such as "Marrano" (swine) were used to label and stigmatize the *conversos* (converts), and of course to identify them as such.

Some converts to Catholicism were sincere in their new faith. From a religious standpoint, some new believers—many encouraged by their Christian neighbors and the Catholic clergy—thought that the ills befalling the Jewish community were proof that God had abandoned the Jewish people and that Christianity was the true religion. However, sincere converts were lumped together with *anussim* (pronounced "ah-new-sim," and meaning those who were forced to convert) under the shadow of suspicion that fell over all new Christians. Once identified as "other," the Inquisition often took over.

The Inquisition

As mentioned above, the first Inquisition was inaugurated in France in the thirteenth century. The Inquisition in Spain began in 1478, when Tomas de Torquemada, Queen Isabella's personal confessor, was appointed Grand Inquisitor. The purpose of the Inquisition, an official department of the Catholic Church, was to ensure that Catholics were not only practicing their religion in the purest way possible, but that converts to Catholicism were neither backsliding into their former religion nor pulling others in that direction. The main currency of the Inquisition was fear, and the second was money.

While converts—both sincere and insincere—were those most likely to experience fear in trying their best to appear as perfect Christians, many around them were encouraged to report their neighbors to the Inquisition as backsliding. Entire lists of behavior were

distributed to Catholics, encouraging them to spy on their neighbors and report if they, for example, washed their clothing or bathed on Fridays (the implication being that they were getting ready for Shabbat), professed an aversion to pork (practically the Spanish national food), or in any way appeared secretive in their behavior.

Once the Inquisition became suspicious of an individual or his or her family, action was often swift and serious. Those accused of heresy, a crime punishable by a torturous death, were arrested, thrown in prison, and their belongings confiscated. Many of these belongings—particularly jewelry and money—were kept by the office of the Inquisition, and used by the Church. Some of the money was given by the Church to the Spanish monarchs of the fifteenth and sixteenth centuries and was used to finance explorations to the New World.[16]

Regardless of whether the suspect was found guilty or not, these possessions were rarely, if ever, returned to the individual or the family. Rather, more money was often given as bribes to the Inquisition with the hope, usually futile, of releasing the suspect. Instead, family members frequently came under suspicion as well, often while the suspect was being tortured in a variety of ways in order to solicit information about other "heretics." Punishments for those accused of various levels of apostasy covered a wide range of penalties. Those not sentenced to death might be forced to wear a bright red or yellow garment festooned with crosses, devils, and flames, called a *sanbenito,* while being paraded through the town to catcalls, flinging garbage, and worse. Those whose crimes warranted death

---

[16] Sue Parker Gerson, *The Financial Structure of the Spanish Inquisition,* unpublished research paper, State University of New York at Binghamton, 1986.

were often consigned to be burned at the stake (public burnings were called *autos-da-fé*, or "acts of faith"), in view of their family and friends who were watched to make sure they did not appear sympathetic to the doomed one.

It is likely that between four thousand and eight thousand Jews (and a smaller number of *Moriscos*, or Muslim converts to Catholicism) were burnt alive during Torquemada's tenure as Grand Inquisitor. The Inquisition continued in Spain for hundreds of years and was instituted in those countries in the New World where Spain established a colonial foothold, ending finally in 1834.

The Expulsion of the Jews from Spain

During the course of the late Middle Ages, beginning with England in 1290, many European countries had forced their Jewish residents to leave, often with few possessions and little or no actual money. In fact, Spain was one of the last countries in Europe to exile its Jews, in the year 1492. It was a shock because for so many centuries, Spain was known as a bastion of tolerance and coexistence. So why, after all that time, did King Ferdinand and Queen Isabella expel the Jews of Spain?

Some clues may be found in the Edict of Expulsion itself. Addressed to the nobility as well as to every Jewish community of the land, the document provides a description of the state of affairs between Jews and Christians in fifteenth-century Spain. The monarchs write that they have watched with dismay as Christians, many of them converts from Judaism, have been swayed by the Jews with whom they have contact—whether business associates, neighbors, or relatives—into "Judaizing" behavior, including:

"achieving that the Christians and their children be circumcised, and giving them books from which they may read their prayers and declaring to them the fasts that they must keep, and joining with them to read and teach them the history of their law, indicating to them the festivals before they occur . . . carrying to them and giving to them from their houses unleavened bread and meats ritually slaughtered, instructing them about the things from which they must refrain . . . and persuading them as much as they can to hold and observe the law of Moses, convincing them that there is no other law or truth except for that one."

The edict goes on to lament that although the purpose of the Inquisition was to eliminate such behaviors among Christians, the Jews with whom they are in contact persist in convincing them otherwise. The monarchs, therefore

"having taken deliberation about this matter, resolve to order the said Jews and Jewesses of our kingdoms to depart and never to return or come back."

After placing the Jews under royal protection, Ferdinand and Isabella granted them until the end of July 1492 (four months, as the edict was dated March 31) to dispose of their possessions, including the ability to export them out of the country, except for "gold or silver or coined money or other things prohibited by the laws of our kingdoms." The edict was to take effect on July 31, 1492—the ninth of Av on the Jewish calendar.[17]

---

[17] Because the secular calendar was in flux between the Julian and Gregorian calendars in the fifteenth century, it's not really possible to pin down the exact Hebrew date of the expulsion (and, the Jews were given a grace period of probably up until August 3 to leave for good). The actual date of expulsion was, however, almost

According to their own words, Ferdinand and Isabella wished to rid Spain of Jews because they were influencing Christians to become Jewish. Why would so many Christians want to become Jewish, especially in the climate that surrounded them in fifteenth-century Spain? The answer seems obvious: because they were really hidden Jews.

With the capture of Granada on January 8, 1492, Spain was entirely under Christian control, and Ferdinand and Isabella wanted to homogenize their population. The Crown and the Church treated these *conversos* as heretics, because they had been baptized as Christians. However, in their hearts and in their behaviors, which they tried and too often failed to hide, many were Jews. Religious Catholics committed to the spiritual purity of their nation and its Christian population, the monarchs felt that with the expulsion of Spain's Jews, their problem would be solved. And so, on July 31, 1492, Spain became officially free of Jews.

A Hebrew account of the exile notes that between 50,000 and 53,000 Jewish families were expelled on that day, leaving cattle, stores, property, houses and vineyards—some of which had been in their families' possessions for centuries. Academies of Jewish learning were abandoned as rabbis fled with their congregants.[18] And while diplomats such as Don Isaac Abravanel, a biblical commentator, historian and council to the monarchy, tried to have the edict overturned by offering arguments and bribes, nothing worked.

Many of the exiled went to Islamic countries in North Africa and the Ottoman Empire, and others went north and east to the more tolerant countries of Holland and Italy. Others went west to Portugal, but were disappointed when there, too, they were expelled in 1497. Some, it is speculated, joined Columbus's voyage to the New World, which left Spain on the same day as the Edict of Expulsion went into effect. Still more converted and remained in Spain and Portugal as hidden Jews; according to one source, after the emancipation of Portugal's Jews in 1910, hidden Jews in Spain and Portugal began practicing Judaism openly once again, for the first time in centuries.

The expulsion of the Jews of Spain closes a chapter in Jewish history, not only in the Iberian Peninsula but for all of Jewry. Many historians, Yosef Hayyim Yerushalmi in particular, mark the Spanish Expulsion as a watershed between the medieval and modern periods in Jewish history. Others believe that the practices employed by the Catholic monarchs and the Inquisition constituted the first systematic example of government-sponsored violent anti-Semitism and were studied and employed by the Nazis in the "final solution" five hundred years later.

Our attention now turns to the Jewish communities that survived and flourished in the Ottoman Empire, Eastern Europe, and the New World.

CONNECTING TO OUR TRADITION

The sage Ben Zoma states in *Pirkei Avot* (4:1): "Who is wise? [The one] who learns from every person." The Golden Age of Spain embodied such tolerance and cooperation between Muslims, Jews, and

---

certainly during the three weeks preceding the commemoration of Tisha B'Av, and is often memorialized on the precise date.
[18] Robert Chazan, *Church, State and Jew in the Middle Ages*, New York: Behrman House, 1980, p. 261. For a portion of the text containing both the Christian and Jewish reports of the Disputation, pp. 319–322.

Christians. This spirit of collaboration and open-mindedness led to unparalleled advances in science, medicine, literature, and philosophy, not to mention advances within the scholarly circles of each group's faith tradition.

DID YOU KNOW?

- One of the reasons many historians speculate that Columbus might have been Jewish is that it's almost too much of a coincidence that his voyage left the same day as the Edict of Expulsion took effect.
- In fact, there is no direct evidence that Columbus himself was Jewish (although, like many in Spain and Italy, where he was from, lots of people—especially those connected to the sciences and wealthy patrons—had Jewish ancestors). However, there is evidence that *conversos* helped to finance the voyage and numbered among his crew. Columbus also hired an interpreter who spoke Hebrew, in order to converse with the natives whom Columbus expected to find in India, where he thought he was headed, and whom he believed to be a remnant of the ten lost tribes.

IMPORTANT TERMS

Sephardic
Auto-da-fé
Converso
Marrano
Morisco
Visigoths
Golden Age of Spain
Umayyads
Almoravids
Almohads
aljama

nasi
The Kuzari
Disputation
Nuevos Christianos
Sanbenito
Forced sermon
Limpieza de sangre
Inquisition
Edict of Expulsion
"judaizing"

Names, Places, and Events

Council of Elvira
Andalusia
Al-Andalus
Abd al-Rahman
Prince Abd al-Rahman III
Reconquista
Hasdai ibn Shaprut
Shmuel Ha-Nagid
Party Kings
Yehudah Ha-Levi
Granada
Tudela
Cordoba
Castile

Moses ben Naḥman (Naḥmanides)
Gerona
Aragon
Pablo Christiani
King James I
King Ferdinand
Queen Isabella
Tomas de Torquemada
Seville
Christopher Columbus
Granada

DISCUSSION QUESTIONS

- In the fourteenth and fifteenth centuries in Spain, the Jewish community was faced with a familiar dilemma: Should they convert, leave their homes for an unknown future in a distant land, or submit to a martyr's death? Unlike their counterparts in earlier centuries in Central Europe, very few Sephardic Jews chose death over conversion, opting instead to convert outwardly but remain Jewish inwardly. Discuss the pros and cons of choosing false conversion over leaving Spain. What do you think motivated each group of Jews to act as they did? What would you have done?
- In 1263, Rabbi Moses ben Naḥman (Naḥmanides) engaged in a public debate with Pablo Cristiani over the validity of Judaism, and won. Today, groups such as Jews for Jesus (Messianic Jews) often try to engage Jews in discussions with a similar purpose: discrediting Jewish thought and winning converts to their side. Engage the class (high school and older students) in a discussion of strategies for managing an encounter with missionaries, such as those that one might encounter on college campuses. In

a synagogue setting, it is highly recommended that you involve the students' rabbi in this discussion. Discuss approaches including close reading of biblical passages and polite disengagement (walking away), among others.

ACTIVITIES

Poetry Reading (E, S, A)

The Penguin Book of Hebrew Verse contains not only information about a myriad of Hebrew poets of all backgrounds from across the centuries, but hundreds of examples of their poetry in Hebrew with English translation. Some of these poems are included in this chapter, but there are many more that are worthy to study, read, and recite. Divide your class into groups and assign one medieval Spanish poet to each group. Have them report on the life of that poet, and recite a selection of his work. You can also turn this activity into a garden party or a café complete with goodies (perhaps Spanish foods such as orange slices and lace cookies) and invite other classes or the students' families.

Jew versus Jew (S, A)

Jews in medieval Spain were faced with the decision of whether to convert to Catholicism and stay, or refuse conversion and flee. Divide the class into teams and stage a debate between a hidden Jew (often a false convert) and a Jew who moves to Turkey in order to practice his or her faith openly. Have the students help their teammates prepare arguments as to why their choice was the best one for them. Vote on who presented the better argument.

Time to Pack: The Edict of Expulsion (E, S)

Help younger students understand the Edict of Expulsion by acting it out. Discuss among students: If you had four months to sell your property and pack only what you could carry but not any silver, gold, or money, what would you choose? How would you decide? Would you bring family items of sentimental value, practical items such as clothes and food, educational items such as books, or things that you could sell easily in order to recoup some of your money?

The Edict of Expulsion: A Close Reading (S, A)

Print copies of the Edict of Expulsion from the Internet. Have students read the edict, and answer the following questions:

- Why did the monarchs want to expel the Jews?
- What behavior was considered "Jewish" in medieval Spain?
- What items were Jews allowed to export and/or bring with them, and what were they forbidden from bringing out of Spain?
- What did the expulsion do to Spain's economy? (For example, did it flood the market of certain precious items? Reduce the price of land and/or property?)
- How easy do you think it was for the Jews to recoup the value of their property when they had four months to sell it, and everyone knew it was "sell it or lose it"?
- What similarities do you think exist between the Spanish Jews and political refugees from other countries today?

TIMELINE (all dates are CE)

c. 300
> Council of Elvira

711
> Muslims conquer Spain

755
> Rise of the Umayyad dynasty; encourage tolerance and cultural advancement

905-975
> Life of Hasdai ibn Shaprut

929
Independent caliphate established in Spain, with center in Cordoba; center of Jewish activity in Spain

993-1056
Life of Shmuel Ha-Nagid

1070-1141
Life of Yehudah Ha-Levi

1094
Invasion of the Almoravids; many Jews flee to Christian Spain

1147
Rise of the Almohads; many centers of Jewish life and culture in Spain are destroyed

c. 1194-1270
Life of Moses ben Naḥman (Naḥmanides)

1391
Anti-Jewish riots and mass conversions of Jews to Christianity

1478
Establishment of Spanish Inquisition

1492
Fall of Muslim Granada; exile of the Jews from Spain; Columbus's voyage to the New World

RESOURCES
Books and Articles

Baer, Yitzhak. *A History of the Jews in Christian Spain.* Philadelphia: Jewish Publication Society, 1971.

Barnavi, Eli, ed. *Historical Atlas of the Jewish People: From the Time of the Patriarchs to the Present.* New York: Schocken Books, 1992.

Carmi, T., ed. *The Penguin Book of Hebrew Verse.* London, England: Penguin Books, 1981.

Chazan, Robert. *Church, State and Jew in the Middle Ages.* New York: Behrman House, 1980.

Gilbert, Martin. *The Routledge Atlas of Jewish History,* 6th ed. London: Routledge, 1995.

Lewy, Hans, ed. *Three Jewish Philosophers: Philo, Saadya Gaon, Jehuda Halevi.* New York: Macmillan, 1969.

Marcus, Jacob Rader. *The Jew in the Medieval World, A Source Book: 315–1791.* Cincinnati, OH: Hebrew Union College Press, 1990.

Pasachoff, Naomi, and Robert J. Littman. *Jewish History in 100 Nutshells.* Northvale, NJ: Jason Aronson, 1995.

Sarna, Jonathan D., and Jonathan B. Krasner. *The History of the Jewish People: A Story of Tradition and Change.* Springfield, NJ: Behrman House, 2006 (see especially chapters 8 and 9).

Stillman, Norman A. *The Jews of Arab Lands: A History and Source Book.* Philadelphia: Jewish Publication Society, 1979.

Stow, Kenneth R. *Alienated Minority: The Jews of Medieval Latin Europe.* Cambridge, MA: Harvard University Press, 1992.

Internet
Visit www.behrmanhouse.com/booklinks for links to Web sites that offer additional resources for this chapter.

Early Modern Period

CHAPTER SIXTEEN
JEWS IN THE OTTOMAN EMPIRE

WHAT'S THE BIG IDEA?
Diaspora
Since the Babylonian exile from Eretz Yisrael in 586 BCE, Jews have lived in a part of the world including much of North Africa, Near East Asia, and Eretz Yisrael that was known for four hundred years— from 1517 until 1917—as the Ottoman Empire. A vibrant Jewish community had thrived in the region for hundreds of years, and after the exile from Spain, large numbers of Sephardic Jewish refugees moved there as well. Ottoman Jews found ways to maintain their own religious observances (and at times, reclaimed their Jewish identity after years of hiding it for fear of reprisals) while adopting the dress, customs, and culture of their new homeland.

BACKGROUND INFORMATION
North African, Turkish, and Palestinian Jewry before the Ottomans
During its height, the Ottoman sultans controlled lands as vast and diverse as sections of Poland and Hungary in Eastern Europe, the Algerian coastline in North Africa, the Balkans, Turkey and Greece in the center of their empire, the Holy Land in the east, and Yemen in the south. Jews had lived in all of these places over the course of the previous two thousand years, ruled by Christians in the north and Muslims in the south.

In 1260, only a few decades after the last Christian crusade to take the Holy Land from the Muslims had ended, the Mamluks—a powerful tribe of slaves who rose up, organized, and wrested power from the Egyptian rulers—conquered vast territories including Eretz Yisrael, Egypt, and coastal Saudi Arabia. The capital of the Mamluk Empire was Cairo, where a strong Jewish community with ancient roots resided. The accepted leader of the Middle Eastern Jewish community—the *nasi*—was also based in Cairo and maintained authority over the Jewish populations of Egypt, Eretz Yisrael, and Syria. While the Jewish communities of the Mamluk Empire enjoyed some autonomy, they were still subject to religious repression by various rulers, including discriminatory legislation in keeping with, and sometimes going beyond, the Jews' status as protected monotheistic people, or *dhimmis* (see chapter 12).

However, because the areas outside Egypt were only nominally under Mamluk control, Jews in Eretz Yisrael and Syria experienced a lesser degree of harassment. Under these favorable conditions, opportunities arose for Jews who sought to come to the Holy Land from the Diaspora. During the Mamluk period, therefore, rabbis and scholars, along with some of their disciples, immigrated to Eretz Yisrael and set up synagogues, schools, and small communities, which were often funded by the Diaspora regions from which they originated. This situation was fortuitous, because by the end of the fifteenth century, one of the largest Jewish communities in the world—that of Spain and Portugal—would once again be looking for a home to call their own. The Ottomans—who overthrew the Mamluks in 1517—found themselves ruling over many minority peoples, including indigenous Jews as well as hundreds of thousands of Jewish refugees from Catholic Spain seeking asylum in the Ottoman Empire.

A Safe Haven

The Ottoman Empire was actually founded in the thirteenth century by the Turkish emperor Osman I, who wrested control away from the Byzantines and began a momentous shift in the character of the region from one dominated by Greek language, heritage, and culture to one of Muslim supremacy. Both Greek- and Arabic-speaking Jewish groups populated the area, making for a well-established and variegated Jewish community even before the absorption of thousands of Sephardic refugees between the late fifteenth and eighteenth centuries.

Jews left Spain in 1492 and Portugal in 1497 in accordance with the edicts of expulsion, and thousands more hidden Jews continued to arrive in the Ottoman Empire for centuries afterward. They immigrated to the major population centers of Eretz Yisrael, Salonika (in what is now modern-day Greece), and Istanbul (in what is now Turkey), as well as to hundreds of other smaller towns and villages. According to one source, by the sixteenth century, so many Sephardic Jews had settled in Salonika that they outnumbered the rest of the city's *total* population.[1]

During the sixteenth century, a period of prosperity came to the Ottoman Empire and the Jews benefited along with everyone else. One reason for this improvement in the lives of so many was the crowning of Emperor Suleiman the

Magnificent. A great military leader, his army conquered vast swaths of land including Hungary, North Africa, the Middle East and Persia, and he incorporated the wealth and achievements of those lands into his own. He rebuilt the walls and many of the structures of the city of Jerusalem, making it more hospitable for Muslims and Jews alike. A poet and scholar as well, Suleiman was a patron of the arts and sciences in the tradition of the Muslim rulers of Spain from centuries before. The Jews therefore found a safe haven in the Ottoman Empire, where they were not only tolerated, but valued for their scholarly and economic contributions.

It should come as no surprise, therefore, that hidden Jews from the Sephardic world continued to flock to the Ottoman Empire during Suleiman's reign as never before. As in the world of Muslim Spain, Jews found themselves perfectly positioned to act as merchants and traders, going back and forth between the Muslim and Christian worlds. They entered industries that were only just beginning to develop, such as weaving and other forms of textile manufacturing, centuries before Jews would be at the forefront of the garment workers' industry in the New World. The value placed by Suleiman on legal advances (in Arabic, he is called "Suleiman the Lawgiver") encouraged Jewish scholars and jurists, such as Rabbi Joseph Caro, whose *Shulhan Aruch* ("The Set Table") is considered even in the modern age to be the most authoritative law code in the Jewish world (see "Joseph Caro and the *Shulhan Aruch*" in this chapter.)

In addition, the emperor was not unsympathetic to the plight of those hidden Jews who sought to leave Europe in order to live openly in the Ottoman Empire. In the mid-sixteenth century, he

---

[1] Naomi Pasachoff and Robert J. Littman, *Jewish History in 100 Nutshells*, Northvale, NJ: Jason Aronson, 1995, p. 149.

was persuaded by the philanthropist Doña Gracia Nasi, who had herself fled Portugal for the very same reason, to grant her a long-term lease on land near Tiberias in order to resettle Jewish refugees. Her nephew, Joseph Nasi, was a court favorite of the Ottoman sultan Selim II, who appointed him as the Duke of Naxos and entrusted him with handling political negotiations and crafting policy on the crown's behalf. Joseph continued Doña Gracia's work in helping to rebuild Tiberias and resettle Jews there, encouraging them to become self-supporting by learning the silk and wool production trades and providing them with employment in those fields. Joseph profited from his good works as well, by introducing competition to the Venetian manufacturers of these textiles at the same time. A Hebrew chronicle of the period, *The Vale of Tears*, by Joseph Ha-Kohen, recounts the story of Joseph Nasi's success in this venture.[2]

As the presence of Jewish favorites in the sultan's court might indicate, Jews prospered throughout much of the Ottoman Empire. The gentile businessman Hans Dernschwarm, an educated German who traveled through the Ottoman Empire in the mid-1500s, recorded in his diary impressions and information about the Jews who lived there at the time. Although he is not complimentary of the Jews as a group or of Doña Gracia or Joseph Nasi in particular, his observations corroborate those in numerous Hebrew sources. An excerpt from his journal reads:

"In Alexandria, in Missr (that is to say, Cairo), in Aleppo, in Antioch in Syria, and in Jerusalem and everywhere else there are many Jews. Those Jews that are old, who have a little money, travel to the Holy Land, to Jerusalem, and still hope that they will some day all come together, from all countries, into their own native land and there secure hold of the government. The well-to-do Jews send money to Jerusalem to support them, for one cannot make any money there. . . .

"There are forty-two or more synagogues in Constantinople. Every Jewish nationality goes to its own synagogue. . . .

"The Jews are allowed to travel and to do business anywhere they wish. . . . There are all sorts of artisans among the Jews who make a living selling their products publicly, for in Turkey every man is free to carry on his trade at home, in a shop, or on the streets. . . . The Jews of Constantinople also have a printing press and print many rare books. They have goldsmiths, lapidaries (gem-cutters), painters, tailors, butchers, druggists, physicians, surgeons, cloth-weavers, wound-surgeons, barbers, mirror-makers, dyers, silkworkers, goldwashers, refiners of ores, assayers, [and] engravers."[3]

While Jews were seemingly included in every imaginable economic venture, they also developed an incredibly rich cultural life. The Ottoman Empire in the sixteenth and seventeenth centuries became the world's center for Jewish scholarship. Rabbinical seminaries flowered in the cities of Jerusalem and Safed in the Holy Land, and in Salonika and other cities in Asia Minor. Unquestionably, one of the most significant advances of these scholars was the preeminent law code by Rabbi Joseph Caro, the *Shulḥan Aruch*.

[2] Jacob Rader Marcus, *The Jew in the Medieval World, A Source Book*, 315–1791, Cincinnati, OH: Hebrew Union College Press, pp. 320–322.

[3] Ibid., pp. 411–417.

Joseph Caro and the *Shulhan Aruch*

While Jewish law codes aplenty existed by the time Joseph Caro wrote his masterpiece, the *Shulhan Aruch* (literally, "the set table"), in the sixteenth century, none was accepted as the standard for the world Jewish community. Moses Maimonides' *Mishneh Torah* (see chapter 14), for example, suffered from a lack of acceptance in the Ashkenazic world and from its lack of source material, even as its clear language and cogent organization were hailed.

The Caro family, like the Maimonides family centuries before, fled Spain because of persecutions against Jews in the wake of the Inquisition. After five years in Portugal, they fled once again to the Balkans, and from there Rabbi Joseph Caro moved to Safed, in Eretz Yisrael. A mystic as well as a Talmudic scholar, Rabbi Caro was a modest man who wanted to include in his work several opinions, before citing what he humbly thought to be the binding point of Jewish law. For this reason, he ultimately decided to base his work on several works, including extensive material from the Talmud as well as Ashkenazic and Sephardic sources. His major work took twenty years to complete. Finished in 1542, its author entitled it the *Beit Yosef* (Hebrew for "house of Joseph"). However, Caro realized that because this work included so many divergent opinions, it wasn't really suited as a quick reference guide. Therefore, he condensed this encyclopedic work into a smaller four-volume *Shulhan Aruch*, or the "set table."[4]

Completed in 1564, the *Shulhan Aruch* had a major advantage over all the law codes that had come before it—the printing press had already been invented. By the time Caro finished his book, the new technology had spread throughout Europe, enabling multiple copies of the work to be distributed to Jewish communities throughout the world. With the additional Ashkenazic commentary by the Polish rabbi Moses Isserles (called, fittingly, the *Mapa,* or "the tablecloth"), the *Shulhan Aruch* became the accepted legal code for world Jewry (as it remains even today).

Kabbalah: Jewish Spirituality in the Sixteenth Century

Today, when one hears the word "kabbalah," one might be just as likely to think of the fascination of Hollywood stars with its mystical teachings as one is to think of Jewish tradition. In fact, the word *kabbalah* comes from the Hebrew word meaning just that—tradition, and refers to the larger subject of Jewish mysticism in general.

Mysticism, which the *American Heritage Dictionary* defines as "immediate consciousness of the transcendent or ultimate reality of God," has been part of Jewish tradition ever since the beginning of the religion. Numerous biblical and Talmudic texts refer to the mystical aspects of Judaism, including encounters with God, angels, and otherworldly phenomena. The Christian and Muslim worlds in which Jews lived also had cultures that accepted the validity of these types of mystical occurrences. Jewish tradition, while accepting the mystical as part of God's creation and embedded within biblical and rabbinic texts, also viewed this esoteric knowledge as dangerous, in a way. Therefore, Jewish men were traditionally prohibited from delving into kabbalah until they were forty years old—an age at which presumably

---

[4] Naomi Pasachoff and Robert J. Littman, *Jewish History in 100 Nutshells*, Northvale, NJ: Jason Aronson, 1995, pp. 173–174.

they would already be well-versed in traditional mainstream Jewish texts, as well as personally grounded in family and community life, and therefore less likely to be swept away completely by mystical studies.

Kabbalah became more popular in the Middle Ages among a group of mystics who emigrated to the city of Safed (or Tzfat) in the Holy Land of Eretz Yisrael. Among other works, these rabbis were engrossed in a mystical book entitled the *Zohar* (Book of Splendor). The *Zohar* was traditionally thought to have been written in Eretz Yisrael during the second century CE by Simon bar Yoḥai. As the legend goes, Simon bar Yoḥai, along with his son, lived in a cave for thirteen years in order to escape capture by the Romans. During their time in hiding, the tradition holds, Elijah the prophet paid them daily visits and instructed them in the deeper mysteries of the Torah.

In Spain during the thirteenth century, a scholar named Moses de Leon claimed to have found the ancient manuscript and began copying and selling passages from the work. After his death, his wife claimed that the work was de Leon's own creation, but its antiquity had already been accepted by the rabbis and their disciples who revered the book as ancient and holy. Scholars today generally believe that the book was in fact written by de Leon, while traditionalists reject that assessment and attribute it to Simon bar Yoḥai.[5]

In any case, when the *Zohar* was first printed in 1556, it found a ready audience in the rabbis of Safed and their students. Safed was close to the tomb of Simon bar Yoḥai, and mystics gravitated there along with large numbers of formerly hidden Jews seeking asylum in this eastern edge of the Ottoman Empire. Mysticism was popular among the Sephardic Jewish refugees because in its very nature of hiddenness, they saw a part of themselves. Just as kabbalah celebrated the esoteric, secret parts of the Torah and Jewish tradition, so, too, these Jews had been in the position of hiding their Jewishness for centuries from their Christian persecutors. These ideas, however, would likely never have taken hold in such a grand way had it not been for the founder of a true system of kabbalah—Isaac Luria.

Rabbi Isaac Luria, known as the Ari ("the lion"), lived only thirty-eight years, but his impact is still felt throughout the world. Although born in Jerusalem to parents of Ashkenazic descent, Luria spent much of his life in Egypt, first studying Talmud and mysticism in Cairo and then on a secluded island on the Nile River. Eventually he moved back to Eretz Yisrael to the city of Safed, where he began teaching an innovative method of understanding kabbalah.

Lurianic kabbalah attempts to explain the mysteries of the universe that plague every questioning Jew: Why is there evil in the world? Where is God? Why are we exiled from our homeland? Rabbi Luria started with the point of creation to develop explanations to these fundamental questions.

In answer to the questions about the existence of evil and the role of God, Lurianic kabbalah presents the idea that in order to create the world, God—who formerly had taken up all the space in the universe—had to contract in order to make room for other creations. (God is referred to in kabbalistic literature as *Ein Sof,* or "without end," and God's withdrawal from the world as *tzimtzum*.)

---

[5] Ibid., pp. 137–138.

Luria developed the idea that once God withdrew from the world, God's essence was contracted into ten "vessels" (in Hebrew, *keilim*). These vessels, according to Luria, represent ten basic qualities of God, or *sefirot,* that we as humans want most to connect with and emulate, including knowledge, strength, and compassion. Of course God and God's light can't be contained into ten vessels, and so Luria explains that these vessels broke, scattering divine sparks of light throughout the world. Our job as humans is to retrieve these holy sparks through the performance of *mitzvot* (observing the commandments, or as some view it, doing good deeds). This retrieval will serve to repair the world (in Hebrew, *tikkun olam*) to the point where God's presence will once again reenter the world, ushering in the Messianic Age and restoring the Jews to their homeland in Eretz Yisrael.

The ideas promulgated by Rabbi Luria achieved immediate popularity in his day and were taken up by disciples both in the Ottoman Empire and in the Ashkenazic world. He and his fellow residents of Safed took *tikkun olam* seriously, seeking to achieve a mystical union with God through the performance of *mitzvot* and introducing a fervor into their prayers that lives on today in the practice of Ḥasidic, Renewal, and other denominations of Judaism.

So, while the term *kabbalah* might be thought of as a catch-all phrase for spirituality or mysticism, truly it refers to an understanding of Judaism on a deeper level, and a commitment to repairing the world through the performance of *mitzvot,* including acts of compassion and kindness to others. How amazing that an idea that was popularized in medieval Israel is so timely today.

CONNECTING TO OUR TRADITION

Our tradition teaches us that Torah study is superior above all. For girls and women, however, Torah study was frequently not an option, or it was discouraged. Often the only girls who received an education were from wealthy families who hired tutors for them. Throughout most of the Ottoman Empire, including in Eretz Yisrael and elsewhere, however, Jewish education for girls was permitted and even encouraged. In sixteenth-century Safed, teachers were hired to teach women and girls to recite prayers and blessings. (One presumes that these may have been Sephardic refugees who had hidden their Judaism and needed a refresher.)

In the Balkans and in North Africa, the creation of the Alliance Israelite Universelle (AIU) in the mid-1800s contributed to the Jewish and secular education of girls, both in separate and coeducational schools. Along with French language and culture and other secular subjects, the students—both boys and girls—learned Hebrew, Bible, and Jewish history. Women were among those trained in the Alliance's teachers' seminary in Paris, and some even rose to the rank of principal.[6]

DID YOU KNOW?

- Years before Theodor Herzl founded the World Zionist Congress and began working actively toward the creation of a Jewish homeland in Palestine (see chapter 23), a rabbi from Sarajevo (now in Bosnia and Herzegovina) named Judah Alkalai became convinced that settling in the Land of Israel was the only solution to anti-Semitism.

---

[6] Shoshana Pantel Zolty, *"And All Your Children Shall Be Learned": Women and the Study of Torah in Jewish Law and History,* Northvale, NJ: Jason Aronson, 1993, pp. 169, 241–242.

- Spurred by the Damascus Affair blood libel in 1840, Rabbi Alkalai roused the ire of the Orthodox rabbinate when he began to urge Jews not to wait for the advent of the Messiah, but to go and settle in Eretz Yisrael regardless. Alkalai published eighteen pamphlets and a number of Hebrew newspaper articles, and visited England and several other European countries advocating this cause.

IMPORTANT TERMS

Diaspora	*Zohar*
Dhimmis	*Ein Sof*
Beit Yosef	*Tzimtzum*
Shulḥan Aruch	*Keilim*
Mapa	*Sefirot*
Lurianic kabbalah	*Mitzvot*
Kabbalah	*Tikkun olam*

Names, Places, and Events

Ottoman Empire	Rabbi Moses
Mamluks	Isserles
Osman I	Doña Gracia Nasi
Byzantines	Joseph Nasi
Salonika	Selim II
Safed	Joseph Ha-Kohen
Suleiman the	Hans Dernschwarm
Magnificent	Rabbi Isaac Luria
Rabbi Joseph Caro	

DISCUSSION QUESTIONS

- Why do you think kabbalah, or Jewish mysticism, has become so popular recently? What conditions do you think exist in the world now that existed five hundred years ago when kabbalah first became popular? Do you agree with Rabbi Isaac Luria's assessment of God's absence from the world and his instructions for repairing the world (*tikkun olam*)? Why or why not?
- Doña Gracia Nasi and her nephew Joseph worked hard to create jobs and opportunities for Jewish refugees in the Ottoman Empire. What examples can you think of

today where opportunities are created to help people resettle after disaster strikes their family and they need to move, often with very little means? (Think of the victims of hurricanes, or the thousands of refugees who emigrate to the United States and to Israel each year.)

ACTIVITIES

A Look at Kabbalah (S, A)

Kabbalah, or Jewish mysticism, has become so popular recently that a search on "Google" turned up over two *million* hits. With your class, explore sites related to kabbalah. How is kabbalah explained? Why do you think there is such a proliferation of "kabbalah centers" that cater to both Jews and gentiles? Ask the students what their opinion is of "kabbalah water" (supposedly blessed by a rabbi) or $20 red strings that bring good luck. Is this Jewish tradition, or something different?

Medieval Aliyah versus Modern Aliyah (S, A)

In the Middle Ages, Jews—primarily Sephardic refugees—began moving back to the Holy Land in numbers not seen since the destruction of the Second Temple fifteen hundred years earlier, despite the danger of the journey and economic hardships they might have encountered. In our day, many Jews choose to move to the modern State of Israel despite the hardships they may face as well as the possible danger of terrorist attacks. Discuss with your class: What common goals and reasons do you see for making *aliyah* in these two groups? What is different?

As a follow-up activity, research the current year's *aliyah* and tourism statistics for the State of Israel. Do you see any trends in the groups moving to or visiting Israel? Is it homogenous or diverse? Compare these trends with those in the Middle Ages stemming from the expulsion from Spain and the openness of the Ottoman Empire to Jewish settlement.

Interview with Doña Gracia Nasi (E, S)

Doña Gracia Nasi was a courageous and fascinating woman who escaped a world of hidden Jews and persecution to influence kings and help scores of her coreligionists. Invite Doña Gracia (an adult in costume) to your classroom and have the students ask her questions about her life and work.

TIMELINE (all dates are CE)

1258–1326
Life of Osman I, founder of the Ottoman Empire

1260
Mamluks overthrow the Christian conquerors of the Holy Land

c. 1280
According to scholars, Moses de Leon composes the *Zohar* (Book of Splendor), major kabbalistic work, in Castile

1488–1575
Life of Rabbi Joseph Caro, author of the *Shulḥan Aruch* law code

1492
Fall of Muslim Granada; exile of the Jews from Spain; Columbus's voyage to the New World.

1510–1568
Life of philanthropist Doña Gracia Nasi

1517
Ottoman Turks defeat the Mamluks, beginning of the reign of Sultan Suleiman the Magnificent

1534–1572
Life of Rabbi Isaac Luria (the Ari), founder of Lurianic kabbalah, in Safed, Israel

1556
First printing of the *Zohar*

1564
First printing of the *Shulḥan Aruch*

RESOURCES
Books and Articles

Barnavi, Eli, ed. *Historical Atlas of the Jewish People: From the Time of the Patriarchs to the Present.* New York: Schocken Books, 1992.

Brooks, Andree Aelion. *The Woman Who Defied Kings: The Life and Times of Doña Gracia Nasi—A Jewish Leader During the Renaissance.* St. Paul, MN: Paragon House, 2002.

Marcus, Jacob Rader. *The Jew in the Medieval World, A Source Book: 315–1791.* Cincinnati, OH: Hebrew Union College Press, 1990.

Sachar, Howard M. *A History of the Jews in the Modern World.* New York: Alfred A. Knopf, 2005.

Sarna, Jonathan D., and Jonathan B. Krasner. *The History of the Jewish People: A Story of Tradition and Change.* Springfield, NJ: Behrman House, 2006 (see especially chapter 9).

Stillman, Norman A. *The Jews of Arab Lands: A History and Source Book.* Philadelphia: Jewish Publication Society, 1979.

Stillman, Norman A. *The Jews of Arab Lands in Modern Times.* Philadelphia: Jewish Publication Society, 1991.

Zolty, Shoshana Pantel. *"And All Your Children Shall Be Learned": Women and the Study of Torah in Jewish Law and History.* Northvale, NJ: Jason Aronson, 1993.

Internet

Visit www.behrmanhouse.com/booklinks for links to Web sites that offer additional resources for this chapter.

CHAPTER SEVENTEEN
EASTERN EUROPEAN JEWRY

WHAT'S THE BIG IDEA?
Diaspora

Since the Jews were forced into exile centuries ago, much of the Jewish community has remained dispersed throughout the world. Once scattered, Jews did not stay in one place but continued to move from country to country, creating communities and developing a distinct culture at each place they stopped.

BACKGROUND INFORMATION

Throughout the Middle Ages, Jews found themselves first welcomed and then expelled from one country after another. While some rulers saw the Jewish people as agents of prosperity, others saw them only as enemies of the Christian faith. Although often persecuted, the Jews managed to prosper in most places. Envied by their Christian neighbors, Jews were often expelled on religious grounds just so their property could be confiscated after they left, as was the case in England, France, and Germany. As monarchs rose and fell due to their own mortality or the winds of war, the fate of Jewish communities also rose and fell. And, when forced out of many Western European countries, Jews looked to the East.

A Jewish Buffer Between Christians and Muslims

Located in the modern region of southern Russia, including the northern Caucasus, eastern Ukraine, Crimea, western Kazakhstan, and northwestern Uzbekistan, the Khazar Kingdom, also known as Khazaria, holds an unusual place in Jewish history as an independent Jewish kingdom. Originally nomads in central Asia, the Khazars were a tolerant people, allowing many religious groups to live with full rights of citizenship within their borders. Jews in other countries recognized the sanctuary promised by such a tolerant community and, as early as 723 CE, Jewish refugees made their way to Khazaria.

To maintain neutrality between his Muslim and Christian neighbors, the Khazar king, Bulan, converted to Judaism, along with much of the nobility, in the late eighth or early ninth century. Later, King Obadiah built synagogues and invited rabbis to settle in Khazaria. With its religious tolerance and Jewish ruler, the Khazar kingdom continued to be a haven for Jews fleeing persecution elsewhere. Khazar monarchs were also known for supporting international Jewry by taking revenge locally on Muslims for persecution of Jews abroad. For example, in 920 a Khazar ruler, hearing that Muslims in Iran had destroyed a synagogue, ordered the minaret of the mosque in the Khazar capital to be broken off and the muezzin executed.

Under the leadership of both Jewish and non-Jewish rulers, the Jewish community of Khazaria continued to grow and prosper. Jewish merchants traveling through Khazaria wrote with astonishment of the Jewish kingdom they visited. Jews governed many key cities and took part in trade. Documents written in Hebrew and Jewish coins have been found dating to this period.

When the Russian-Byzantine expedition destroyed Khazaria in 1016, three hundred years of religious tolerance came to an end. Although it is not clear what happened to Khazaria's Jews, it is likely that they dispersed into neighboring countries including Russia and Poland.

Jewish Life Under the Czars

While life had been good for the Jews centuries earlier during the reign of the Khazars, under the Russian czars, their life was not easy. Cycles of persecution followed by acceptance and then another wave of persecution were frequent, primarily due to the tension between economics and religion. At times when Russian rulers were influenced by the Catholic Church, Jews were despised. However, when a strong economy was uppermost in the ruler's mind, Jews were often invited to live within the realm and help it prosper.

In 1526, Moscow's ambassador to Rome stated that the Muscovite people despised the Jews and would not allow them within their borders because they were a bad influence on Christians. Later, in 1550, Ivan IV (also known as Ivan the Terrible) made this position even clearer when he forbade Jewish merchants to enter the country because he believed they were importing poisonous herbs and that they would lead Christians away from their faith.

A few years later, he had all Jews who would not submit to baptism drowned. The rulers of Kiev and Lithuania, however, realized that Jewish merchants could be good for the economy and invited them to live within their borders. Showing the true nature of the tension between religious-based anti-Semitism and the realities of the market-place, Czarina Katherine I expelled all the Jews from

Russia in 1727 and then, realizing her mistake, compromised by allowing them to enter only for commercial purposes.

The Golden Age of Poland

As Jews were expelled from many Western European countries, Polish rulers saw the economic benefits of having Jews establish homes and businesses within Poland. With this realization, many Polish rulers began to invite Jewish traders who had been expelled from Germany to settle in Poland. These traders joined Jews who had fled from Western Europe during the Crusades.

In 1264, King Boleslaw the Pius issued a charter, known as the Statute of Kalisz, which gave equal protection to Jews and Christians alike. The most unprecedented part of this charter was that it forbade charges of ritual murder against Jews. If such charges were brought, six witnesses—three of whom had to be Jews—were required to testify to the crime. The Statute of Kalisz went a long way toward securing the place of Jews in Poland.

For many years Jews prospered in Poland, building businesses, creating a system of self-government, and developing a unique culture. Jewish entrepreneurs helped Polish landowners develop eastern Poland by transporting wheat to the new markets in Western Europe. Jews managed the estates, collected tolls on roads, built mills, and owned riverboats for transporting the wheat. In addition to their involvement in the wheat trade, Jews were also involved in businesses including soap manufacturing, glazing, tanning, and the fur trade. Jews also had their own guilds (associations of merchants or craftsmen).[1]

---

[1] Paul Johnson, *A History of the Jews*, New York: HarperCollins, 1987, p. 252.

Although Jews were involved in commerce with their Christian neighbors, and often oversaw the estates of Polish nobles, Polish Jews still lived very separate lives within their *kahal,* or Jewish community. The *kahal* was originally established for the collection of taxes owed to the king from the Jewish community, but it also gave the Jews autonomy to govern themselves. As long as the taxes were paid, the Polish rulers allowed the *kahal* complete autonomy.

Within the *kahal,* Jewish values taught in the Torah and Talmud became the basis for everyday life. The *kahal* took care of the poor and sick, the widow and the orphan. Justice was overseen by a *beit din* (Jewish court), and business was transacted according to the laws of the Talmud. There was a system of universal education for boys at a time when most Polish peasants were uneducated.

Council of the Four Lands

While each local *kahal* functioned similarly to the corporate system of government found in Western Europe (see chapter 20), unique to Poland was the development of the Council of Four Lands (in Hebrew, *Va'ad*), a federation of Jewish communities in Great Poland, Little Poland, Volhynia, and Lithuania. Like the *kahal* itself, the Council of Four Lands acted primarily as a taxing agency, dividing the taxes due to the king among the different *kehillot.* The council also acted as an intermediary between Polish Jews and the Polish government. In this capacity, it acted as a defender of Jewish rights. The council also helped to oversee the social, educational, and business needs of the *kehillot.* Rarely did the council involve itself in the matters of individual communities, but when it did it generally supported the leaders of the *kahal* against the common people. This position is not surprising, considering that the council members were elected by a small minority of Jewish landowners.

Neither the Council of Four Lands nor the *kahal* was a democracy. In many ways the hierarchy of the *kahal* reflected that of Poland itself, with the wealthy minority at the top, supported by the poor majority at the bottom. It is interesting to note that Jewish peasants working for Jewish landowners replicated in a microcosm the system of Polish peasants unhappily working for Polish landowners. Eventually, tensions between poorer Jews and their wealthier governors arose as taxes increased and much of their burden was placed on those least able to afford it.

Yiddish

The laws of the *kahal* would have been enough to separate the Jews from other Poles, but the Jewish community had also developed its own language. Yiddish, German with a Jewish accent and a smattering of Hebrew thrown in, reflects a rich Jewish heritage. Brought to Poland by German Jews, Yiddish became the primary language of Polish Jews for oral communication. In writing, Yiddish existed alongside Hebrew, with Hebrew being the language used for religious study by the educated, and Yiddish used for religious and secular purposes by the masses.

Much early Yiddish literature was based on Hebrew scriptures. One very popular book first published near the end of the sixteenth century was the *Tze'enah U-Re'enah,* a Yiddish interpretation of the Bible that also included midrashim and commentaries. It was intended for the use of both men and women, but became mainly a text that women read on Shabbat. Over time, many different Yiddish genres developed including ethical writings, epic poems based on the Bible, historical songs and narratives that told of events that had recently befallen the Jewish community, and plays based on the Scriptures. Yiddish literature helped bind the local Jewish community together and also helped Jews all across Europe communicate. Later, during the periods of great emigration in the nineteenth and twentieth centuries, Yiddish language and culture would spread to many different corners of the world.

Chmielnicki Insurrection and the Fall of Polish Jewry

One of the many positions a Polish Jew could hold was that of steward, or manager, on a Polish estate with an absentee landlord. As stewards, Jews collected the often burdensome taxes from peasant farmers. Their role in the oppressive feudal system only increased the hatred with which many Catholic Poles viewed the Jews. In 1648, the Ukrainian Cossacks, led by Bogdan Chmielnicki, rebelled against their Polish oppressors. Chmielnicki's great ambition was to become the leader of the Ukraine and he used the peasants' hatred of the Jewish stewards to help him incite an uprising. During the one-and-a-half years of the Cossack terror, known as the Deluge, it is estimated that half the Jewish population of Poland was killed in horrible and unspeakable ways.

Life for the remaining Jews in Poland changed drastically after the Chmielnicki massacres. No longer did they hold a protected place in Polish society. The kings who came to power just after the Chmielnicki massacres did not see the economic benefit in maintaining a Jewish community that their predecessors had recognized. They allowed the Polish nobles to claim Jewish labor and earnings

as their own, just as they claimed ownership of the work and income of their serfs. No longer could Jewish merchants act as independent businessmen. When there was unrest among the peasants, Jews were a handy target for their violence. The Polish nobles would incite the peasants to attack the Jews in order to protect their own positions and property.

Under the Saxon kings, the Catholic Church also held more power, and the nobles allied themselves with the Church against the Jews. At the same time, the *kehillot* were on the verge of bankruptcy, and the Council of Four Lands had been disbanded by the government in 1764. As a result, there was little that the Jews could do for themselves as the old trumped-up charges of ritual murder, and the resultant atrocities against Jews, reappeared.

CONNECTING TO OUR TRADITION

Jewish tradition teaches that a convert is to be treated as any other Jew, even to the extent that it is impolite to mention it. Thus, members of the Khazarian Jewish community who had converted to the faith were accepted by their coreligionists worldwide as Jews, in accordance with this precept. In turn, the kings of Khazaria felt responsible for fellow Jews who lived elsewhere in the world, opening their borders as a refuge to those seeking asylum and meting out justice to those who would hurt Jews elsewhere. As it says, "All Israel is responsible one for the other" (Tractate Sanhedrin 27b).

IMPORTANT TERMS

Conversion	Pogrom
Czar	Yiddish
The Deluge	*Beit din*
Diaspora	Steward
Kahal	

Names, Places, and Events

Bogdan Zinovi Chmielnicki

Cossacks

Khazar Kingdom/ Khazaria

King Bulan

King Obadiah

Statute of Kalisz

King Boleslaw the Pious

Czar Ivan IV

Czarina Katherine I

Ukraine

Tze'enah U-Re'enah

DISCUSSION QUESTIONS

• While the *kahal* clearly benefited the Polish rulers by generating revenue, how did the *kahal* benefit Polish Jewry?

• What laws and cultural and/or religious practices separated Jews from their Christian neighbors in Poland? Did this separation make it easier or more difficult to remain Jewish? Are there laws and cultural and/or religious practices that separate you from your non-Jewish neighbors? Do you think this is a good thing? Why or why not?

• In Khazaria and Poland, Jews lived within a thoroughly Jewish environment and had greater or lesser degrees of self-rule. Is there anywhere that this is possible today? What are some differences and similarities between these Jewish communities of the Diaspora and the Jewish communities of Israel?

ACTIVITIES

Track the Diaspora (S, A)

Using a world map, track the movement of Jews from Western Europe to Eastern Europe during this period. Also track the movement of Jews within Eastern Europe.

Jewish Pen Pal (S)

You are a traveling Jewish merchant. Write a letter home to your community about the Khazar Kingdom or your travels to other places in Eastern Europe. What events are taking place?

Community Research (S)

Many institutions found in our Jewish communities today can trace their roots back to the Polish *kahal*. As a class, learn about Jewish organizations found in your community and find parallels, if not the exact same institution, in the Polish Jewish community. Some examples might include *ḥevrah kadisha,* Jewish Federation, and religious schools. Have students design a museum exhibit, write essays, or do class presentations comparing the modern and historic organizations.

DID YOU KNOW?

• *Po'lin*, the Hebrew name for Poland, can be read as two Hebrew words that, when taken together, mean "rest here." To many Jews fleeing Western Europe, this play on words seemed like a sign from God that they should go to Poland.[2]

• The word *"kehillah,"* found in the names of many synagogues worldwide, comes from the same root as *kahal* and means "community."[3]

TIMELINE (all dates are CE)

723

Jewish fugitives from Greece flee to the Khazar Kingdom

1016

Russian-Byzantine expedition conquers the Khazar Kingdom and Jews disperse to other Eastern European countries

1264

Statute of Kalisz gives religious protection to Jews and Christian living in Poland.

---

[2] Benjamin Blech, *The Complete Idiot's Guide to Jewish History and Culture* (New York: Alpha Books, 2004), p. 161.
[3] Ibid.

1388

Grand Duke Vitovt of Lithuania grants privileges to Jews

1399

First persecution of Jews in Poland; the rabbi and thirteen elders who are charged with desecration of church property are tortured and burned alive

1494

First Polish ghetto established in Cracow

1545

Jews are forbidden to visit or trade in Moscow

1563

Russian Jews who refuse to be baptized are drowned

1648

Cossack rebellion against the Poles leads to the slaying of hundreds of thousands of Jews

1708

Peter the Great halts a pogrom and allows Jews to settle in St. Petersburg

RESOURCES
Books and Articles

Blech, Benjamin. *The Complete Idiot's Guide to Jewish History and Culture.* New York: Alpha Books, 2004.

Blech, Benjamin. *Eyewitness to Jewish History.* Hoboken, NJ: John Wiley & Sons, 2004.

Gilbert, Martin. *Atlas of Jewish History.* Dorset Press, 1976.

Johnson, Paul. *A History of the Jews.* New York: HarperCollins, 1987.

Sachar, Howard M. *The Course of Modern Jewish History.* New York: Vintage Books, 1990.

Internet
Visit www.behrmanhouse.com/booklinks for links to Web sites that offer additional resources for this chapter.

CHAPTER EIGHTEEN

SHABBETAI TZVI, FALSE MESSIAH

WHAT'S THE BIG IDEA?
Covenant

Jews have traditionally understood the events that befell them to be the will of God, part of God's overarching plan for Jewish history in particular and human history in general. Intrinsic to this view is the concept of the Jews as God's chosen people, singled out for a special covenant that promises Eretz Yisrael as a heritage and prosperity for the Jewish people. During the years that the Jews have lived in Diaspora, particularly in times of turmoil, the Jewish community has held on to faith in this covenant, particularly with regard to God's pledge that we would once again be free to live in the Land of Israel, led there by God's appointed representative—the Messiah.

A Jewish Concept of the Messiah

The term "Messiah" (in Hebrew, *mashi'ah*) literally means "anointed one" and has its roots deep in Jewish tradition and history. The concept of a Messiah as an anointed ruler descended from King David who will herald an age of peace and prosperity for all of mankind, ushering in the World to Come (in Hebrew, *Olam Ha-Ba*, or the Messianic Era), is expressed by the biblical prophets. The first kings were referred to as "*Mashi'ah Adonai*," or "anointed one of God." When no descendant of David came to the throne after the Babylonian exile, the people began to dream of a time when an anointed king from the House of David would again sit on the throne of Israel. The more Judah was oppressed,

particularly by the Roman Empire, the stronger the belief grew in the coming of the Messiah, who would bring salvation and freedom to the Jewish people, while the Roman Empire would be replaced by the Kingdom of God on earth.

When Judah fell in 70 CE and the Temple was destroyed, the Jewish people's longing for the Messiah intensified. In their last revolt against Rome from 132 to 135 CE, the leader of the Jews in Israel was a man by the name of Shimon, son of Koziba. Rabbi Akiva called Shimon "God's Anointed," or Messiah, and changed his name from *Bar Koziba* to *Bar Kochba*, "the son of a star." (See chapter 9 for more about Bar Kochba.)

With the defeat of the Jewish army and the torture and murder of Bar Kochba by the Romans, resulting in the end of Jewish autonomy in the Holy Land until 1948, it became clear that Bar Kochba had not, in fact, been the Messiah. Thus began a period of time when the Jewish people yearned for the Messiah more than ever, and this figure began to be surrounded with mystery. The concept of Messiah from this point on has referred to a sort of divinely inspired deliverer, perhaps with some supernatural powers, whose arrival would be announced by the prophet Elijah. Upon the arrival of the Messiah, traditional Jews believe, the dead will rise again, the Day of Judgment will begin, and the righteous will be rewarded.

During the long centuries of exile, the Jewish people continued to dream of the Messiah and the return to Israel. Many false Messiahs arose, both mystics who really believed in themselves and impostors who took advantage of the people's despair. Each false Messiah brought suffering and disillusion in his wake, yet each new "Messiah" found many followers anxious to believe that the Return was at hand.

According to Jewish tradition, some real litmus tests exist to determine whether an individual who poses as the Messiah—or whom others believe to be the Messiah—actually is that person. These include a lineage from the House of King David, the capability to garner support from the people, and the ability to usher in an era of peace and prosperity. However, because tradition states that this era will be preceded by a period of upheaval and suffering, it has sometimes been difficult for the Jewish community to assess clearly whether or not an individual really is the Messiah. Such a dilemma faced the world Jewish community in the seventeenth century with the arrival on the scene of Shabbetai Tzvi.

Who Was Shabbetai Tzvi?

In the seventeenth century a charismatic leader named Shabbetai Tzvi arose, claiming to be the Messiah. Eventually, a significant number of the world's Jews believed him to be God's anointed one. The story of Shabbetai Tzvi's life and times, his relationship to the Jewish community and its rabbinic leadership, and his brief reign as the supposed Messiah had ramifications far beyond the scope of his life and actions and influenced Jewish beliefs and practices for centuries afterward.

Shabbetai Tzvi was born in Smyrna in 1626 to Spanish immigrants. His parents provided him with a traditional Jewish education, and he studied Talmud and Jewish law with rabbis in his hometown, becoming known as a talented pupil and rising star. Also fascinated with kabbalah (see chapter 16), Shabbetai Tzvi found the ascetic strains of Jewish mysticism to be particularly appealing, along with mystical calculations about when the "end of days" heralding the Messiah would begin.

A small number of mystics who were adherents of this methodology claimed that through mortification of the body one could communicate with God and the angels, predict the future, and perform miracles. Shabbetai Tzvi spent a lot of time alone, and his first two marriages ended in divorce purportedly due to his unwillingness to engage in marital relations. However, this solitude did not extend to his rabbinic and kabbalistic colleagues, among whom he garnered quite a following.

The year 1648 was a year thought by some to be the herald of the World to Come due to mystical calculations in both the Christian and Jewish communities. Not coincidentally, it was that year that Shabbetai Tzvi announced to his friends and family that he believed himself to be the Messiah and that part of his role would entail overthrowing the secular governments of the world and bringing the Jewish people back to Eretz Yisrael.

After this pronouncement, Shabbetai Tzvi continued to live the life of a mystic, garnering followers and impressing them primarily through pronouncing God's four-letter holy name, the Tetragrammaton. (Traditional Jews do not pronounce God's name, represented in English by the letters Y-H-V-H, substituting instead the title "Adonai," literally, "my Lord.") Due to these actions, the rabbinic community excommunicated Shabbetai Tzvi and his followers in 1651, whereupon the entire group left for Salonika, in Greece.

In Salonika, a center of kabbalistic learning, Shabbetai Tzvi again proclaimed himself to be the Messiah and staged many unusual events designed to encourage his followers in this belief, for example, a wedding ceremony betrothing himself to God and a Torah scroll. Not surprisingly, the rabbis of Salonika also banished him from their city, and he and his followers continued to roam around the Ottoman Empire, practicing their version of mysticism and heralding the Messianic Era in cities far and wide, ultimately arriving in Eretz Yisrael.

During his travels, he was married a third time, to a young woman named Sarah, a survivor of the Chmielnicki massacres (see chapter 17) who had visions that she was going to marry the Messiah. Rumors that she had been a prostitute during her teenage years only served to make Shabbetai Tzvi seem more authentic to his followers, because he was seen to emulate the prophet Hosea, who himself married a prostitute (as a metaphor for the Jewish people's unfaithfulness to God). Shabbetai Tzvi and Sarah's marriage introduced the practice of sexual licentiousness to his movement, and this behavior would become a cornerstone of later groups that spun off from Shabbetai Tzvi's followers.

After traveling to Eretz Yisrael, Shabbetai Tzvi met a man who was to be his most influential follower and the organizer of his movement, Nathan of Gaza. Nathan, who claimed to be the risen prophet Elijah who thereby would herald the Messiah's

advent, not only believed that Shabbetai Tzvi was in fact the Messiah, but he began formulating a plan in order to gain worldwide support for their campaign. In 1665, Shabbetai Tzvi and Nathan of Gaza made a bold announcement in synagogue on Rosh Hashanah that the Messianic Era would begin the following year—complete with the blowing of the shofar and a heralding of Shabbetai as the "King Messiah." Christians and Jews worldwide supported this claim; they believed that the year 1666 was in fact foretold to be the end of the millennium and so were encouraged by the news that came of Shabbetai Tzvi's activities. By the time Shabbetai Tzvi entered the city of Constantinople in 1666, much of the Jewish world was primed for the beginning of the Messianic Age.

False Hopes and Dashed Dreams

An obvious question is why such a significant number of the world's Jews believed that an individual who appeared to be a madman and who flouted Jewish law was in fact the Messiah. (For example, he circulated a flyer abolishing the fast of the Tenth of Tevet, substituting instead a day of feasting in honor of the Messianic Era.) The answer is based in the climate of the times, the efforts of Nathan of Gaza in spreading his message, and a dichotomy between the rabbinic leadership and the communities that they led.

In 1648, the same year that Shabbetai Tzvi proclaimed himself to be the Messiah in the Ottoman Empire, Eastern European Jewry was experiencing the worst persecution to befall the Jewish people since the Spanish Inquisition 150 years earlier—the Chmielnicki Massacres (see chapter 17). Led by Bogdan Chmielnicki, a Cossack soldier and minor Ukrainian noble, troops seeking independence for the

Ukraine tortured and massacred tens of thousands of Polish Jews and wiped out entire villages, signaling the end of a four-hundred-year period of relative safety, prosperity, and autonomy for the Polish Jewish community. Compounded by this enormous calamity was a sea change in the relationship of the Church to the Jewish communities of Eastern Europe. Jews were accused by the priests of interfering with the Church's activities on the estates that they managed for Polish nobles, and they were branded with the old charge of blood libel (false accusations of murdering Christian children in order to use their blood in making Passover matzah, among other allegations).

Then, less than a decade after the Chmielnicki massacres, the Russo-Swedish War brought Russian troops to the region of Poland and Lithuania, and Jews—accused by the local population of collaborating with both the Russians and the Swedes—were subjected to more massacres, forced conversions and deportations.[1]

In the minds of Eastern European Jews, and in fact the world Jewish community, such a series of events certainly qualified as the predicted upheaval that would precede the End of Days and the Messianic Era. And while the mainstream rabbinate in general opposed Shabbetai Tzvi's movement, the kabbalistic community, who had computed the days of the Messiah to concur with Shabbetai Tzvi's rise, saw in him a true savior, fomenting Messianic hopes throughout the Ottoman Empire in particular.

---

[1] Eli Barnavi, ed., *A Historical Atlas of the Jewish People: From the Time of the Patriarchs to the Present*, New York: Schocken Books, 1992, p. 146.

In 1666, this Messianic fervor began to alarm the Ottoman authorities, for the same reason it had concerned the Roman authorities fifteen centuries earlier during the Bar Kochba era: true Messianism in the Jewish community also included a military goal of overthrowing the secular authorities. Ottoman soldiers threw Shabbetai Tzvi in jail where his followers bribed the guards to allow him to entertain guests and have conjugal visits with his wife, and ultimately summoned him to appear before the sultan. The Ottoman sultan gave him the option of death or conversion, and to the initial amazement of his followers and indeed world Jewry, Shabbetai Tzvi—the presumed Messiah—submitted to the sultan and converted publicly to Islam.

Nathan of Gaza immediately began a campaign to explain Shabbetai Tzvi's actions in the context of his claim to be the Messiah. In kabbalistic language familiar to his followers, Nathan claimed that Shabbetai Tzvi had converted to Islam in order to descend into the depths of evil in order to liberate the divine sparks trapped there and effect *tikkun olam* (repair of the world) (see chapter 16 for a more in-depth discussion of this concept in particular and kabbalah in general). Not only did this explanation resonate with some of Shabbetai's mystical adherents, but the whole idea of hiding one's true self by outwardly converting to a different faith was familiar and understandable to the Sephardic community, which had dealt with the issue of *conversos* (see chapter 14) for two centuries.

Nathan's explanation and Shabbetai's actions were accepted by a number of their closest followers, who failed to be disabused of their belief that he was the Messiah either by Shabbetai's conversion or by his death in 1676 (Nathan of Gaza died four years later). The descendants of these believers named themselves the Dönmeh (the Turkish word for "religious convert"), a sect that survived in Greece and Turkey until the twentieth century.

In Europe during the eighteenth century, a man named Jacob Frank continued this trend by claiming to be the reincarnation of Shabbetai Tzvi and, therefore, the Messiah. Frankism advocated the outward conversion to Catholicism while remaining inwardly Jewish (albeit with unorthodox practices, including sexual licentiousness), in order to emulate Shabbetai Tzvi's methodology of descending into the depths by flouting the laws of the Torah in order to collect divine sparks. Spreading from Germany to Poland to Lithuania, small numbers of Frankists remained active throughout the eighteenth and nineteenth centuries.

Aside from these small numbers of adherents, however, the rest of world Jewry utterly rejected Shabbetai Tzvi's Messianic claims following his conversion to Islam. However, the disastrous effect of Shabbetai Tzvi's apostasy on a Jewish population that was prepared to drop everything and go to Eretz Yisrael to greet the Messianic Era on a moment's notice is difficult to describe. Not only Jewish writers, but gentile diarists and historians of the period as well chronicled the events leading up to and following Shabbetai Tzvi's conversion. The British diplomat Sir Paul Rycaut, who lived from 1628 to 1700 and traveled extensively throughout the Ottoman Empire, wrote:

"All the cities of Turkey, where the Jews inhabited, were full of the expectation of the Messiah; no trade or course of gain was followed. Every one imagined that daily provisions, riches, honors and government were to descend upon him by some unknown and miraculous manner. An example of which is most observable in the Jews at Thessalonica, who now full of assurance that the restoration of their kingdom and the accomplishment of the times for the coming of the Messiah was at hand . . . applied themselves immediately to fastings; and some in that manner beyond the abilities of nature, that having for the space of seven days taken no sustenance, were famished. [The Jews did penance to speed the coming of the Messiah.] Others buried themselves in their gardens, covering their naked bodies with earth, their heads only excepted, and remained in those beds of dirt, until their bodies were stiffened with the cold and moisture. [They believed that they would miraculously be transported to Israel for the Messianic Era.]"[2]

The English diarist Samuel Pepys wrote, on February 19, 1666, of gossip concerning bets being placed on the likelihood of Shabbetai Tzvi's authenticity as he shopped at his bookseller:

"Here I am told for certain, what I have heard once or twice already, of a Jew in town, that in the name of the rest do offer to give any man £10 to be paid £100, if a certain person now at Smyrna be within these two years owned by all the Princes of the East, and particularly the grand Signor as the King of the world, in the same manner we do the King of England here, and that this man is the true Messiah. One named a friend of his that had received ten pieces in gold upon this score,

---

[2] Sir Paul Rycaut, *History of the Turkish Empire*, quoted in Jacob Rader Marcus, *The Jew in the Medieval World: From the Time of the Patriarchs to the Present*, New York: Schocken Books, 1992, pp. 263–264.

and says that the Jew hath disposed of £1,100 in this manner, which is very strange; and certainly this year of 1666 will be a year of great action; but what the consequences of it will be, God knows!"

Most moving, perhaps, is the entry written by Glückel of Hameln, a seventeenth-century businesswoman living in Germany who penned a moving and informative family history that included her own father-in-law's involvement with the events of 1666:

"Our joy, when the letters [proclaiming the Messiah's arrival] arrived [from Smyrna] is not to be told. Most of them were addressed to the Sephardim who, as fast as they came, took them to their synagogue and read them aloud; young and old, the Germans too hastened to the Sephardic synagogue.

"The Sephardic youth came dressed in their best finery and decked in broad green silk ribbons, the gear of Sabbatai Zevi . . . many sold their houses and lands and all their possessions, for any day they hoped to be redeemed. My good father-in-law left his home in Hameln, abandoned his house and lands and all his goodly furniture, and moved to Hildesheim. He sent on to us in Hamburg two enormous casks packed with linens and peas, beans, dried meats, shredded prunes and like stuff, every manner of food that would keep. For the old man expected to sail any moment from Hamburg to the Holy Land.

"More than a year the casks lay in my house. At length the old folks feared the meat and other edibles would rot; and they wrote us, we should open the casks and remove the foodstuffs, to save the linens from ruin. For three years the casks stood ready, and all this while my father-in-law

awaited the signal to depart. But the Most High pleased otherwise."[3]

The Legacy of Shabbetai Tzvi

The Shabbetai Tzvi affair had lasting consequences for world Jewry. The first was that the rabbinic community closed ranks, unwilling to accept any deviation from mainstream Jewish practice. The result of this crackdown was to suspect any Jewish group that moved in a direction—even in custom, if not Jewish law—away from accepted traditional practice. The fledgling Hasidic movement, therefore, met with much more resistance from the mainstream Orthodox community than it might have if the rabbis had been of a mind to accept alternative expressions of religious joy, for example, the storytelling, dancing, singing and table-banging that characterized Hasidic gatherings.

The Hasidic community, moreover, became the bastion of continued Messianic hopes, (characterized most recently by the supporters of the late Lubavitcher Rebbe, Menachem Mendel Schneersohn, many of whom believing that he will in fact return as the Messiah), even as most traditional Jews continue to include prayers for the arrival of the Messiah in daily worship up until the present time.

In the end, a crackdown on differences has meant that the observant community, particularly its rabbinate, continues even in the modern era to be less tolerant of change and alternative expressions—even within the bounds of *halachah*—than it might otherwise have been had not the Shabbetai Tzvi affair occurred, and taken

---

[3] Marvin Lowenthal, trans., *The Memoirs of Glückel of Hameln,* New York: Schocken Books, 1977, pp. 46–47.

in so many believers who, it turns out, misplaced their trust.

CONNECTING TO OUR TRADITION
Maimonides' (see chapter 14) twelfth principle of faith is belief in the coming of the Messiah. This Hebrew sentence, *"Ani ma'amin b'emunah shleimah b'viyat Ha-Mashi'aḥ"* ("I believe with perfect faith in the coming of the Messiah") is most easily recognizable to modern Jews as a song. In Eastern Europe, these words were set to a mournful tune and said to have been sung by those entering the gas chambers during the Holocaust. Recently, they have been set to more upbeat music and sung in religious schools and Jewish summer camps in happier settings.

DID YOU KNOW?
Even today, a group called "Dönmeh West" exists in California. The group's leader is Reb Yakov Leib HaKohain, who considers Jacob Frank to be his namesake and claims to be the last in a chain of Shabbetai Tzvi's spiritual descendants. HaKohain advocates a particularly radical spin on kabbalah and "Jungian spirituality." The group refers to its movement as interfaith and nonsectarian.

IMPORTANT TERMS
Kabbalah
Dönmeh
Messiah/*Mashi'aḥ*
Olam Ha-Ba (World to Come)
Tetragrammaton
Tikkun olam
K'lipot
Conversos

Names, Places, and Events
Ottoman Empire	Jacob Frank
Shabbetai Tzvi	Russo-Swedish War
Nathan of Gaza	Sir Paul Rycaut
Salonika	Samuel Pepys
Smyrna	Glückel of Hameln
Bar Kochba	Menachem Mendel
Chmielnicki	Schneersohn/The
Massacres	Lubavitcher Rebbe
	Jacob Frank

DISCUSSION QUESTIONS
- Why do you think that Shabbetai Tzvi was able to garner such a large following into believing that he was the Messiah? What qualities do you look for in a leader—spiritual as well as secular? Did Shabbetai Tzvi possess any of these qualities?
- Moses Maimonides and traditional Jews for centuries have held a belief in the Messiah as an unshakable tenet of Jewish faith. While most traditional Jews continue to believe in the Messiah as a real figure, many liberal Jews have different ideas of what Messianism means. Do you believe in the coming of the Messiah? What does the Messianic Age mean to you? Do you believe that the Messiah will be a real person, or do you believe that the Messianic Age signifies something different?

ACTIVITIES
False Messiahs (S, A)
By one count, Shabbetai Tzvi was the *twenty-seventh* in a series of false Messiahs that arose during the Middle Ages and the early modern period. Working in pairs or small groups, have your class research some of these false Messiahs. Examples include Solomon Molcho and David Reubeni, who lived in sixteenth-century Europe, and others. What do they have in common? How did they influence their followers? What traits of the Messiah did they claim to have? How did their movements end?

Interview with Shabbetai Tzvi (E, S)
Invite someone charismatic to come into
your class dressed as Shabbetai Tzvi. Have
the students prepare questions in advance,
and ask "Shabbetai" to answer them. The
goal of this activity is to help the students
understand how Jews the world over could
be taken in by a false Messiah.

TIMELINE (all dates are CE)
1626
      Birth of Shabbetai Tzvi in Smyrna
      (Izmir), Turkey
1648
      Shabbetai claims to followers that
      he is the Messiah; excommuni-
      cated by the Smyrna rabbis
1648
      Chmielnicki massacres
1651–1666
      Shabbetai Tzvi and followers
      wander around the Ottoman Empire
c. 1658
      Marriage of Shabbetai Tzvi to
      Sarah in Cairo
1665
      Shabbetai Tzvi meets Nathan
      of Gaza
1666
      Shabbetai Tzvi's arrest and
      conversion to Islam
1676
      Shabbetai Tzvi dies (according to
      some, on Yom Kippur)
1726–1791
      Life of Jacob Frank

RESOURCES
Books and Articles

Gilbert, Martin. *The Routledge Atlas of
Jewish History,* 6th ed. London:
Routledge, 1995.

Lowenthal, Marvin, trans. *The Memoirs of
Glückel of Hameln.* New York: Schocken
Books, 1977.

Marcus, Jacob Rader. *The Jew in the
Medieval World, A Source Book: 315–
1791.* Cincinnati, OH: Hebrew Union
College Press, 1990.

Sachar, Howard M. *A History of the Jews
in the Modern World.* New York: Alfred
A. Knopf, 2005.

Sarna, Jonathan D., and Jonathan B.
Krasner. *The History of the Jewish
People: A Story of Tradition and Change.*
Springfield, NJ: Behrman House, 2006
(see especially chapter 10).

Scholem, Gershom, and R. J.
Werblowsky, trans. *Sabbetai Sevi.*
Princeton, NJ: Princeton University Press,
1973.

Schreiber, Mordecai, ed. *The Shengold
Jewish Encyclopedia.* Schreiber
Publishing, 1998.

Stillman, Norman A. *The Jews of Arab Lands:
A History and Source Book.* Philadelphia:
Jewish Publication Society, 1979.

Stillman, Norman A. *The Jews of Arab
Lands in Modern Times.* Philadelphia:
Jewish Publication Society, 1991.

Internet
Visit www.behrmanhouse.com/booklinks
for links to Web sites that offer additional
resources for this chapter.

CHAPTER NINETEEN

ḤASIDISM AND OTHER RELIGIOUS DEVELOPMENTS

WHAT'S THE BIG IDEA?
Jewish Culture and Thought

Despite repeated devastation to Jewish communities over the centuries, a creative, rich Jewish culture and religious life have continued to flourish. The flexible and resilient nature of the rabbinic-based religious system has enabled Jews to successfully respond to and thrive in new environments and circumstances. Many changes to Jewish thought and practice that grew out of Ḥasidism, an eighteenth-century Polish grass-roots movement, are still with us today.

BACKGROUND INFORMATION

As seen in chapter 17, the Chmielnicki massacres of the mid-seventeenth century decimated the Jewish community of Poland and left the remaining Jews in a precarious position, holding little power or position in a rapidly declining situation. Within the *kahal* (Jewish community), Jewish life was governed by an authoritarian social hierarchy in which well-educated Jewish merchants held most of the power. The majority of Jews, however, were common laborers with little education, wealth, or status who had few options when it came to matters of day-to-day life or religious expression.

Over the years, Jewish religious life had become the bastion of the well-educated. Community Elders often made judgments based upon how much time one spent in prayer, study, and exploring the finer points of Jewish laws. Scholars of the day engaged in highly intellectual Talmudic debates that often had little to do with the realities of daily life. Therefore, while Judaism had evolved in a way that held meaning and promise for many, for some of the Jewish masses who found themselves unable to participate due to their lack of education, it held little solace.

Jewish practice and culture have rarely remained stagnant. Throughout history there have been Jews who have rebelled against the strictures imposed by external or internal forces. Jewish life in Poland in the late eighteenth century required a new outlook, a new perspective to meet the needs of the Jewish populace. Just as the Christian world began to experience a rise in spiritualism and evangelical religion, so too did the Jewish community. The Christian and Jewish worlds were separate enough that they probably did not exert much influence over each other, but rather both worlds were suffering from similar political, economic, and religious issues.

Ḥasidism and the Ba'al Shem Tov

Described as having a spiritual soul and great charisma, a new Jewish leader was gaining the attention of poor Jews throughout Poland. His name was Israel ben Eliezer, and he became known as the Ba'al Shem Tov (literally, "master of the good name") or by the acronym "the Besht." The Ba'al Shem Tov was an orphan from the western Ukrainian town of Okup. In every way, he was a man of the people, having little learning, no connection to a line of rabbis, and often working as a common laborer in the clay pits or ritual slaughterhouse. On the side, the Besht had begun to do the work of a holy man connected to kabbalah (Jewish mysticism; see chapter 16 for more details), making amulets, performing cures and miracles, and foretelling the future through his dreams.

Gradually, the Ba'al Shem Tov developed his own religious principles and guidelines for a Jewish way of life that would become the foundation of the Hasidic (from the ancient Hebrew word meaning pious) movement. First, from the text "the whole earth is full of His glory" (Isaiah 6:13) came the idea that goodness and Godliness could be found in all things, both sacred and secular. It also allowed one to appreciate all the pleasures in the world. For example, the Besht said, "Don't deny that a girl is beautiful. Just be sure that your recognition of her beauty brings you back to its source—God." Second, the Besht believed that one's ultimate goal should be "cleaving to" or "communion with" God (in Hebrew, *deveikut*). This "clinging" was done not through study or asceticism, as suggested by the mainstream Judaism of the time, but through heartfelt devotional prayer, religious ecstasy, a joyful disposition, *nigunim* (songs without words), and dancing as part of worship.[1] Third, the Ba'al Shem Tov revived the idea of the *tzadik* (Hebrew for "a righteous individual"), a person who can cleave to God in the closest way possible for a human being. Therefore, there could be many *tzadikim* at one time, and these

would eventually become the leaders who helped spread Hasidism. The Ba'al Shem Tov popularized his teachings through secular stories that had a message about how to live a Jewish life. Originally the Besht's stories were passed on from storyteller to storyteller. It was only after the Ba'al Shem Tov's death that many of these stories were written down. One tale told by the Besht focused on the issue of who is a better Jew:

"Two Jews lived next door to each other. One was a scholar, the other a poor laborer. The scholar would rise every day at the break of dawn, go to the synagogue, study a page of Talmud, and say the morning prayers quietly and slowly until almost midday. His neighbor, the poor laborer, also rose early and went to work in order to feed his family, having no time to go to the synagogue to pray with the congregation at the proper hour.

"Precisely at midday, the scholar left the synagogue to return home, filled with a sense of satisfaction. He would invariably meet his neighbor, the poor laborer, hurrying to the house of worship with great anguish and regret for his tardiness. The laborer would utter a mournful groan, bemoaning his inability to have fulfilled his religious obligations properly. At the same time, the scholar would look with scorn at his simple, working neighbor, and a smirk would form on his lips as he considered his superiority.

"For many years it was so, until both of them eventually passed on to be judged by the Heavenly Court. For the scholar, they brought forth the scales and on one side put all of his good deeds, all of his study of Torah, and all of his brilliance. On the other they placed the smirk of contempt he had for a fellow Jew. Behold, the weight of the smirk turned the scale to guilty! For the poor laborer, they put his few failings

---

[1] Elijah Judah Schochet, *The Hasidic Movement and the Gaon of Vilna*, Northvale, NJ: Jason Aronson, 1994, p. 5.

on one side: coming late to the synagogue, not studying enough Torah. But on the other, they put the groan that issued from the depths of his soul, a groan that showed how much more he wanted to do had his poverty not prevented him. And the weight of the groan of the poor worker turned the scale to innocent!"[2]

Mitnagdim

With its emphasis on spirituality over scholarship, feeling over habit, the importance of the heart over the head, and joy in all things, Hasidism gained large numbers of followers throughout Poland. Hasidism's principles were somewhat antithetical to traditional Judaism, and it was a popular movement that did not require the leadership of learned rabbis. It should come as no surprise, therefore, that Hasidism threatened those who were part of the Jewish establishment, and that many Jews were opposed to the Hasidic movement. Soon, these Jews became known as *mitnagdim* (Hebrew for "opponents").

Chief among the opponents of Hasidism was Elijah ben Solomon Zalman, also known as the Vilna Gaon. Born in 1720, Elijah ben Solomon Zalman was a child prodigy (*gaon* literally means "genius" in Hebrew) who gave his first public sermon at the age of six or seven, and no longer needed a teacher by the age of ten. He went on to become well versed in both religious and secular subjects; he is particularly known for his commentaries on the Talmud. As a scholar himself, the Vilna Gaon believed that *halachah* (Jewish law) and scholarship were of primary importance. Furthermore, the Vilna Gaon felt that the visions and miracles of Hasidism were lies, and that venerating the *tzadik* was a form of idolatry. According to the Vilna Gaon, "It is

the duty of every believing Jew to repudiate and pursue them [Hasidim] with all manner of afflictions and subdue them because they have sin in their hearts and are a sore on the body of Israel."[3] The Gaon followed through on his pronouncement with two *herem*s (excommunications) in 1772 and 1781. The first *herem* also involved publicly burning books related to Hasidism. As part of the second *herem*, Hasidic Jews were expelled from Jewish communities and people were told not to give them lodging, marry them, or do business with them. Despite his efforts, however, the Hasidic movement continued to flourish.

Compromise and Coexistence

When the Ba'al Shem Tov died in 1760, he left behind many disciples, some of whom were acclaimed as *tzadikim* in their own right, to carry on the Besht's work. It is interesting to note that within one generation of the death of the Ba'al Shem Tov it was acceptable, and even laudatory, for Hasidic masters also to be Talmudic scholars, an indication of the movement's growing acceptance in the mainstream. Unfortunately, however, some Hasidic leaders took advantage of the trust put in them by their followers and used their position to gain wealth and social standing. One such *tzadik* was the Besht's own grandson, Baruch of Miedzyboz, who lived in the grand manner of Polish nobles. Such exploitation of the masses was one of the serious concerns that the *mitnagdim* had with Hasidism.

At the same time, other changes were also taking place elsewhere in the religious and secular communities. The Vilna Gaon encouraged secular studies, which helped move mainstream orthodoxy away from a myopic view of the world seen only through

---

[2] Benjamin Blech, *Eyewitness to Jewish History*, Hoboken, NJ: John Wiley & Sons, 2004, pp. 171–172.

[3] Paul Johnson, *A History of the Jews*, New York: HarperCollins, 1987, p. 298.

Talmudic study (against which the Ḥasidim had originally reacted). In addition, *Haskalah* (Hebrew, meaning "enlightenment") was viewed by religious Jews of all types as a new common enemy.

Many evangelical, superstitious, and naïve elements of Ḥasidism were purged, and learning in its proper context was brought into the movement. These reforms continued into the second quarter of the nineteenth century, allowing Ḥasidism—an adaptation of traditional Judaism by the common people—to become more acceptable in mainstream Judaism.

CONNECTING TO OUR TRADITION

The stories told by the Ba'al Shem Tov and passed down among his followers originally were quite novel and promulgated views often at variance with the Orthodox Judaism of the time. However, over time, these same stories and their values became part of the Jewish library of texts drawn upon by different contemporary movements. Many modern liberal synagogues regularly include texts about or by the Ba'al Shem Tov as readings during worship services. Some High Holy Day greeting cards include illustrations based on Ḥasidic tales.

IMPORTANT TERMS

Ḥasidim	*Deveikut*
Mitnagdim	*Tzadik*
Gaon	*Ḥerem*

Names, Places, and Events

Israel ben Eliezer	Vilna Gaon
Ba'al Shem Tov	Vilna
Besht	Okup
Elijah ben Solomon Zalman	

DISCUSSION QUESTIONS

- During the time that the Ḥasidic movement developed, a tension existed between structured study of Torah and more free-flowing expressions of joyous prayer. How is this tension still present in Judaism? In what ways have compromises been reached? In what ways is there still a standoff?
- What do you think is more important—study of Torah or nurturing the soul? This was of primary importance to the Ḥasidim and the *mitnagdim,* and it is no less relevant today. Explain your answer.

ACTIVITIES

Character Interview (E, S)

Invite someone to come to the classroom to play the part of the Ba'al Shem Tov or the Vilna Gaon. Ask the character to talk about his life and teachings, and give the students the opportunity to ask questions. After the interview, have the students write letters to the character saying what they found most interesting about his life.

A Great Debate (S, A)

Invite two people to the classroom to play the roles of the Ba'al Shem Tov and the Vilna Gaon, to present their philosophies, and engage in a debate. Students may also be given an opportunity to ask questions and get responses from both the Besht and the Vilna Gaon. After the debate, the students can determine who gave a better argument supporting his position.

Ḥerem Trial (S)

Convene a court of the *Va'ad* (Council of Four Lands—see chapter 17 for more information) to determine whether or not the Ḥasidim should be excommunicated. Break the students into three groups and give them material to read about the *herem* (excommunication). One group will take the Ḥasidic position against the *herem.* One group will take the position of the *mitnagdim.* The third group will play the part of the *Va'ad* court and make a final decision between the groups. At the end of the activity, present the actual verdict in which the Ḥasidim were excommunicated.

Stories of the Ba'al Shem Tov (E, S, A)
Choose stories of the Ba'al Shem Tov for the students to read and discuss; you can find such tales in the book, *In Praise of the Ba'al Shem Tov,* listed in the "Resources" section of this chapter. Depending on the age of the students, you may want to have the group illustrate the stories (for younger children) or discuss the relevance of these stories in our Jewish community today (for older children or adults). Some students may already be familiar with some of these stories even if they did not know they were from the Ba'al Shem Tov. What does that teach us about the acceptance of Ḥasidic concepts and values in mainstream Judaism today?

Hasidism as a Popular Movement (S, A)
Ḥasidism began in part because some of the common people in eighteenth-century Poland had certain needs and desires that weren't being met by traditional Judaism. Throughout history there have been popular movements, both secular and religious, that have changed society. Examine folk music, labor unionism, Jewish renewal, and/or other movements or countercultural expressions. Compare and contrast these cultural expressions with the development of the Ḥasidic movement.

TIMELINE (all dates are CE)
1700
        Birth of the Ba'al Shem Tov
1720
        Birth of the Vilna Gaon
1760
        Death of the Ba'al Shem Tov
1772
        First *herem* against the Ḥasidim
1781
        Second *herem* against the Ḥasidim
1797
        Death of the Vilna Gaon

RESOURCES
Books and Articles

Bank, Richard D., and Julie Gutin. *The Everything Jewish History and Heritage Book.* Avon, MA: Adams Media Corp., 2003.

Ben-Amos, Dan, and Jerome R. Mintz. *In Praise of the Ba'al Shem Tov.* New York: Schocken Books, 1984.

Blech, Benjamin. *Eyewitness to Jewish History.* Hoboken, NJ: John Wiley & Sons, 2004.

Johnson, Paul. *A History of the Jews.* New York: HarperCollins, 1987.

Sachar, Howard M. *The Course of Modern Jewish History.* New York: Vintage Books, 1990.

Sachar, Howard M. *A History of the Jews in the Modern World.* New York: Alfred A. Knopf, 2005.

Schochet, Elijah Judah. *The Hasidic Movement and the Gaon of Vilna.* Northvale, NJ: Jason Aronson, 1994.

Internet
Visit www.behrmanhouse.com/booklinks for links to Web sites that offer additional resources for this chapter.

Enlightenment Period

CHAPTER TWENTY
EMANCIPATION FOR THE JEWS OF EUROPE

WHAT'S THE BIG IDEA?
Assimilation

The people with whom Jews have lived have often held Jews at arm's length, even when not persecuting them. However, throughout history there have been times when Jews have been allowed to enter mainstream society. The period we call Emancipation (from the late eighteenth century to the late nineteenth century) was the first time in hundreds of years that European society was open enough that assimilation became a concern.

BACKGROUND INFORMATION

For centuries the Jews of Europe were forced to live separately from those in the dominant culture because Christians feared them and considered them to be non-European. Jews were often separated physically into walled ghettoes. They were not allowed to own land or participate in most commercial enterprises. Travel restrictions kept Jews from moving freely between and within countries. Often, special taxes were imposed on Jewish individuals or communities by the reigning monarch or local government.

Jews were also considered to be a separate group or "corporation." Within this system Jews, like other corporations, had the right to govern themselves. However, this right brought with it the responsibility of providing all social services such as education, health care, and sanitation. Jewish leaders imposed taxes on the community to support these social services, and taxes had to be paid to the local and national governments as well. This system both enforced double taxation on the majority of Jews and helped to keep them separate from the larger society.

Many Jews were satisfied to live separate lives from their Christian neighbors because it allowed them to keep and maintain their religion. Jewish laws concerning *kashrut* (dietary regulations), intermarriage, and Shabbat would have kept Jews separate from the larger community even if walls and secular laws had not. Living together in a tightly knit enclave also meant that one could depend on the community to provide moral support in the face of religious persecution.

"Exception Jews"

Even as the majority of Jews lived separate lives limited by discriminatory laws, a few Jews found a way to subvert those restrictions by becoming exceptions to the general rules and were granted special status either for financial or intellectual reasons. Those Jews who were given special privileges due to their financial standing were often referred to as "Court Jews." Court Jews were merchants or financiers who provided goods and money to the emperors or princes of Europe in their wars against each other. It could be a tenuous position and some Court Jews fell into disgrace as a result of political intrigue. However, most Court Jews also enjoyed special privileges such as being able to travel freely, not having to wear a Jew's badge, being able to slaughter animals according to Jewish ritual without penalty or persecution, and not having to pay higher taxes than their Christian neighbors. During their tenure, short as it might be, Court Jews often acted as the intercessors for their coreligionists, bringing petitions on their behalf to court. This is not to say that they were well loved in the Jewish community; envy of their position and the power they wielded over Jewish corporate life due to their financial position tended to put them at odds with other Jews. However, petitioning the Court Jew was often the only chance the Jewish community had to be heard by the reigning monarch.

Other "exception Jews" held positions of favor because of their great learning. Often sponsored by an emperor or prince, these Jews might be accepted into the leading salons of the city, although such acceptance did not extend to their coreligionists.

Moses Mendelssohn (1729–1786), born to a traditional Jewish ghetto family in Dessau, Germany, was one such "exception Jew" whose work had a significant impact on European Jewry. Mendelssohn was a short, hunchback man who had an amazing mind that he turned to both Jewish and secular subjects. As a boy, he studied with Rabbi David Hirschel Frankel, and when Rabbi Frankel moved to Berlin, Mendelssohn (though only fourteen) followed. In Berlin, Mendelssohn had the opportunity to study with many great teachers and learned German, Hebrew, French, Italian, English, Latin, and Greek, in addition to mathematics, logic, philosophy, and the continuation of his Jewish studies.

Mendelssohn wrote works on many secular subjects as well as numerous philosophical essays in support of the existence of God and the special nature of Judaism. One such treatise, "Evidence in the Metaphysical Sciences," earned him a prize from the Prussian Academy of Sciences in 1763. His writings also brought him to the attention of Emperor Frederick the Great who gave him the status of "Jew under extraordinary protection."

Despite all of Mendelssohn's secular studies and recognition, he remained a committed Jew. He believed in Judaism as a rational, humane theology, yet he realized that daily life in the Jewish ghetto was often perceived as backward and isolating. Mendelssohn wanted to make German literature and culture accessible to all Jews. In his pursuit of this goal, Mendelssohn wrote a very unusual and important translation of the Bible in 1783. Written in German using Hebrew characters, this version of the Pentateuch allowed literate Jews who were well versed in the Bible to learn German. Within a generation, almost all Jewish homes in Europe had a copy of Moses Mendelssohn's translation of the Bible on their bookshelves.

Moses Mendelssohn's bridging of the gap between Jewish religious culture and German secular culture, paired with the expansion of Emancipation through much of Western Europe, set the stage for the *Haskalah* (Jewish Enlightenment). Mendelssohn's writings and his activism in this regard helped Jews to become knowledgeable about secular culture, and his followers—as well as others—continued to expand on his work after his death. (See chapter 21 for more information about the *Haskalah*).

The French Revolution and the Jews

The French Revolution and the emancipation of the Jews would greatly change life for the majority of Jews living in Western Europe. For the first time since the rise of

Christianity, all Jews, not just a select few, would have choices about where and how to live. These choices would lead some Jews to assimilate, some Jews to remain separate, and others to search for ways to live in both the Jewish world and the modern world simultaneously.

The late eighteenth century saw the growth of many new philosophies including humanism, which asserts the dignity and worth of people and their capacity for self-realization through reason, and rationalism, which sees reason itself as the superior source of knowledge. These philosophies led many people to question old beliefs and seek changes in government. Nowhere did this have a more explosive impact than in France.

In 1789, the French people overthrew the government and the monarchy and wrote the Declaration of the Rights of Man. Similar to the Declaration of Independence in America, the Declaration of the Rights of Man put forth the idea of equality and the right of all people to participate in government. Using this document as a starting point, the French revised their government from a corporate system into a system of departments and districts in which each individual, rather than each group or corporation, had a direct relationship with the state.

With the Declaration of the Rights of Man, all groups including the Jews lost their political autonomy but in theory gained greater rights. The reality was a little different. At first only non-Catholic Christians were declared citizens and granted these rights. Then in 1790, Sephardic Jews residing in France were emancipated, and finally in 1791 all French Jews received full rights. Not all French citizens believed that Jews should

have the same rights as all other citizens, but many gradually came to realize that the philosophy expressed in the Declaration of the Rights of Man needed to be applied consistently if it was to carry any weight at all.

As French citizens, Jews began to serve in the army and make financial contributions to support the military. They took roles in public office and began to send their children to public schools where they learned secular subjects and were exposed to Christianity in a systematic way. Even with the changes to their status as French citizens and their participation in French culture and society, most French Jews remained connected to Judaism.

The violence of the French Revolution grew as more and more people thought to be a danger to the new society were beheaded until there was a backlash to the Revolution itself. With this backlash also came renewed anti-Semitism. This response was most pronounced in Alsace, in the northeastern region of France, where Jews had continued to be money-lenders even as opportunities had opened in other businesses. Those opposed to the Revolution began to circulate stories about Jews and Protestants buying up holy places and desecrating them. They used this and other old arguments about Jews to try to have them disenfranchised.

Napoleon Bonaparte Convenes a Sanhedrin

While Napoleon Bonaparte, who came to power as emperor in 1799, was aware of the spread of anti-Semitism, he had found that gaining the favor of minority groups was a useful way to build a support base. He continued this practice with French Jewry.

In 1806, in an attempt to gain Jewish loyalty to the state and to bring about change in the Jewish community, Napoleon called an Assembly of Jewish Notables. Composed of 112 Jewish businessmen, financiers, rabbis, and scholars handpicked by the French government, the assembly was meant to represent the Jews of France and help prove their worthiness as French citizens. The assembly was asked to reply to twelve questions that, if answered appropriately, would help ensure that the emperor would protect their rights. The questions included:

1. Are the Jews permitted to have more than one wife?
2. Does Judaism permit divorce?
3. Can Jews and Christians marry?
4. In the eyes of the Jews are the French brothers or strangers?
5. What behavior does Jewish law prescribe toward French Christians?
6. Do Jews born in France consider France their country and are they willing to defend it and obey its laws?
7. Who appoints the rabbis?
8. What police jurisdiction do the rabbis exercise over the Jews?
9. Are Jewish electoral forms and police jurisdictions prescribed by Jewish law or merely by custom?
10. Does Jewish law prohibit the Jews from entering the professions?
11. Does Jewish law encourage Jews to practice usury among Jews?
12. Does Jewish law encourage Jews to practice usury among Christians?[1]

Having given the questions to a committee of rabbis and laymen, the Assembly was able to return answers to the twelve questions in about a week. Knowing how much was at stake, they hedged or were evasive on certain issues, yet Bonaparte

[1] Howard M. Sachar, *The Course of Modern Jewish History*, New York: Vintage Books, 1990, p. 48.

was satisfied with the statements of loyalty. Wanting to do something that would impress the Jewish community and help guarantee their support, on September 3, 1806, Napoleon issued a summons for a Sanhedrin.

The Sanhedrin had been the Supreme Court of the Jews in ancient times, but had not been convened since the destruction of the Temple in Jerusalem over seventeen hundred years earlier. When Napoleon convened the Sanhedrin, the Jews of France were stunned by the apparent generosity of this act, which recognized Jewish history and law. The Jewish community was told that the Sanhedrin would confirm and turn into Jewish law the answers to the twelve questions prepared by the Assembly of Jewish Notables. The Sanhedrin did and, in doing so, had a far-reaching impact. By renouncing separate Jewish nationhood, this decision would set the tone for Jewish life in Western Europe for over a century.

Napoleon had many reasons for convening the Sanhedrin, most of which had to do with building support for his government within the French Jewish community, as well as other Jewish communities in Europe that he was in the process of conquering. One other reason was to divert attention from the fact that he planned to take back some rights given earlier to the Jews of France. In 1808, the "Organic Regulation on the Mosaic Religion" was enacted, making Judaism one of the official religions of France and placing rabbis under the supervision of the Ministry of Religion. This designation allowed the government to use rabbis to police certain issues such as conscription of youth into the military, loyalty to France, and an official stance against usury. Along with this measure, Napoleon began to regulate the commercial activity of French Jews and turn them away from certain businesses such as money lending, while also forcing them into the field of agriculture. This regulation has become known as the "Infamous Decree," because it struck at the heart of Emancipation by restricting the freedoms for Jews that had so recently been granted.

Emancipation Elsewhere in Europe

Jews in other parts of Europe watched what was happening in France and looked toward a day when they might also gain equal citizenship in their own countries. As early as 1792, the Jews of the Holy Roman Empire petitioned their local governments for many of the same rights being granted the Jews of France. However, the various dukes who ruled in what would eventually become Germany wanted to retain their power and were not willing to share the rights of citizenship with their serfs or with the Jews.

As the war with Napoleon continued, German hatred of Jews was further combined with their fear of Jews as "other" and possible traitors who would side with the French. The Jewish community in Germany would have to wait until Napoleon's armies conquered the country to gain the same rights as French Jews. When Napoleon's forces finally arrived in Germany, the army literally tore down the walls of the Jewish ghettoes and led the occupants out into the cities. After dealing with the physical division of the Jewish and Christian communities, laws were also rewritten and Jews gained full citizenship. One exception was Bavaria where Napoleon never quite found the time to deal with the Jewish issue; for this reason, Bavarian Jews were the last in Germany to receive citizenship, on April 22, 1871.

Prussia, also once part of the Holy Roman Empire, experienced a slightly different situation because Napoleon's armies did not occupy the country. Once the Prussian army had been defeated by the French, King Frederick William III made some reforms but did not at first see any reason to grant Jews the rights of citizenship. However, as Prussia went on to lose more than half her territory to Napoleon, the fear of French occupation became real and Prussian leaders realized that in order to defend the country they would need to reform their government into something akin to that of the French. As changes were made to bring different groups into direct relationship with the government, as had been done in France, individual Jews were given more freedoms and the Jewish community as a whole was placed under the authority of the government.

Even in lands that Napoleon did not conquer, changes could be seen as the philosophy behind the French Revolution traveled to other countries. One example of this phenomenon was the change in status of the Jews in England. By the middle of the nineteenth century, most restrictions on British Jews had been lifted. However, they could not hold a seat in Parliament because anyone elected to Parliament had to swear an oath on a Christian Bible, and that oath included the words "upon the true faith of a Christian." Since a Jew could not swear these words without lying, thus nullifying the oath, a Jew could not serve in Parliament. This situation was challenged repeatedly by Baron Lionel Rothschild between 1847 and 1858. During this time, Rothschild ran for Parliament as a Liberal candidate for the City of London and was elected six times. Each time Baron Rothschild was elected, he, with the help of others in Parliament, would try to amend the oath of office so that he could swear on a Hebrew

Bible and delete the Christian words. Parliament was hesitant to change the wording of the oath since an attempt to do this more than one hundred years earlier led to riots and great anti-Semitism. Finally, on July 26, 1858, the oath was changed for the House of Commons and Baron Lionel de Rothschild was able to take his rightful place in Parliament. It would take nearly another thirty years before a Jew—Nathaniel May de Rothschild, Lionel's son—would be allowed to take a seat in the House of Lords, which he did on July 9, 1885.

The Alfred Dreyfus Affair—The Backlash of Emancipation

In 1894, suspicious papers were found in the wastepaper basket of a German attaché in France. These papers appeared to indicate that a French soldier was providing military secrets to the German army. Alfred Dreyfus, a French Jew from Alsace, immediately came under suspicion. Those investigating the case claimed that the handwriting on the papers resembled Dreyfus's handwriting, even though the two handwriting samples were not at all alike. Dreyfus's real crime was being the only Jewish officer working in the midst of the primarily Catholic military.

Dreyfus was tried in a secret military court where he was not given the opportunity to examine the evidence or to protest his innocence. Found guilty of treason, he was stripped of his military rank in a humiliating public ceremony and sent to spend the rest of his life at Devil's Island, a penal colony off the coast of French Guiana. In the media of the day, Dreyfus's case was connected to an "international Jewish conspiracy," as French anti-Semitism again came to the surface.

Dreyfus probably would have lived out the rest of his days on Devil's Island if not for Lieutenant Colonel Picquart, the Chief of Army Intelligence. Although a strong anti-Semite himself, Picquart did not want the actual offender to go free, so when he discovered evidence that Dreyfus could not have written the note found in the German attaché's wastebasket, he brought it to the attention of members of the Senate. A new court-martial was held, this time to try the actual perpetrator who was a member of the aristocracy. However, the army did not want to turn over the original ruling of "Jewish treason," and the perpetrator was acquitted.

Other events then conspired to keep the Dreyfus Affair in the news and many began to call for a new trial. On January 13, 1898, an article titled "*J'Accuse*" ("I accuse") by Émile Zola, one of France's greatest writers, was published in a French newspaper. Taking up the full front page of the paper, "*J'Accuse*" spoke out against the crimes committed against Alfred Dreyfus and the manner in which the whole affair had been handled. Addressed to the president of the republic, this outcry by one author helped bring about the rightful conclusion to the Dreyfus Affair. Finally, in 1899, Dreyfus was pardoned and allowed to return to France, although he had to wait until 1906 before his military rank was restored to him.

Conclusion

Emancipation opened many doors for Europe's Jews. For the first time, Jews needed to make choices about how to live, not only within the Jewish community, but within the larger world around them. This freedom would have a far-reaching impact upon Jewish thought and culture. Yet in the midst of emancipation, not all Europeans truly took to heart the philosophies upon which emancipation rested. The presence of anti-Semitism continued, as can be seen in the Dreyfus Affair, and still limited the lives of Jews living in Europe, prohibiting full integration.

CONNECTING TO OUR TRADITION

The convening of a Sanhedrin, like the idea of a return to Zion, was for Diaspora Jews symbolic of their acceptance as a legitimate people, at home in their own nation rather than a scattered people living at the mercy of other nations.

When Napoleon convened a new Sanhedrin in 1806, he tapped into this part of the Jewish psyche and used it for his own political reasons. The French Jewish community, and others as well, came to believe that they might not need to return to Israel to become a nation again, but that they could have that nationhood where they currently lived.

IMPORTANT TERMS

Rationalism	Infamous Decree
Secularism	Usury
Humanism	Court Jews
Nationalism	*Haskalah*
Ghetto	Emancipation

Names, Place, and Events

Declaration of the Rights of Man	House of Lords
	Parliament
Assembly of Jewish Notables	Alfred Dreyfus
	Lieutenant Colonel
Sanhedrin	Picquart
Napoleon Bonaparte	Émile Zola
Holy Roman Empire	Moses Mendelssohn
House of Commons	

DISCUSSION QUESTIONS

• What were the choices Jews had to make about how to be Jewish before Emancipation? How did these choices change after Emancipation? What choices do we have today?

• Anti-Semitism can take many forms. What was different or the same about anti-Semitism before Emancipation and after Emancipation? What forms of anti-Semitism are present in our society today? Does this discrimination limit our lives as Jews? If so, how?

• Emancipation opened the doors for Jews to enter the common culture and society in new ways. This opportunity raised the specter of assimilation. Can assimilation ever be good for the Jewish people? Explain your answer.

ACTIVITIES

Mock Assembly of Jewish Notables (S, A)
Provide the class with copies of the twelve questions that Napoleon Bonaparte asked the Assembly of Jewish Notables. In small groups, have the students determine how the questions might be answered to satisfy the French government and yet not give up too much that is important to the Jewish people. Each group can share their answers with the class. Then give the students a copy of the actual answers the assembly developed. Ask the class some of the following questions: How are the answers different or the same? Do you think it was difficult for the assembly to come up with satisfactory answers? Why or why not? Why were the questions and answers so important to the Jewish people? Did the Assembly of Jewish Notables help lead to the possibility of assimilation? How?

Friend or Foe? (E, S)
Using *The History of the Jewish People: A Story of Tradition and Change* by Jonathan D. Sarna and Jonathan B. Krasner, have students do the Napoleon's Questions exercise on page 12. You might expand on this activity by asking the students what they think are some of the

consequences of seeing the French people as relatives, or as strangers.

Character Interview (E, S)

Invite several people to come to the classroom as Alfred Dreyfus, Lieutenant Colonel Picquart, and Émile Zola. Each visitor should share part of the story from his perspective. Then give the students a chance to ask questions. After the visit, have the students write newspaper articles about the Dreyfus Affair from different perspectives—military, Jewish, anti-Semitic, and as a citizen desiring the truth.

Create a bulletin board or newspaper using the articles. Provide the students with a copy of Emile Zola's "*J'Accuse*" and discuss its importance in the Dreyfus Affair. Discuss the effects of the Dreyfus Affair in what was supposed to be an emancipated society. Did the Jewish people have full equality? Why or why not? How does anti-Semitism limit Jewish freedom? Is this condition still true today?

Museum Exhibit (E, S)

After studying Jewish life before Emanci-pation and Jewish life after Emancipation, have the students design a museum exhibit that compares and contrasts life before and after Emanc-ipation in Western Europe. Use the discussion questions at the end of this chapter to help the students think about how to arrange their exhibit. Pictures and primary documents for the exhibit can be found in books and online. Students can write labels and headings for the exhibit. Parents and/or other classes can be invited to view the exhibit.

DID YOU KNOW?

In 1808, Napoleon made all Jews take last names. Many took names derived from that of their hometown (such as Berliner or Frankfurter) or their trade (such as Cantor).

TIMELINE (all dates are CE)

1729
    Moses Mendelssohn is born

1786
    Moses Mendelssohn dies

1789
    French Revolution

1791
    Napoleon establishes the Sanhedrin for the Jews of France

1835
    Moses Montefiore knighted by Queen of England

1858
    Baron Lionel Rothschild inducted into the House of Commons

1885
    Nathaniel Mayer de Rothschild inducted into the House of Lords

1894
    Alfred Dreyfus found guilty of treason

1899
    Alfred Dreyfus cleared

1906
    Dreyfus's army rank restored

RESOURCES

Books

Pasachoff, Naomi, and Robert J. Littman. *Jewish History in 100 Nutshells.* Northvale, NJ: Jason Aronson, 1995.

Sachar, Howard M. *The Course of Modern Jewish History.* New York: Vintage Books, 1990.

Sarna, Jonathan D., and Jonathan B. Krasner. *The History of the Jewish People: A Story of Tradition and Change.* Springfield, NJ: Behrman House, 2006.

Internet

Visit www.behrmanhouse.com/booklinks for links to Web sites that offer additional resources for this chapter.

CHAPTER TWENTY-ONE
JEWISH ENLIGHTENMENT AND RELIGIOUS RESPONSES TO EMANCIPATION

WHAT'S THE BIG IDEA?
Jewish Culture and Thought

Despite repeated devastation to Jewish communities over the centuries, a creative, rich Jewish culture and religious system enabled Jews to successfully respond to and thrive in new environments and circum-stances. European Enlightenment and Emancipation offered Jews the possibility of full citizenship and a new context within which to be Jewish. Such changes required new responses, many of which continue to shape the way Jews live today.

BACKGROUND INFORMATION

As discussed in the previous chapter, following the French Revolution Napoleon Bonaparte extended his rule across the continent and granted the rights of citizenship to many groups that had previously been excluded, including the Jews. When the ghetto walls came tumbling down in Western Europe, both literally and metaphorically, the Jewish community was left with the question of what it meant to be a Jew and how to be Jewish in the modern world.

In determining the answers to these questions, people looked to the models of "exception Jews" like Moses Mendelssohn, to the lessons of Jewish history, and to the philosophy of the European Enlightenment. Their varied responses included assimilation and conversion, Jewish secularism, and new approaches to Jewish religious life.

Assimilation and Conversion

While Jews gained many basic rights in the late eighteenth and early nineteenth centuries, this did not mean that they were suddenly accepted by all their neighbors. For many Jews, it seemed like the only way to truly become part of the world outside the ghetto walls was to become Christians. Between 1800 and 1850, a quarter of a million Jews in Western Europe voluntarily converted to Christianity.

Often, the decision to convert was not so much a religious choice as a practical one for those who wished for greater acceptance. Unfortunately, many who made this decision found that, in the end, conversion to Christianity didn't result in the warm reception to the larger community that they sought. For example, Heinrich Heine, one of Germany's greatest poets, chose this route, only to realize at the end of his life that he had in reality cut himself off from his own people without ever really being accepted by Christians either.

Haskalah

While some Jews were trying to become Christians, others were adapting the philosophy of the Age of Reason to Jewish life. The *Haskalah* (from the Hebrew word *sekhl,* meaning "reason") refers to the Jewish Enlightenment, which lasted from the late eighteenth century through the late nineteenth century. Beginning in Western Europe, especially Germany, the ideas central to the *Haskalah* later moved into

Eastern Europe. Advocates of the *Haskalah,* known as *maskilim,* followed in the footsteps of Moses Mendelssohn, a great Jewish intellectual who believed that the acquisition of secular culture and learning could help the Jewish community leave the backwardness of the ghetto (see chapter 20 for more information). Through education—including instruction in the national language—and job training, the *maskilim* worked to help their coreligionists elevate themselves, live within the modern world, and yet retain their cultural Jewish identity.

Education

Under the old corporate system, the Jewish community had provided a religious-based education centered around the study of Torah and Talmud to its children. Memorization and debate were the primary teaching methods at these schools, known as *heder*s. After Emancipation, the *maskilim* sought to add secular studies, modern language, and practical training to the school curriculum to help students gain access to the world outside the ghetto.

In many cases, the *maskilim* had help achieving their educational goals because the laws of the land required secular education. For example, in the late 1780s Joseph II ruled that Jewish children must be sent to "normal" schools provided by the Jewish community or to state-run schools, at least for their elementary education. Once students had completed their secular studies they were allowed to engage in the study of Talmud.

As a result of these laws, many communities established new Jewish schools with modern teaching methods and a secular curriculum in addition to Jewish subjects.

Like many Haskalah schools, the Freischule ("Free School") or Ḥinuch Ne'arim ("Youth Education") that opened in Berlin in 1778 provided a free education for poor Jewish students (other Jewish schools often charged tuition). The curriculum included German, French, arithmetic, geography, history, art, Hebrew, and Bible. Talmud was noticeably absent from the curriculum.

While the "Free School" enrolled only boys, following the traditional Jewish system of schooling, other *Haskalah* schools trained poor girls whose families could not afford to hire a tutor. Focusing mainly on vocational and domestic training rather than academics, these schools also offered Hebrew, German, arithmetic, and some religious classes on subjects such as ethics and prayer.

Whether in Breslau, Dessau, Frankfurt, or elsewhere, *Haskalah* schools provided only primary education. Those students who wished to continue their education beyond elementary school went to non-Jewish state-sponsored schools. Between the curriculum of the *Haskalah* schools and/or attendance at state schools, many European Jewish children during the nineteenth century were exposed to and educated in a completely different world from that of their parents and grandparents a few short decades before.

Language and Literature

The everyday language of the Jewish ghetto in Germany and parts of Eastern Europe had been Yiddish, a dialect of German that also incorporates many Hebrew words and phrases. Hebrew was considered a holy language used only for study and prayer. By the late seventeenth century (if not earlier) those Jews who were involved in business or politics had acquired the national language of the countries they lived in so that they could pursue their livelihood. As Emancipation opened the gates of the ghetto to all Jews, many came to view Yiddish as a backward language that separated Jews from their non-Jewish neighbors. Some Germans had also suggested that Yiddish was employed by Jews as a secret language in order to mislead non-Jews in business.

Based on these allegations, many local governments required that all business documents be written in German. Again, state law and a Jewish desire to enter mainstream culture came together to bring about change. As explained above, *Haskalah* schools included the study of language in the curriculum, thus widening the circle of Jews who could speak German and French.

With their interest in Jewish culture, the *maskilim* did not wish to abandon all Jewish language, just that which they deemed backward and restrictive. During the *Haskalah* in Western Europe there emerged a Hebrew renaissance that focused on the purer Hebrew language of the Bible.

Using biblical Hebrew as its basis for grammar and vocabulary, the writers of the *Haskalah* began to publish journals and books written in Hebrew. Published from 1783 to 1797, *Ha-Me'assef* (meaning "the literary collection") was the primary magazine of the *Haskalah,* transmitting many of the ideals of the Jewish Enlightenment to a broad audience.

Within its pages, Hebrew became a secular language used to express nonreligious ideas for the first time in the modern world. Jewish writers also began publishing popular Jewish fiction set in Palestine that conveyed the message that

Jews could improve their lot if they took positive action.

New Jobs for Jews

As seen in chapter 20, some anti-Semitic sentiment in Europe sprung from the Jews' role in business. Money lending, criticized in the Bible, was particularly repugnant to many Christians, as were the Jews who made their living through this activity. With Emancipation, many governments tried to restrict the kind of work Jews could do and move them into agriculture and a variety of trades.

The *maskilim* often supported such changes, offering skilled training at their schools and making suggestions to the government on how to help "improve" the Jews. They believed that manual labor could help improve both the Jewish character and the place of Jews in society. In 1812, a society for the Promotion of Industry was established in Berlin to support and promote the "creative spirit" among Jews while refuting the idea that they could only be involved in commerce. This labor-oriented attitude, combined with an interest in Palestine, would eventually help lead to the Zionist movement and the establishment of *kibbutzim* (collectives) in Eretz Israel.

Reaction Within the Jewish Community

While many Jews in western and Eastern Europe supported the *Haskalah* and were helped by the educational system developed by the *maskilim,* not all Jews advocated a secular Jewish lifestyle. The *mitnagdim* and Ḥasidim (see chapter 19) in particular opposed the *Haskalah* because of its focus on secularism and culture at the expense of religious study, prayer, and ritual. They believed that the *Haskalah* posed a threat to their religious way of life. This belief helped bring the two opposing movements closer together in a fight against a common enemy: non-Orthodox Jewish leaders and intellectuals.

Multiple Religious Responses to Emancipation

Reform Judaism

While many of the responses to Emancipation discussed above focused on a primarily secular approach to the *Haskalah,* Europe's religious Jewish community responded in different ways. Some Jews tried to reform religious practice, making it, in their opinion, more relevant, more dignified, and more rational.

One area of concern was the worship service. Many acculturated Jews viewed the traditional Jewish worship service with distaste with its selling of *aliyot,* chatter in the women's gallery, and cacophony of individuals worshipping each at their own pace. If the worship service could be reorganized along the same lines as a German church service, perhaps more Jews would return to the synagogue, theorized some early reformers.

Israel Jacobson (1760–1828), a banker in Seesen, Prussia, and founder of a *Haskalah* school for girls and boys, began putting "reform" ideas into practice. In 1810, approximately nine years after his school opened, Jacobson added a chapel, which he called a "temple," to the school. Previously, the word "temple" had only been used to refer to the Temple in Jerusalem and Jacobson's usage reflected an anti-Messianic philosophy that would become prevalent, along with the term "temple," in Reform Judaism.

Jacobson introduced a number of innovations commonly found in German churches into services at the temple, such as an organ and choir, prayers in German,

and a sermon delivered in the vernacular. His services were also shorter than traditional Jewish services. When leading services, Jacobson wore a clerical collar similar to those worn by German ministers. Many parents began attending services with their children at the school. Concerned that such modest changes might lead to more drastic changes, Orthodox leaders petitioned the Prussian government to close the temple. Israel Jacobson later went on to open another temple in Hamburg, Germany.

Initially concerned with aesthetic changes like the ones described above, Reformers eventually turned their attention to liturgy, theology, and history. Many Jews in Germany, like their coreligionists in France, believed that they had found their true homeland and no longer needed to look to a day when the Jewish people would return to Zion and again bring sacrifices to the Temple.

With such beliefs, Messianic theology and liturgy no longer seemed relevant. The Hamburg temple prayer book, which incorporated these ideas into its prayer service, became the first example of Reform liturgy. The book opened from left to right like a German book rather than a Hebrew book, included a German translation of the prayers, and eliminated prayers that referred to Jewish sovereignty.

These changes, especially the elimination of passages related to the Messianic return to Zion, outraged many rabbis who brought suit against the Hamburg temple and its leaders. Legal action was possible because the German state controlled religion as well as politics. However, in this case the government ruled that the temple could organize itself any way it wished. The rabbinic authorities did eventually condemn the Hamburg Temple and issued a proclamation forbidding any alteration to liturgy, prayer in any language other than Hebrew, or the use of musical instruments in a synagogue. The Reformers responded with their own attacks, drawing on *halachah* (Jewish law) to defend their arguments.

When the early Reformers found it necessary to defend their innovations, they developed new approaches to Judaism based on the scientific study of Jewish history. As part of the emphasis on rational thought and study that gave rise to the European Enlightenment, the science of history and its impact on human affairs emerged as a discipline at many universities.

By the nineteenth century, many Germans—both Christians and Jews—had adapted this approach to religion. Yomtob Lipmann (Leopold) Zunz (1795–1886), a great intellectual, was the foremost Jewish authority on what came to be known as *Wissenschaft des Judentums,* the science of Judaism. *Wissenschaft* defined Judaism as an evolving civilization.

According to Zunz, by knowing what had come before in Jewish history, one could know how Judaism ought to be practiced now. In his *Studies of Rabbinical Literature,* published in 1818, Leopold Zunz proved that scientific method and criticism could be applied to Jewish literature. He later went on to write the *History of the Jewish Sermon* in response to a Prussian law that forbade changes to the sermon in a Jewish worship service. Zunz's defense of this practice provided evidence that a sermon in the vernacular wasn't a modern innovation but rather a

historic part of Judaism that had fallen into disuse.

As Reform Judaism continued to evolve and organize, Reform rabbis trained at universities in the discipline of *Wissenschaft des Judentums* emerged. These rabbis became the leaders of the Reform movement. Samuel Holdheim (1806–1860) was one of the most radical Reform rabbis in Germany. Not only did Holdheim believe in the idea of reason and historicism (the thought that ideology needs to progress with the changes in history), but he also believed in progressive revelation.

Significantly, Holdheim was quoted as saying, "The Talmud speaks with the ideology of its time, for its time it was right. I speak from the higher ideology of my time, and for my time I am right." This philosophy effectively eliminated the notion of binding *halachah* in segments of the emerging Reform rabbinic community.

Not all Reform rabbis agreed with Samuel Holdheim, however. Many felt that a less radical stand and a stronger connection to *halachah* were appropriate. Beginning in the 1840s, Reform rabbis organized four rabbinic synods to clarify their ideological and theological positions. The Frankfurt Synod, convened in 1845, became an important turning point for Reform Judaism and marked the split between Reform Judaism and the Positive Historical School, which would become known as Conservative Judaism.

Conservative Judaism
Thirty-one rabbis attended the conference in Frankfurt, among them Zacharias Frankel, a moderate reformer. Born in Prague, Frankel was both yeshiva and

university educated. In 1843, two years prior to the Frankfurt Synod, Frankel coined the term "positive-historical" to connect the "positive" aspects of Judaism, which included elements such as faith and the revelation at Sinai, with the "historical" aspects of Judaism, which change over time. While Frankel, like many other rabbis at the Frankfort Synod, believed that history was proof of Judaism's endurance, he also believed that one could not dispose of all parts of the religion without damaging Judaism itself. It was this latter idea that set him apart from many of the Reform rabbis in Frankfurt.

One topic under discussion at the Frankfurt Synod was the use of Hebrew in worship services. While the Hamburg Temple prayer book included the prayers in Hebrew, with the German translation below, many wished to see the prayers themselves recited in the vernacular so that everyone would understand them. Frankel could not argue that the Talmud did not support prayer in other languages, but he believed that Hebrew was so intrinsic to Judaism that praying in another language would diminish Judaism in the modern era.

The discussion of Hebrew prayer so affected Frankel that he came to see it as indicative of the Reformers' entire approach, and became so disenchanted that he left the conference. A number of other rabbis followed him. This group went on to separate themselves from the Reform movement and establish the "Positive-Historical" school, or Conservative movement.

The Conservative movement, under Zacharias Frankel's leadership, took a balanced position between the positive and the historical approaches. The movement maintained traditional Jewish law, but also allowed for personal interpretation. As a standard for which aspects of tradition to keep or reject, the movement decided to eliminate only those practices that had ceased to have meaning for most Jews. The focus on the positive aspects of Judaism led Conservative rabbis to encourage much more adherence to tradition and ceremony than in the Reform movement, which found many of these aspects to be irrational and thus worthy of elimination.

Orthodoxy

While Reform and Conservative Judaism may be considered radical religious reactions to Emancipation, the *Haskalah* had an impact on Orthodoxy as well. As discussed in chapter 19, under the leadership of Jewish scholars such as the Vilna Gaon, the Orthodox community was beginning to move away from an exclusively Talmudic-centered educational system that relied on *pilpul* (Talmudic "hairsplitting") to embrace a dual approach that included both secular studies and religious studies.

Samson Raphael Hirsch (1808–1888) was an Orthodox rabbi influenced by the *Haskalah* and the spirit of the Reformers, but who adhered more closely to a trad-itional understanding of Judaism. Hirsch is responsible for reforming the Orthodox Judaism of his day and developing modern Orthodoxy.

Born in 1808 in Hamburg, Germany, Samson Raphael Hirsch attended public schools where he received a secular education that included German philosophy and culture. At home, he learned about Judaism from his observant father, his grandfather who founded the Hamburg Talmud Torah, and some of the finest German Jewish scholars of the time. After studying Talmud for six years, Hirsch attended the University of Bonn where he studied alongside the future Reform leader, Abraham Geiger.

As a rabbi, Samson Raphael Hirsch adopted some aspects of Reform Judaism but was also concerned with the assimilationist tendencies he saw around him. While he wore clerical robes, accepted a (male-only) choir, and delivered sermons in German, he also helped build Jewish schools and *mikva'ot* (ritual baths), and supported kosher ritual butchers (*shohets*).

Like other Jewish religious leaders and intellectuals of the time, Hirsch also published writings that outlined his religious principles, such as *Neunzehn Briefe über Judenthum* (The Nineteen Letters of Ben Uziel), which defended traditional Judaism. He also published a commentary of the Torah that is still used today in the Modern Orthodox community.

Hirsch believed that the ideal Jew cleaved to God and Torah but was also a citizen of the modern world and should have knowledge of its culture and language. Yet he was a vocal opponent of both the Conservative and Reform movements of Judaism. He believed that Conservative Judaism was relativistic in its attitude toward the Torah (because it accepted a historical approach) and he could not abide the rejection of ritual found in Reform Judaism. Hirsch's motto was "*Torah u'mada,*" or "Torah together with science."

CONNECTING TO OUR TRADITION

Modern Hebrew, a cultural Jewish identity, and a variety of religious practices can all trace their roots back to the secular and religious responses to Emancipation. Reform, Conservative, and Orthodox Judaism have helped Judaism remain vibrant and relevant. These movements have not stagnated in their original stages but continue to evolve in response to a changing modern world based on the needs of their constituents.

For example, Reform Judaism, realizing that it had possibly become too rational and dry in its practice, has returned to many Jewish traditions. In the modern age, all movements have responded to changes in societal issues such as gender equality, more open attitudes toward homosexuality, and intermarriage in their own unique ways.

IMPORTANT TERMS

Haskalah
Maskilim
Emancipation
Enlightenment
Reform
Conservative
Orthodox
Wissenschaft des Judentums

Names, Places, and Events

Israel Jacobson
Leopold Zunz
Samson Raphael Hirsch
Samuel Holdheim
Abraham Geiger
Zacharias Frankel
Frankfort Synod
Freischule/*Hinuch Ne'arim*
Ha-Me'assef
Hamburg Temple Prayer Book
History of the Jewish Sermon
Neunzehn Briefe über Judenthum

DISCUSSION QUESTIONS

- How did the flexibility of Jewish culture and thought help Judaism remain relevant after Emancipation?
- In what ways are the different responses to Emancipation still present in Jewish life today?
- How would you define your identity? What about living as a Jew in the modern world makes it difficult or easy to define your identity?
- The *maskilim*, Reform, Conservative, and Orthodox, all had different ideas about what would help Judaism survive in the modern world. What were the core values of each group? Which group do you think has done the most for Jewish survival? Why?

ACTIVITIES

Different Schools for Different Times (S, A)

Provide the class with two lists. One list includes the curriculum for a *heder* in the Jewish ghetto. The second list includes the curriculum for a *Haskalah* school. Discuss the lists. What are the major differences? What are the similarities? What are the skills students will acquire at the different schools? What will these skills prepare them to do as adults?

Compare the two lists to the curricula at a local public school and a local Jewish Day School. How do they compare? Based on the students' experience in their own schools, what might have been some of the secular influences on Jewish students attending a *Haskalah* school? Why might those adhering to a traditional Jewish life in the nineteenth century been concerned about the *Haskalah* based just on the issue of education?

Biography (E, S)

Assign each student to research an important historical figure, for example, Heinrich Heine, Hannah Rachel Werbermacher, Moses Mendelssohn, Abraham Geiger, Leopold Zunz, or Samuel Holdheim. Brief biographies of these figures, appropriate for fifth to seventh graders, can be found in *The History of the Jewish People: A Story of Tradition and Change* by Jonathan D. Sarna and Jonathan B. Krasner, which is listed in the Resources section at the end of this chapter.

Have students dress up as their character and address the class. Provide the class with research questions to get them started, such as: What kind of educational background did this person have? Did he or she think change was important? Why or why not? What kinds of changes did this person help establish? Would you nominate this person into a Jewish Heroes Hall of Fame? Why or why not?

Compare-Contrast (S, A)

Divide the class into small groups. Provide each group with copies of a few pages from your synagogue's prayer book and those from some of the groups described in this chapter. Ask the students to compare and contrast these different documents. Which are the most similar? Which are the most different? What differences in language do you find? What are some themes found in each?

Debate (S, A)

Invite three adults to come to your classroom in the roles of Samuel Holdheim, Zacharias Frankel, and Samson Raphael Hirsch. Each historical personality should briefly introduce himself before entering into a debate on the issue of using Hebrew for worship. At the end of the debate, students may ask them questions related to the different Jewish movements they helped create.

DID YOU KNOW?

- In Bohemia, Moravia, Hungary, and Galicia in the late nineteenth century it was necessary to have a certificate of school attendance (at a secular school) in order to get married.
- One change that some reformers made to Jewish practice was to hold worship services on Sunday rather than Saturday in order to fit in with their Christian neighbors.
- Charles Darwin's theory of evolution, which came after Leopold Zunz's work, helped strengthen the feeling of many reformers that change was necessary for continuity.

TIMELINE (all dates are CE)

1778
First *Haskalah* school founded in Berlin; called either the Freischule ("Free School") or *Ḥinuch Ne'arim* ("Youth Education")

1780s
Joseph II issues edict requiring Jews to attend "normal" schools or state schools

1798
Together Christians and Jews in the city of Bonn literally tear down ghetto walls

1801
Israel Jacobson founds school in Seesen, Prussia

1810
A "temple" is added to Jacobson's school

1818
Leopold Zunz publishes *Studies of Rabbinical Literature*

1838
Abraham Geiger becomes Associate Rabbi of temple in Breslau

1844
First rabbinical synod to clarify Reform position on theology and ritual

1845
Frankfurt Synod

RESOURCES
Books and Articles

Blech, Benjamin. *The Complete Idiot's Guide to Jewish History and Culture.* New York: Alpha Books, 2004.

Blech, Benjamin. *Eyewitness to Jewish History.* Hoboken, NJ: John Wiley & Sons, 2004.

Borowitz, Eugene B., and Naomi Patz. *Explaining Reform Judaism.* New York: Behrman House, 1985.

Mendes-Flohr, Paul, and Jehuda Reinharz, eds. *The Jew in the Modern World: A Documentary History.* New York and Oxford: Oxford University Press, 1980.

Meyer, Michael A. *Response to Modernity: A History of the Reform Movement in Judaism.* Detroit, MI: Wayne State University Press, 1988.

Meyer, Michael A., and W. Gunther Plaut. *The Reform Judaism Reader.* New York: UAHC Press, 2001.

Sachar, Howard M. *The Course of Modern Jewish History.* New York: Vintage Books, 1990.

Sarna, Jonathan D., and Jonathan B. Krasner. *The History of the Jewish People: A Story of Tradition and Change.* Springfield, NJ: Behrman House, 2006.

Internet
Visit www.behrmanhouse.com/booklinks for links to Web sites that offer additional resources for this chapter.

CHAPTER TWENTY-TWO
JEWISH LIFE IN EASTERN EUROPE

WHAT'S THE BIG IDEA?
Diaspora
Since our people were first exiled from Eretz Yisrael centuries ago, much of the Jewish population has remained dispersed throughout the world. Once scattered, we did not stay in one place but continued to move from country to country. Some of our moves were forced, others were chosen. Sometimes we stayed put, but the national boundaries around us changed, placing us in a new and often precarious position. Without a land to call our own, the Jewish community was often vulnerable to the larger powers under which they lived.

Building Community
Regardless of the reasons for Jewish migration, when a few Jews settled somewhere, they sought out each other and established Jewish institutions to help support the community and a Jewish way of life. These charitable organizations often took the place of state aid and were sometimes the envy of the non-Jewish community.

BACKGROUND INFORMATION
Emancipation, the breaking down of ghetto walls and the gradual inclusion of Jews into national life as full citizens, as described in chapters 20 and 21, had little or no effect in Eastern Europe. Napoleon's reach did not extend this far and eastern rulers, most notably the czars of Russia, were ambivalent in their adoption of western values and philosophy.

When Russia annexed part of Poland in 1772, it also acquired most of Poland's Jews. As seen in previous chapters, Poland had been a cultural center where Judaism flourished for centuries. The Czars felt very differently about the Jews than earlier Polish rulers had, and while they were happy to gain Polish land and peasants, they were not so happy about acquiring millions of Jews. Part of the "Jewish problem" for Russia's leaders from the time of Catherine the Great onward was how to absorb the Jews into Russia. Unlike other cultural groups, the Jews clung to their ethnic traditions, religious rituals, and distinctive way of dress. Their religion was also clearly a problem in a signifi-cantly Christian country.

For approximately twenty years, beginning in the year 1772 with the first partition of Poland, the official policy of Czarina Catherine the Great was to tolerate the Jews living in the areas that Russia had annexed. However, in later years when Catherine the Great decided to begin a process of Russification (indoctrination into Russian culture and language), and not knowing yet how Jews would fit into that policy, she decided to separate the Jews from greater Russia by creating the Pale of Settlement in 1794.

Ninety percent of the population already living in this area was Jewish. Over subsequent years and rulers, the majority of those Jews living in greater Russia were moved into the Pale of Settlement unless they had special protection or privileges.

In 1804, Alexander I issued the Constitution of the Jews. According to these new rules, Jews were forbidden from owning or leasing land, making it impossible for them to be farmers, nor could they operate taverns. Furthermore, they were expelled from larger villages and hamlets. In 1835, the Charter of Disabilities drove Jews out of Kiev and the surrounding countryside, and deeper into the Pale of Settlement. Confined to residing and earning their livelihood in small towns or *shtetls* (Jewish villages), life was very hard for the Jews. Golda Meir, a future prime minister of Israel, spent her childhood in Russia where she recalled a life of constant poverty, cold, hunger, and fear.[1]

While poverty and hunger were by-products of the severe limitations placed on Jews living in the Pale of Settlement, fear was a by-product of laws and activities meant to destroy individual Jews and/or their communities. One adviser to Czar Alexander III suggested a "triple play" approach to dealing with Russia's Jews: one-third should be forced to convert to Christianity, one-third should be expelled, and one-third should die of starvation. From the late eighteenth century through the mid-twentieth century, the Czars of Russia applied different parts of the triple play, with disastrous results for Eastern European Jews.

Cantonist Decrees

Nicholas I believed in the importance of a strong military to protect Russia and the throne. He also saw the military as a tool for acculturating minority groups such as the Jews, since it removed soldiers from their culture of origin and placed them in a largely homogenous Russian military context in which differences were not accepted.

In 1827, Nicholas I established a series of laws known as the Cantonist Decrees, due to their connection with military training camps, which he believed would help crush the Jewish spirit by absorbing Jewish children into the Russian majority through military conscription. The Cantonist Decrees were among the harshest laws directed at Russian Jews. Jewish children between the ages of twelve and eighteen were drafted into the Russian army for a period of twenty-five years. During this time, they were likely to die in battle or due to harsh treatment. Even if they survived twenty-five years in the army, most of these children would long since have given up their connection to Judaism.

Making these laws even more crushing, the Jewish community was expected to enforce them by gathering up their own children. Wealthier members of the Jewish community might protect their sons by bribing local officials or by paying poor families to enlist their own children in place of the richer ones. Poorer families sought other methods, including chopping off their child's right index finger so he could not pull the trigger of a gun. Such desperate acts increased tensions between richer and poorer members of the same community.

Pogroms

As seen in previous chapters, Jews living in Eastern Europe were often convenient scapegoats for national leaders or revolutionaries, and it was no different in czarist Russia. At the beginning of the twentieth century, pogroms—organized orgies of rape, pillage, murder, and

---

[1] Benjamin Blech, *Eyewitness to Jewish History*, Hoboken, NJ: John Wiley & Sons, 2004, p. 209.

torture—were so prevalent that between 1903 and 1907, there were 234 recorded pogroms, accounting for fifty thousand casualties. These events were not widely publicized in newspapers of the time since such stories were often censored by the government, yet personal narratives of travelers occasionally made their way to Western Europe and further abroad.

One of the worst pogroms, and one that gained public attention in the West, was the Kishniev Pogrom on Easter Sunday 1903. Wanting to dispel national tensions (tensions that would ultimately lead to a failed revolution), the czarist government organized a pogrom. News of this pogrom did in fact make it into western newspapers that described the horrific scenes of rioting, looting, and beatings. Jews and non-Jews in Western Europe and America were outraged, but their protests had little effect.

Irrational Accusations
As tensions continued to increase under the czarist governments at the beginning of the twentieth century, Jews were falsely accused of many crimes. Blood libel charges, prevalent in the past, were revived. According to such charges, Jews were accused of killing Christian children in order to use their blood to make matzah for Passover. In 1911, Mendel Beilis was charged with murdering a twelve-year-old boy and using his blood for ritual purposes. Despite the outcry of Jews around the world who put pressure on their governments to encourage the czar to intercede, Beilis would have been executed had not the real murderer confessed at the last minute.

The Russian government developed a new charge against the larger Jewish community in 1903 in the guise of a forged document known as *The Protocols of the Elders of Zion.* According to Russian secret police who circulated the fictitious document, *The Protocols* were actually minutes of a secret meeting of Jewish leaders plotting to control the world over the next century. This document and its allegations helped stir up the Russian population against the Jews. Although proven to be a forgery, *The Protocols* has had its anti-Semitic supporters throughout history and the world, including in the United States where auto magnate Henry Ford translated it into English and helped distribute the pamphlet.

Jewish Response
In the midst of all this pain and hardship, many Russian Jews found joy in their relationship with God. This religious connection gave rise to a rebirth in Jewish study and the development of important Jewish charitable organizations.

In Russia, as in Poland earlier, Jewish study had become primarily the bastion of the wealthy elite who had the time to study Torah and Talmud, while poorer Jews spent their time trying to eke out a living. Two Russian rabbis helped change both what was studied and how it was studied. In 1803, Rabbi Chaim ben Isaac of Volozhin (1749–1821) envisioned and created a large yeshiva supported not just by one community for itself, but supported by many communities for anyone who wanted to attend.

The Volozhin Yeshiva was staffed by some of the top teachers in the land and offered a curriculum focused on Torah and Talmud. Some secular subjects were also offered, but not enough to please the Russian authorities who were trying to secularize Jewish education by teaching Russian language and culture. In 1892, the

Volozhin Yeshiva was closed by the Russian government, but in its almost ninety-year history it had become a model for other *yeshivot*.

While interest in Torah study had been revived in part by Rabbi Volozhiner, some Jews were questioning the focus of that Torah study. Previously, many Jewish scholars had concerned themselves with the intricate debate of legal aspects of the Talmud. Rabbi Israel Lipkin of Salant (1810–1883), also known as Rabbi Israel Salanter, believed that the morality and ethics found in the Torah should be the ultimate focus of all Torah study. His vision gave rise to the *Mussar*—or Morality—movement. While many in the Orthodox community were at first skeptical, believing this was another kind of Reform, others were won over and the *Mussar* movement has become part of the curriculum at many *yeshivot*.

Perhaps it was due to the revived emphasis on Torah study or the new emphasis on values and ethics that Jews in the Pale of Settlement came together to form institutions that would help support members of their community who could not support themselves—and there were many. Statistics show that by 1900, at least 14 percent of the Jews living in every province in the Pale of Settlement received some type of economic assistance. In some cities the numbers were even worse. For example, in Vilna, 80 percent of the Jews did not know where their next meal was coming from. The Jewish community established charitable organizations such as fuel charities and cheap eateries in order to help fellow Jews survive. Other charitable entities provided clothes for poor students, kosher meals for soldiers, free medical treatment, and dowries for poor or orphaned brides.[2]

CONNECTING TO OUR TRADITION

Life in the Pale of Settlement was difficult, yet our people survived by turning to God and their community, supports that have served us well throughout our history. Out of this connection to God grew the model still used for present-day *yeshivot* and the present-day *Mussar* movement. A sense of Jewish community, and a romanticized picture of the *shtetl* that still pervades Jewish cultural life today, has its roots in the Pale of Settlement.

IMPORTANT TERMS

Emancipation
Czar
Mussar
Pogrom
Blood libel
Shtetl
Russification

Names, Place, and Events

Russian Annexation of Poland	Charter of Disabilities
Pale of Settlement	Alexander I
Catherine the Great	Alexander III
Constitution of the Jews	Protocols of the Elders of Zion
Nicholas I	Kishniev Pogrom
Cantonist Decree	Mendel Beilis

DISCUSSION QUESTIONS

* What techniques did Jews living in the Pale of Settlement use to help them survive under the oppressive Russian regime? Which of these techniques have been used by Jews elsewhere in time or place? Which are still used today?

---

[2] Martin Gilbert, *Atlas of Jewish History*, Dorset Press, 1976, p. 72.

- How did Jewish institutions help preserve a Jewish way of life in the Pale of Settlement? What Jewish institutions can you think of in your community that help Jews in need?

ACTIVITIES
Torah Scholars (E, S, A)
Assign students to read a particular passage in the Torah with the goal of understanding the plain meaning of the text, its deeper level, and its *mussar* or ethical level. Examples could be the story of Abraham and the angels, or Abraham arguing with God over the fate of the wicked of Sodom (Genesis 18) or that of the daughters of Zelophehad, who petitioned Moses for equal property rights in the absence of male relatives (Numbers 27). Have the students divide into two groups—the "plain reading" group and the *mussar* group—and have them debate the true meaning of the text.

You're in the Army Now (E, S, A)
Have students read the Cantonist decree What were the particular goals of this type of discrimination toward Jews? Discuss: What benefit might there be for a country to erase differences and create a homogenous military force?

Have students explore regulations for soldiers in the in different branches of the armed forces in the country in which they live, particularly those that deal with religious and cultural expressions.

A follow-up activity for older students could include an exploration of news articles dealing with the United States Air Force Academy's struggle in 2005 with the overwhelming preponderance of Christian activities, and questions about tolerance. How can a country's military create a unified force while at the same time allowing for personal expressions of culture and faith in a nondiscriminatory way?

Protest! (E, S, A)
Many examples of unfair, discriminatory, and violent treatment of Jews during the 1800s and 1900s in Eastern Europe reached the West, yet it was very difficult for Jews (and ethical and concerned Christians) to effect any real change. Yet, sometimes the community did protest—either by going directly to their country's leaders to ask for intervention, or by staging an actual protest.

Have your students choose one example of discriminatory behavior against the Jews (the Beilis trial, the Kishniev pogroms) and have them create a protest plan. Would they send a delegation to their representatives in Congress? Would they march in protest? Discuss: Which methods do you think would be most effective? Which methods, if any, have been effective in the past? What can you do now to protest discriminatory and violent behavior that oppresses people in the modern world?

DID YOU KNOW?
Rabbis in the Pale of Settlement decreed that no Christians could convert to Judaism. The rabbis were concerned that some of their Christian neighbors, observing how well Jews took care of their own poor, might consider conversion to take advantage of the Jewish welfare system since neither the Russian government or Church took care of the Christian poor very well.

TIMELINE (all dates are CE)

1772

First Partition of Poland

1794

Catherine the Great establishes the Pale of Settlement

1804

Constitution of the Jews

1827

Cantonist Decree

1835

Charter of Disabilities

1844

Jewish schools in the Pale of Settlement abolished

1855

Pale of Settlement shrinks

1903

Protocols of the Elders of Zion and the Kishniev Pogrom

1903–1907

Total of 284 pogroms take place in this four-year period, with fifty thousand casualties

1911

Mendel Beilis blood libel

RESOURCES

Books and Articles

Blech, Benjamin. *The Complete Idiot's Guide to Jewish History and Culture.* New York: Alpha Books, 2004.

Blech, Benjamin. *Eyewitness to Jewish History.* Hoboken, NJ: John Wiley & Sons, 2004.

Gilbert, Martin. *Atlas of Jewish History.* Dorset Press, 1976.

Sachar, Howard M. *The Course of Modern Jewish History.* New York: Vintage Books, 1990.

Internet

Visit www.behrmanhouse.com/booklinks for links to Web sites that offer additional resources for this chapter.

CHAPTER TWENTY-THREE
EARLY ZIONISM AND THE *YISHUV*

WHAT'S THE BIG IDEA
Covenant

Jews have traditionally understood that they are God's chosen people, singled out for a special covenant promising us the Land of Israel. For the Jews of the Diaspora, this covenant between God and the Jewish people was central to religious practice and tradition but was not something they expected to see in their lifetime, until the nineteenth century brought together streams of nationalism, *Haskalah* (the Jewish enlightenment), anti-Semitism, and passionate leadership. Zionism arose from this potent mix, creating the context for the Jewish people to fulfill its longed-for covenantal goals.

BACKGROUND INFORMATION

"Next year in Jerusalem!" cry Jews around the world as they conclude their Passover seders. This hopeful phrase sums up the aspirations of a dispersed people. Jews living all over Europe and Russia in the nineteenth century were familiar with the religious notion of returning to Jerusalem or Zion, one biblical name for the Land of Israel. Three times a day they prayed for God to return the Jewish people to its homeland.

After meals, when they recited *Birkat Ha-Mazon* (the Grace After Meals), they included a prayer for the rebuilding of Jerusalem. These religious aspirations may have given the Jewish people a sense of cohesion over time, and something to hold onto in the face of anti-Semitism, so that, in a sense, Jews have always been

Zionists. However, in the nineteenth and twentieth centuries, this age-old Jewish dream finally became a reality.

Zionism: What Is It?

While rationalism and the Enlightenment had given rise to the emancipation of Jews in Western Europe in the eighteenth century (see chapter 20 for more information), a new "ism" came along in the later part of the nineteenth century, focusing on emotions, history, and a sense of peoplehood. Jews, who had always considered themselves to be a distinct people with a common history, now discovered that in the wake of the creation of independent nations in Central Europe, Germans, Italians, Russians, and others were developing nationalistic feelings of their own. Nationalism, a sense of a common history, language, and culture, often did not allow much room for "others," and in places like Russia it added fuel to anti-Semitic violence.

As part of the Jewish Enlightenment, or *Haskalah*, many Jewish writers used Hebrew language, wrote about Palestine, and employed historical themes in their literature (see chapter 21). Having observed anti-Semitism firsthand, and having been influenced by the nationalistic fervor of the countries within which they lived, some *maskilim* (Enlightenment thinkers) began talking about Jewish nationalism, or Zionism. One such person was Dr. Leon Pinsker, a Russian physician. He published a pamphlet called *Auto-Emanzipation* (Self-Emancipation) in 1882, in which he stated his scientific belief that anti-Semitism was deeply rooted in human nature and would not go away, no matter how "enlightened" the people of the host nation happened to be. Pinsker also realized that the success of the German and Italian national movements was that each had an ancestral land. The idea of a nationalistic Jewish movement focused on its own ancestral land gave rise to a practical Zionism with the goal of rebuilding a Jewish homeland in what was then Palestine.

In 1884, Dr. Pinsker became the president of *Hovevei Zion* (the Lovers of Zion), a Russian Zionist organization that had begun two years earlier. Organizing courses in Hebrew, Jewish history, and Jewish music, *Hovevei Zion* helped build cultural awareness and pride, but it also had the goal of sending Russian Jews to Palestine in order to escape persecution and work the land. Since Zionism was illegal in Russia, most of the group's meetings were held in secret; in fact, its national meeting in 1884 was held out of the country, in Germany. Even so, by 1892 *Hovevei Zion* had approximately fourteen thousand members committed to its mission of enabling Jews to settle in Eretz Yisrael.

Theodor Herzl

Although Theodor Herzl is widely considered to be the father of Zionism and the modern State of Israel, Zionism as a movement had already existed for about sixteen years before Herzl called the First World Zionist Congress. However, it was Herzl who gave a practical form to the Zionist vision and created the diplomatic connections that would make the creation of the State of Israel possible a little more than fifty years later.

Theodor Herzl was born in Budapest, Hungary, in 1860 into an assimilated Jewish family. His parents provided him with a general Jewish education and Shabbat and holidays were celebrated at home. However, Herzl's identity was more that of a European intellectual than a strongly connected Jew. While Herzl studied to become a lawyer, he eventually gave up the law to become a journalist. It was as a foreign correspondent of the *Neue Freie Presse* (The New Free Press), a liberal Viennese newspaper, that he covered the Dreyfus trial in France in 1894, in which a French Jewish army officer was falsely accused of treason (see chapter 20). Witnessing firsthand the anti-Semitism surrounding Dreyfus's trial and remembering his own painful experiences as a Jewish college student in liberal Vienna, Herzl came to the realization that there would always be anti-Semitism unless Jews had a country to call their own.

In 1896, Herzl published *Der Judenstaat* (The Jewish State), in which he outlined his ideas. The book was very practical, detailing the steps necessary to build and develop a viable state, including the establishment of a Jewish assembly or congress that would help plan and organize the new state. Interestingly, nowhere in the book did Herzl indicate that this homeland must be in Palestine. For Herzl, Zionism was about solving the very real problem of anti-Semitism; it was not about nationalism. Therefore, the location of a Jewish homeland was not as important as the political reality of a sovereign country ruled by Jews themselves.

As a journalist, writer, and intellectual, Herzl had many contacts in political and diplomatic circles. In planning for a Jewish homeland, he made the most of all of these contacts. Many thought him crazy, like the

Jewish philanthropist Baron de Hirsch, who, after hearing Herzl's plan for a Zionist congress, thought his ideas shocking. But others, like Dr. Max Nordau, a Jewish publicist, wholeheartedly supported Herzl's ideas, stating, "If you are insane, we are insane together. Count on me!"[1] Eventually Herzl realized that most wealthy Jewish leaders were not interested in his proposed Zionist Congress. Instead, Herzl turned to the masses—to the Russian and Eastern European Jews who had responded enthusiastically to his book and filled railroad stations when they heard he was coming to town. In fact, after the publication of *Der Judenstaat,* most branches of *Hovevei Zion* in Russia aligned themselves with Herzl.

Having finally found his support base, Herzl called the First World Zionist Congress in 1897. Initially he planned to convene the Congress in Germany, a major center of Jewish life at the time. However, German Jews, and many other Western European Jews, were horrified by Herzl's crazy idea that Jews were not simply a religious group but rather a separate nation.

For those Jews living in relative safety and comfort in Western Europe and who supported the statements of the French Sanhedrin (see chapter 20), Herzl's philosophy was an anathema. Instead, the First World Zionist Congress met in Basel, Switzerland, with 204 delegates from around the world, including 80 from Russia. The meeting succeeded in achieving its primary goals of establishing an international Zionist organization (the World Zionist Organization), adopting a Jewish flag, and adopting a national anthem ("*Hatikvah*"). Herzl later wrote in

his journal, "In Basel, I created the Jewish state." In many ways, his statement was true.

The World Zionist Congress continued to meet on an annual basis, discussing different matters and developing the tools necessary for the building of a Jewish homeland in Palestine, such as establishing the Jewish National Fund, which would raise money with which to buy land. Between meetings, Herzl and other members worked tirelessly, pursuing their dream. Further outlining what a Jewish homeland in Palestine would look like, Herzl wrote *Altneuland* ("Old-New Land") in 1902. In it, he painted a picture of a totally modern country with the best in modern technology and transportation systems, and a socialist-based government under which Jews and Arabs could live in peace.

At the same time, Herzl was taking practical steps to gain support for a Jewish homeland in Palestine from foreign leaders. With this goal in mind, he visited Kaiser Wilhelm II of Germany and the sultan of the Ottoman Empire. He even met with the pope, who merely indicated that the Vatican would not stand in the way of such a homeland, but offered no support. Rather, the pope indicated that if the Jews went to Palestine, the Church would be prepared to baptize all of them.

With little or no support from other sources, Herzl eventually turned to the British, who controlled the area at the time. Meeting with Joseph Chamberlain, a former member of the House of Commons, in 1903, Herzl found his first sympathetic listener. Chamberlain understood the plight of the Jews, made even more serious by the Kishniev Pogrom that had occurred that year. Seeing a way that a Jewish homeland

---

[1] Howard M. Sachar, *The Course of Modern Jewish History,* New York: Vintage Books, 1990, p. 315.

could be beneficial to the British Crown, Chamberlain offered Herzl land in the British territory of Uganda, in central Africa, where the Jews could till the soil and grow sugar and cotton.

Herzl continued to hold onto the idea of a permanent homeland in Palestine, but felt that Uganda might be a temporary solution for Jews in Russia who needed to escape immediate danger. With these thoughts in mind, Herzl raised the issue of the Uganda Program at the Sixth World Zionist Congress in 1903, where it was met by a storm of protest from many delegates. While the Uganda Program was adopted by a very narrow margin, some delegates walked out, a move that threatened to divide the Zionist movement. Interestingly, the Russian and Eastern European delegates were the most outspoken against the Uganda Program even though it was designed to help people in their communities. Ultimately, the Uganda Program came to naught as the offer was revoked by the British and voted down in 1905 at the Seventh World Zionist Congress. If nothing else, the debate surrounding this issue proved just how vitally important the Land of Israel still was to the Jewish people.

Herzl expended much of his time and energy pursuing the dream of a Jewish homeland in Palestine. The battle proved to be greater than he was, and on July 3, 1904, at the age of forty-four, he died quite suddenly. Herzl's funeral in Vienna attracted ten thousand Jews who followed his Zionist flag–draped coffin to the cemetery. Many years later, when the dream he helped give shape to was finally fulfilled, his body was reinterred on Mount Herzl in Jerusalem. His life's work had truly embodied the rabbinic principle: "It is not yours to finish the work, but

neither may you desist from it" (*Pirkei Avot* 2:21).

Ahad Ha'am

While Theodor Herzl was one of the primary Zionist leaders whose work helped create the modern State of Israel, he was by no means the only Zionist leader. Many others believed in the importance of building a Jewish homeland in Palestine, but sometimes with an emphasis that was different from Herzl's brand of Zionism and its primary focus on the practical and political aspects of creating a state. Ahad Ha'am (Hebrew meaning "one of the people"), the pen name of Asher Ginsberg, was one such Zionist leader. His vision has become known as spiritual Zionism, as opposed to Herzl's political Zionism.

Born into a Hasidic family in the Ukraine in 1856, Asher Ginsberg had both a traditional Jewish and a secular education. Like many of his generation in Russia, he became involved in Jewish nationalism and joined the *Hovevei Zion* movement. However, where *Hovevei Zion* was primarily focused on sending Jewish pioneers to Palestine, Ginsberg became more interested in how Judaism's unique culture could help rebuild the Jewish character and promote national unity.

Eventually, Ginsberg came to believe that Palestine could best serve the Jewish people not as a homeland for all Jews, but as a cultural center that would support Jewish civilization in the Diaspora. This vision of Zionism became the basis for his article *"Lo Zeh Ha-Derech"* (This Is Not the Way), which he wrote under the pen name Ahad Ha'am. Ahad Ha'am's vision influenced a new generation of Zionists including Chaim Weizmann, the first

Israeli president, and Ḥayim Naḥman Bialik, a preeminent Jewish author.

Rav Kook

Throughout history, a few religious Jews had always continued to live scattered throughout Eretz Yisrael. Their notion had never been to rebuild a Jewish homeland; rather, they were eking out an existence in the land of the Bible and waiting for the Messiah to restore Jews to Zion. There were enough religious Jews in some places to make hiring rabbis from Europe to serve their communities feasible. One such rabbi, who helped to create a new flavor of Zionism and had a profound impact on both religious and secular Jews in Palestine, was Abraham Isaac Kook, known simply as Rav Kook.

Abraham Isaac Kook was born in Latvia in 1865 to a family with strong roots in the ultra-Orthodox community. His maternal grandfather was a follower of the Ḥasidic movement and his father had studied with the *mitnagdim* (see chapter 21). Kook himself had a very traditional upbringing, but also followed his own interests in philosophy. In 1904, he moved to Palestine and became the rabbi in Jaffa (located near present-day Tel Aviv). Here he was responsible not only for his community of religious Jews, but also for a growing number of secular Zionists. Unlike many members of his community, Kook was not put off by the nonreligious lifestyle of the Zionists. While he tried to bring Torah and *halachah* to the agri-cultural settlements, he also viewed their Zionist passion as a form of Messianism.

Based on what he had seen in Palestine, Kook believed that one could be religious and a Zionist, merging the two ideas into the Religious Zionist movement. He returned to Europe to bring these ideas to

the traditional Jewish community and got caught there by the beginning of World War I. After the war, in 1921, Rav Kook returned to Palestine and became the first Ashkenazic chief rabbi of its Jewish community. During his many years as chief rabbi, Kook wrote on *halachah* and Jewish thought, and helped bridge the gap between secular Zionists and religious Zionists. However, his belief that God's covenant with the Jewish people would finally be fulfilled by a mixture of Jews from different points on the religious spectrum did not sit well with many in the traditional Jewish community who became suspicious of his practices and motives. Rav Kook died in Jerusalem in 1935, but his influence still continues through his many books and writings.

Ideas Are Great, But Let's Get Practical

While leaders like Theodor Herzl, Aḥad Ha'am, and Rav Kook were creating visions of what Zionism could look like, thousands of Eastern European Jews were anxious to turn those visions into a reality. Between 1882 and 1914, approximately sixty-five thousand Jews made *aliyah* (Hebrew, literally "going up," a term that has come to mean emigration to Israel) and laid the foundation for the modern State of Israel.

First Aliyah

In 1882, approximately seven thousand Russian Jews who were involved with *Hovevei Zion* went to Palestine. These Jews brought with them the ideals of the Zionist movement, particularly that Jews needed to return to Eretz Yisrael and work the land. Politically, they were influenced by socialist ideas about building communities that would work together for the common good.

Yishuv, "settlement" in Hebrew, was the term used by the early Zionists when referring to the Jewish residents of Eretz Yisrael who began to flock there from Europe in the 1880s. "The *Yishuv*," therefore, refers to both these individuals as well as the areas where they resided from that time until the establishment of the State of Israel in 1948.

Most of these early Zionists arrived in Palestine with no real plans for what they were going to do or how they would support themselves. Many found work in agriculture and eked out an existence. While full equality between men and women was part of their socialist ideology, it sometimes took a while for the reality to catch up with the theory. Techiah Lieberson, an early pioneer, arrived in Petach Tikva in 1905. She wanted to do her part to help reclaim the land, but found that very few people wanted to hire a woman for heavy agricultural work. Even among fellow Zionists, most people thought women should be doing piecework (sewing) or other jobs that kept them indoors.[2]

Gradually, the new immigrants bought up land and created rural settlements of their own. Degania, near the Kinneret (a large lake, also known as the Sea of Galilee, located in northern Israel), was one of the very first settlements. It was later followed by Rosh Pinah and Zichron Ya'akov. These early *moshavim* (cooperative communities) helped pave the way for further immigration and settlement. Many are still in existence today.

---

[2] Benjamin Blech, *Eyewitness to Jewish History*, Hoboken, NJ: John Wiley & Sons, 2004, pp. 224–227.

Birth of Modern Hebrew

The *maskilim* in Europe began developing a modern version of the Hebrew language based on the biblical Hebrew they knew, in order to write Jewish literature in Hebrew. However, this language was used in the context of Eastern European literary circles and did not require an entire vocabulary for all that happens in daily life. The settlement of Palestine, however, required a new language for a new land, at least according to some Zionists. Chief among the proponents of spoken Hebrew was Eliezer Ben Yehuda, who became the father of modern Hebrew.

Born in 1858 in Lithuania, Eliezer Ben Yehuda learned Hebrew as a child, but this was the Hebrew of the Torah and prayers. In later years, he became interested in Hebrew as a modern language. Ben Yehuda and his family went to Palestine in 1881, and once there, he would speak only Hebrew. This situation required the development of many new words for items that had no names in Hebrew. Adapting new words from old ones by using the traditional Hebrew grammatical system based on the three-letter root words, Ben Yehuda formed the foundation for modern Hebrew. This system of creating new words continues today and the Bible's influence can be found in many everyday terms. Eventually, Ben Yehuda created a dictionary of modern Hebrew. By the end of the First Aliyah, more and more pioneers were speaking Hebrew, and Hebrew elementary schools were established to teach a new generation of Jews a language that was modern and ancient at the same time.

Second Aliyah

A combination of factors led to the Second Aliyah (1904–1914). First, the controversy over the Uganda Program at the Sixth Zionist Congress helped refocus people's attention on the need to establish a Jewish homeland specifically in Palestine. Second, the Kishniev Pogroms of 1903 and other pogroms a few years later made it clear that Jews needed to leave Russia. By 1914, forty thousand Jews—mostly from Russia—had moved to Palestine.

The ḥalutzim, or pioneers, of the Second Aliyah made many significant contributions to the Zionist movement and helped shape the young country. Most of the ḥalutzim worked as hired laborers on Jewish agricultural settlements or in the cities. As laborers, they soon realized they needed to organize and work together, and so they formed Po'alei Zion ("workers of Zion") and Ha-Po'el Ha-Tza'ir ("the young workers"), some of the first labor unions in Palestine. These labor unions still exist today and many Israelis belong to them. Regular strikes for changes in working conditions are something of an annual event in the modern State of Israel. Unlike in America, where unions are made up of people employed in specific lines of work, for example, a teachers' union or the Teamsters' union, Israeli unions are often composed of workers in many different industries. When a strike is called in Israel, it might affect such disparate businesses as banking and transportation, bringing much of daily life to a standstill.

In some cases, the pioneers created entirely new cities. In 1909, Tel Aviv became the first true "Jewish city." Originally a suburb of Jaffa, an Arab city, Tel Aviv has become a bustling metropolis along the Mediterranean that dwarfs Old Jaffa. The city was meant to connect the old with the new and thus was given the name Tel (a hill built on the remnants of older civilizations) Aviv (meaning spring, a time of rebirth). This name is also found in the Bible in Ezekiel 3:15.

CONNECTING TO OUR TRADITION

The Jewish people longed to return to its home in Israel ever since the very first dispersions to Assyria and Babylonia. Our texts are filled with references to that return, whether in the Psalms, the prayer book, popular Jewish music, or Jewish poetry. Yehudah Ha-Levi (1070-1141), the famous Jewish poet from Spain (see chapter 15), wrote "A Longing to Return to the Land of Israel," which sums up the Jewish people's feelings about Israel:

"My heart is in the East, and I in the uttermost West.
How can I find savor in food? How shall it be sweet to me?
How shall I render my vows and my bonds, while yet
 Zion lieth beneath the fetter of Edom, and I in Arab chains?
A light thing would it seem to me
To leave all the good things in Spain—
Seeing how precious in mine eyes
To behold the dust of the desolate sanctuary."

IMPORTANT TERMS

Zionism	Moshav
Yishuv	Aliyah
Covenant	Halutzim
Kibbutz	Socialism

Names, Places, and Events

Dr. Leon Pinsker	Jewish National
Hovevei Zion	Fund
Theodor Herzl	Palestine
Joseph Chamberlain	Uganda
Aḥad Ha'am	First Aliyah
Rav Abraham Isaac Kook	Second Aliyah
Eliezer Ben Yehuda	Der Judenstaat
First World Zionist Congress	"Hatikvah"
	Lo Zeh Ha-Derech
Sixth World Zionist Congress	Tel Aviv

DISCUSSION QUESTIONS

- What impact has the idea of covenant had on the history of Zionism?

- For the Jews of the Diaspora prior to the establishment of the modern State of Israel, hoping for and praying for a return to Israel made sense. In an age when a modern State of Israel exists, what does it mean for us to pray for a return to Zion, even if we don't intend to move there ourselves?

- Do you think the creation of the modern State of Israel by Jewish men and women fulfills God's covenant with the Jewish people? Why or why not?

- Theodor Herzl said, "If you will it, it is no dream." How did the Jewish people turn this dream into a reality? Can you think of other events in history that would support this quote?

- Many Jews today take pride in the vision of leadership and strength of character that brought about the modern State of Israel. However, some very religious Jews refuse to recognize the modern state as the fulfillment of the covenant because it was not brought about directly by God. What do you think?

- Now that we have a Jewish state, and can freely return to our homeland, why do you think so many Jews choose to remain in the Diaspora?

ACTIVITIES

An Interview with Herzl (E, S)

Assign your students to portray newspaper and radio reporters from different countries. Have an adult come into the classroom in the role of Theodor Herzl. Using questions the students have formulated prior to the visit, have the students interview Herzl. After the interview, the students can write newspaper articles and record radio reports based on their experience. A neat twist on this activity could be that since Herzl himself was a reporter, he could come in and interview the students on their views about Zionism!

Hatikvah (E, S, A)

Teach the students to sing "*Hatikvah,*" the Israeli national anthem. Share with them the English translation of the words. With older students, discuss the title, what it refers to, and the connection between the words of the song and Jewish tradition. Have students listen to the song again and illustrate what they think of when they hear "*Hatikvah.*"

Sixth World Zionist Congress Debate (S, A)

At the Sixth World Zionist Congress, there was a significant debate about the location of the Jewish homeland. Provide the class with background information about the pogroms in Russia. Also provide information related to building a homeland in Uganda or in Palestine. Assign the students roles as delegates from different countries with different backgrounds. Have the class debate whether or not the British proposal of a homeland in Uganda should be accepted. After the debate, discuss what actually happened at the Sixth World Zionist Congress. Discuss why the delegates, especially those from Russia and Eastern Europe, were so set on Palestine as the only possible homeland for the Jewish people.

World Zionist Organization Museum (E, S)

The World Zionist Organization that was created in Basel, Switzerland, still exists and represents Jewish people around the world. Have the class research the organization, its history, and some of its significant projects. If you are teaching this subject during a year when the World Zionist Organization meets, have the students learn about the important topics that will be voted upon during the meeting. Students can share what they have learned with parents or other classes by developing a museum exhibit.

Changes on the Kibbutz (S, A)

The early pioneers had many socialist ideals that they put into practice on the early *moshavim* and *kibbutzim*. Some of the original communities still exist, but life there has changed quite a lot over the years. Have groups of students research different collective communities in books and articles and on the Internet. Each group can either give a class presentation or design a small exhibit on a trifold presentation board. Parents or other classes can be invited to view the exhibits.

Primary Source Text Study (S, A)

Have students read the story of Techiah Liberson in *Eyewitness to Jewish History* (see "Resources" at the end of this chapter) and discuss her situation. What can they learn about the early pioneers? What were Liberson's goals? What were the obstacles she faced? How did she, and people like her, help to actualize God's covenant with the Jewish people in Eretz Yisrael?

DID YOU KNOW?

- The word "Zionism" comes from the Hebrew word "Zion," a biblical name for Jerusalem (and Israel).
- The Israeli flag is based on the *tallit,* or prayer shawl, with a Jewish star added in the middle, perhaps to symbolize the shield of King David.
- The words to "*Hatikvah*" were written by Naftali Herz Imber. He based the melody on a theme found in an old Eastern European folk song called "The Moldau."

TIMELINE (all dates are CE)

1856
    Aḥad Ha'am (Asher Ginsberg) is born

1860
    Theodor Herzl is born

1865
    Abraham Isaac Kook is born

1882
    First Aliyah to Israel begins

1897
    First Zionist Congress is convened in Basel, Switzerland

1904
    Theodor Herzl dies at age forty-four

1904
    Second Aliyah to Israel begins

1927
    Aḥad Ha'am (Asher Ginsberg) dies

1935
    Abraham Isaac Kook dies

RESOURCES
Books and Articles

Blech, Benjamin. *The Complete Idiot's Guide to Jewish History and Culture.* New York: Alpha Books, 2004.

Blech, Benjamin. *Eyewitness to Jewish History.* Hoboken, NJ: John Wiley & Sons, 2004.

Pasachoff, Naomi, and Robert J. Littman. *Jewish History in 100 Nutshells.* Northvale, NJ: Jason Aronson, 1995.

Sachar, Howard M. *The Course of Modern Jewish History.* New York: Vintage Books, 1990.

Sachar, Howard M. *A History of Israel from the Rise of Zionism to Our Time.* New York: Alfred A. Knopf, 1996.

Internet

Visit www.behrmanhouse.com/booklinks for links to Web sites that offer additional resources for this chapter.

Modern Period

CHAPTER TWENTY-FOUR

ANTI-SEMITISM AND THE HOLOCAUST

WHAT'S THE BIG IDEA?
Diaspora

Since the Jewish people was first exiled from Eretz Yisrael centuries ago, much of the Jewish population has remained dispersed throughout the world. Once scattered, we did not stay in one place but continued to move from country to country, often to find a safer haven. While our history includes periods of peace and prosperity among the peoples of the world, there have been many times when we were vulnerable to the larger powers under which we lived. Having no homeland, we could not count on anyone to take our part and speak out on our behalf. At no point in our history were the limitations of being a dispersed people more apparent than during the Holocaust.

BACKGROUND INFORMATION

Jews have lived in Europe since before the destruction of the Second Temple in 70 CE. In the countries where Jews resided, they coexisted with other minority groups as well. One difference between the Jews and other ethnic minorities was religion; being Jewish had been a liability for centuries in much of Christian Europe. Another difference was that the Jews did not have a homeland that could offer protection. These differences made them particularly easy targets, often placing Jews on the lowest rung of society and thereby lacking protection and advocacy afforded to the majority population.

Anti-Semitism

One can trace the history of anti-Semitism back to the earliest arrival of Jews into Europe. Seen as Christ-killers by their neighbors, Jews were viewed with suspicion and/or hatred by many (see chapters 11 and 13). When religion became a significant factor in determining governmental policy, Jews often faced murder, expulsions, or forced conversion. In many countries, including Poland and Italy, Jews lived in ghettoes, separated from the rest of society. While Jewish life often thrived in the ghetto, it was also a place of poverty and hardship. Ghetto residents had little or no hope of changing their lot in life because the outside world was closed to them.

The nineteenth century dawned on an enlightened age, in which science and rational thinking were expected to explain the nature of all things. In this environment, Western European governments gradually changed and all residents, including Jews and other minorities, began to acquire new rights. In many areas, the ghetto walls came down and Jews gained access to new opportunities (see chapters 20 and 21 for more information). They could choose how to practice their Judaism or whether to assimilate. More jobs and professions were open to them. Jewish philosophers and scientists became members of high society.

Many Jews believed that their identity was truly French, Italian, or German rather than primarily Jewish, and that there was no longer any reason to look toward a day when Jews would be restored to Zion.

Periodically, events would occur, such as the Dreyfus Affair, that served to remind world Jewry that anti-Semitism still lurked in the hearts and minds of their neighbors. Still, life was better for Western European Jews at the beginning of the twentieth century than had it been for generations, or than it was at the same time for their cousins in Eastern Europe.

In Eastern Europe, constantly changing borders led to national instability. Rulers often found it wise to suppress the many ethnic groups living within their borders. Nationalism led Poles and Russians to view the "other" with contempt or worse. Among all the minority groups found in Eastern Europe, Jews were at the bottom. Thus they were often the targets for persecution, which took the form of local or state-sanctioned killings, restrictive laws, and/or severe taxation. The Enlightenment never really reached Eastern Europe, and life was still difficult for Eastern European Jews at the beginning of the twentieth century.

The Impact of World War I

As the result of World War I, many of Europe's borders were redrawn, and once again Jews found themselves in new countries. They hadn't moved, but the borders had. Two of the most significant effects of World War I on Jewish history were (1) Germany's sense that they had been humiliated by the Allies during the peace process that ended the war, and (2) the rebirth of Poland, which, following World War I, included many different ethnic groups and the largest Jewish population in Europe. Both factors would be instrumental in the eventual destruction of European Jewry during the Holocaust.

Germany

Before World War I, Germany had a history of culture and civilization that could be seen in its great composers, philosophers, and scientists. German Jews felt that they had long been part of German society, holding positions in the professions, in business, and in government. Many German Jews believed that, first and foremost, they were Germans; after all, they had lived in Germany for generations. They were proud to be part of such a great civilization.

At the end of World War I, Germany felt humiliated by the terms of the peace treaty engineered by the Allied forces who won the war. Germany lost much of the territory it had previously claimed during the war. Seen as the instigator of the war, Germany took much of the blame and was saddled with enormous war debts that undermined the national economy. In this environment, a culture of nihilism (viewing traditional values as unfounded and existence as senseless) grew.

Many small nationalistic parties developed with the goal of helping a proud Germany rise again. These parties played upon the fears of their constituents and looked for an outside source to blame. The National Socialist German Workers Party (or Nazi Party) was one such small group that became active in the 1920s. Its leader, Adolf Hitler, aroused anti-Semitic feelings among Germans (and other groups), and eventually used terror to gain power, imposing his vision of a "new Germany" on the world.

Poland

From the twelfth through the eighteenth centuries, Poland was a great center of Jewish learning and culture (see chapter 17). However, due to its history as a nation ruled by many different powers over the years, Poland had become a country comprised of various ethnic groups, many of whom held little love for the Jews. After World War I, Poland regained her sovereignty but also recognized that many of her neighbors would like to swallow her up again.

In this suspicious and tenuous environment, a strong Polish nationalism grew that did not support other ethnic groups living within its borders. Financial aid to Jewish groups was cut and Jews were forced out of jobs when many businesses were nationalized and taken over by the government. Unfortunately, government control of businesses was not effective and led to an economic depression.

As in the past, poverty led to the search for a scapegoat and the Jews handily filled this role yet again. By the 1930s, anti-Semitism in Poland had increased widely. Schools were segregated, with Jewish students forced to sit on separate benches from Polish students. Poland also enthusiastically observed widespread German anti-Semitism and began to copy some of Hitler's policies even before the German invasion in 1939.

The Rise of Adolf Hitler
Long before annexing the Sudetenland, the name for the parts of Czechoslovakia with a significant German-speaking population, Adolf Hitler thought of Germany as a great world power. Born in Austria in 1889, Hitler moved to Vienna to try his hand as a painter. Unfortunately, his talent was not great. Forced to eke out an existence, Hitler filled his time forming his own vision of a strong and great Germany. During these years, he also developed a growing hatred for both socialists and Jews. He fought with the Kaiser's army in World War I, hoping to

see his visions fulfilled, but these hopes were dashed when Germany lost the war.

After World War I, Hitler became part of the Nazi Party and initiated a failed attempt to overthrow the German government in 1923. Jailed for treason, Adolf Hitler used his time behind bars to write *Mein Kampf* ("My Struggle"), which outlined his view of the world and his vision for Germany. Most significantly, the book voiced his great hatred of Jews and his desire to rid Germany of them so that it could once again rise to greatness. When Hitler was released from prison, he continued working toward these goals.

By the early 1930s, Adolf Hitler and the Nazi Party began to gain followers as inflation and unemployment became serious challenges for Germany. With growing allegiance, Hitler used provocative oratory to inflame old hatreds and gain greater support. Intimidation of people on the street by thugs operating as a militarized arm of the Nazi Party helped them gain the remainder of votes needed to take over the German parliament legally. In 1933, Adolf Hitler became chancellor of Germany and began putting his twin goals of taking over the world and destroying the Jewish people into practice.

Over the next two years, German Jews were subject to every type of harassment. In some cases, Nazi acts were reminiscent of state-sanctioned anti-Semitism of the past. In other situations, the violence of these events hinted at what was to come later. In 1933, the Nazis called for a boycott of all Jewish stores. They burned Jewish books and forced Jews out of civil service jobs. In 1934, expanding their focus, Nazis began entering small German villages to destroy Jewish property and kill Jews.[1] Still, many German Jews, feeling that Germany was their home, refused to see Hitler's true nature and with each event believed the worst was past.

Nuremberg Laws

Initially, the Nazis' anti-Semitism consisted of randomly organized events that, while carried out by the government, had no real legal backing. That changed in 1935 when the Nuremberg Laws codified into law the basis for all further deprivation and violence. Some believed that these laws were based on the anti-black "Jim Crow" segregation laws of the American South in the late nineteenth and early twentieth centuries, since both sets of legislation called for separate, but not equal, societies. Hitler's government legalized racial segregation by denying Jews all rights of citizenship and prohibiting marriages between Jews and non-Jews, among other restrictions.

As the 1930s continued, Jews were subject to further restrictions based on the Nuremberg Laws. They were required to carry identification cards. They could not vote. Signs began appearing in public places indicating that Jews were not welcome. The racial views outlined in the Nuremberg Laws became part of the German school curriculum. While Jewish children were segregated into special seats or special classrooms, teachers taught their students that the Jews comprised a lower race. Many German children, raised on these principles, became part of the Nazi Children's Party, and later—as older adolescents and adults—helped to carry out some of the greatest atrocities the world has ever seen. The Nuremberg Laws also became the backbone of Nazi policy, and they were often some of the first laws implemented in

any area or country that Germany conquered in the coming years. Some countries in which anti-Semitism was already prevalent, such as Poland, started enacting similar laws before the German invasion. Even in areas where anti-Semitism was not as obviously rampant, many Eastern European countries were only too willing to comply with the Nuremberg Laws once they were conquered by Germany.

From Segregation to Annihilation
Kristallnacht

Not all German Jews accepted what was happening to them. Some realized that segregation was likely only the beginning and found ways to leave Germany for other European countries, America, or Palestine. Others tried to focus world attention on what was happening by taking action. One such individual was Herschel Grynszpan, the seventeen-year-old son of a German family of Polish descent. When Herschel's family, along with many others, was expelled from Germany across the Polish border, Herschel wanted to fight back. Since he was living in Paris, there was not much he could do directly, so he struck out by killing Ernest vom Rath, a German diplomat in Paris.

Germany retaliated for this incident against the Jews under their jurisdiction in Germany, Austria, and the Sudetenland. On November 9 and 10, 1938, the Nazis organized a pogrom and encouraged mobs to attack Jews and destroy their property. The local police were instructed not to interfere with these actions. Synagogues and Jewish businesses were destroyed. Some Jews were killed, while others were rounded up and sent to concentration camps that had been established earlier in the 1930s to house political prisoners. These nights of destruction came to be known as *Kristallnacht,* the "night of broken glass." In a further humiliation, the Jews themselves were blamed for the events and forced to pay fines for the damage.

[1] Martin Gilbert, *The Holocaust: A History of the Jews of Europe During the Second World War,* New York: Henry Holt and Co., 1986, p. 42.

Kristallnacht was also a turning point in German policy toward the Jews. No longer was it enough to oppress the Jews through laws or expel Jews into Poland. The Nazis had concluded that Jews must be totally excluded from the economy. As a result, new laws were passed requiring Jews to turn over most of their assets to the government, making it easy to evict Jews from their homes and to restrict Jewish movement. Physical violence against Jews also increased from this point on, and some consider *Kristallnacht* to be the true beginning of the Holocaust.

After *Kristallnacht,* Nazi brutality against the Jews increased dramatically. Not only were Jews humiliated by being forced to do menial labor in the streets or spit on the Torah, but these events were paired with beatings and shootings. This brutality grew out of Nazi propaganda that categorized Jews as "subhuman." The Nazis had also discovered, through the lack of world response to *Kristallnacht,* that other countries did not seem to care much what they did to the Jews living under their control, emboldening them even further.

World War II
In 1939, Germany invaded Poland. This military action again Poland was also seen as act of war by the Allies. No longer could they ignore Hitler's land-grabbing. World War II had begun. With the annexation of Poland, the Nazis suddenly had hundreds of thousands of Jews under their jurisdiction. As they marched into Poland, they destroyed Jewish villages and killed Jews. While partly an act of war, there was greater destruction in these areas than in areas where there were no Jews. The Poles had already instituted many anti-Semitic laws along the lines of the Nuremberg Laws and were only too happy to hand over Polish Jews to the German authorities.

Ghettoes
With so many Jews living scattered through all of Poland, the Germans decided it would be easier to deal with the "Jewish Problem" if the Jews were all living in consolidated areas. With this in mind, the Nazis began a systematic process of rounding up Jews from the countryside and relocating them to walled ghettoes in Polish cities. Jewish councils were established in each ghetto, and the responsibility of carrying out German orders was given to the council leaders and Jewish police officers. Jewish policeman helped support the councils. This system of administration put great stress and pressure on the Jewish community as councils were forced to collect outrageous taxes and help determine who would be sent to do forced labor for the Germans (and later, who would be "selected" to be deported to death camps).

Living in ghettoes, the Jews tried to maintain as normal a life as possible. Jewish synagogues and schools were established. Cultural groups that performed plays and music provided the community with distractions as life became more and more unbearable. Death and illness became constant companions since food was scarce. The Nazis often entered the ghettoes at night and raided apartments, dragging people from their beds to be humiliated, beaten, and or taken away. Many never returned.

In the spring and summer of 1941, Germany continued to pursue its expan-sionist goals by invading Yugoslavia, Greece, and the Soviet Union. With the invasion of the first two, the Nazis continued their general pattern of randomly shooting and beating Jews in their path. However, the invasion of the Soviet Union marked a turning point in the Holocaust. Hitler realized that the local hatred of Jews could be used to further his own goals by providing willing executioners. As the German army moved into the Soviet Union, entire Jewish villages were rounded up and led into the forests where they were lined up and shot by killing squads composed primarily of local collaborators.

Wannsee Conference
On January 20, 1942, with Germany ruling over much of Eastern Europe and still fighting on several fronts, fifteen top Nazi officials met at Wannsee, in a villa in a suburb of Berlin, to discuss the "final solution." This very vague term was used by the Germans to refer to the systematic destruction, or genocide, of all Jews in Europe. The "final solution" had begun earlier with the development of death camps and the organized killings of Jews in the Soviet Union and elsewhere. At Wannsee, the discussion centered on the details of carrying out the "final solution" on a larger scale by building more concentration camps, developing gas chambers where Jews would be killed, and obtaining and scheduling trains that would bring the Jews from all parts of the German empire to the extermination centers.

By the time of Wannsee, the Jews of Eastern Europe had no way out. The borders of the German Empire were closed, and few if any countries were willing to admit large numbers of Jewish refugees. While Jews living in the Diaspora had faced many bad situations in the past, none had ever affected so many communities concurrently, and none has been so scientifically calculated.

There would be little or no relief for Eastern European Jewry until 1945 when the Allies defeated Germany and began to liberate the concentration camps throughout Eastern Europe. By that time, approximately six million Jews had been murdered by the Nazis along with at least five million others that the Germans deemed unworthy of living, such as Gypsies, homosexuals, mentally and physically disabled individuals.

It was a crime of such magnitude that the world at that time did not know how to grasp what had happened. Neither did they know exactly how to deal with its aftermath. Many Jews liberated from concentration camps went into displaced persons camps because they did not have homes to which to return. Others looked for ways to emigrate, but few countries would take them.

In 1946, the Nuremberg Trials were convened to bring Nazi leaders involved in carrying out the "final solution" to justice. Adolf Hitler was not among them because he had committed suicide in the final days of World War II. The testimony given by survivors at these trials gave the world a glimpse of the atrocities carried out by the Nazis during the war. The defendants were found guilty. Some were hanged and others imprisoned.

Many significant Nazi leaders hid under assumed names elsewhere in the world. Simon Wiesenthal, a Holocaust survivor, became instrumental in tracking, locating, and bringing these criminals to justice. In 1962, he helped Israeli intelligence locate Adolf Eichmann, the Nazi officer who coordinated the "final solution" for Hitler. The Israelis kidnapped Eichmann and brought him to Israel to stand trial. While the trial brought one of the key Nazis to justice, it also served to help heal the emotional wounds of many Holocaust survivors living in Israel and to show that Jews now had a voice and legal system with which to defend themselves.

Resistance
As the "final solution" gained momentum, the Germans rounded up increasingly larger

numbers of Jews, sending them to their deaths at several concentration camps designed for the specific purpose of killing Jews, collecting their possessions, and disposing of their bodies. Word of these atrocities eventually filtered out to the Jews living in the ghettoes. Slowly, some realized that at least an attempt at resistance had to be made.

Sometimes, it was resistance on a small, individual scale such as when a person jumped from a train on its way to one of the camps, or when forced laborers sabotaged the building and repair of train tracks to the camps. Sometimes, Jewish leaders resisted by refusing to turn Jews over to the German authorities. There was even spiritual resistance such as when concentration camp inmates sang Shabbos songs. These acts helped save a few lives and souls, sparking hope in others.

Warsaw Ghetto Uprising
Perhaps one of the most significant acts of resistance was the Warsaw Ghetto Uprising in 1943. Of all the ghettoes in Poland, the Warsaw Ghetto was the largest. Residents of the ghetto, with the help of underground resistance groups who operated in the Polish forests, obtained a small number of grenades and firearms. When the Germans entered the ghetto in January 1943 to round up more Jews for deportation, the resisters attacked. The Germans were temporarily stunned, and halted deportations. Believing that their armed attack had been responsible for ending the roundups, the Jews of the Warsaw Ghetto prepared for an even larger revolt.

Their opportunity to put this plan into action came on Passover of 1943 when the Germans returned to the ghetto, planning to deport the remaining Jews. The ensuing

battle lasted for almost a month. In the end, the Germans completely destroyed the ghetto, killing close to seven thousand Jews. Another seven thousand were transported to the death camp of Treblinka, and fifty-six thousand others were captured and transported to additional camps.

Though the outcome was pretty much a foregone conclusion, the acts of courage by the resisters of the Warsaw Ghetto became a symbol for Jews elsewhere that revolt was a possibility. As Tuvia Borzykowski, a resistance fighter, wrote about the smaller uprising in January:

"Though the unit was destroyed, the battle on Niska Street encouraged us. For the first time since the occupation we saw Germans clinging to the walls, crawling on the ground, running for cover, hesitating before making a step in the fear of being hit by a Jewish bullet."[2]

World Response
As trainloads of Jews sped toward certain death, the world looked on and did little. When Hitler first came to power, some Jews managed to leave Eastern Europe, but as the Nazis put pressure on Jewish communities through restrictive laws and terror, many foreign gates also closed. Due to Arab pressure, the British cut off all immigration to Palestine in the 1930s. The United States hardly filled its immigration quota from Eastern Europe during the war years, and in one case even turned away those who possessed documents giving them permission to enter the country.

The passenger ship *St. Louis* left Germany in 1939 with 1,128 refugees headed for the

---

[2] Martin Gilbert, *The Holocaust: The Story of the Jews of Europe During the Second World War*, New York: Henry Holt and Co., 1985, pp. 523–524.

United States. Seven hundred of the passengers held U.S. immigration quota numbers, but for three years hence. Docked in Cuba, the United States refused to allow the refugees to enter, and Cuba refused to let them in as well. Negotiations went back and forth among the nations. Finally, the ship was forced to sail back across the Atlantic to Europe. A few passengers were able to find refuge in Paris, Brussels, and Amsterdam. The remainder returned to Germany and eventually were killed.[3]

Righteous Gentiles

Although many Germans, Poles, and Eastern Europeans helped the Nazis or looked the other way, there were exceptions. Individuals in many countries did their part to save Jews, through acts both large and small. These individuals have become known as Righteous Gentiles and have been honored by Yad Vashem, Israel's national Holocaust museum. Two of the most notable Righteous Gentiles were Oskar Schindler and Raoul Wallenberg.

Oskar Schindler

Oskar Schindler, an ethnic German businessman, followed the Nazis into Poland when they annexed the Sudetenland in 1939. He was looking to make a profit, and succeeded by purchasing an enamel works factory formerly owned by a Jew and using Jews as cheap labor. Gradually Schindler came to see the Nazis' true intentions and felt compelled to do something. Using all types of deceit—bribery, blackmail, and lies—and his good relations with German officials, Schindler saved approximately fifteen hundred Jews from certain death.

He looked out for the Jews who worked in his factories, supplementing their meager food rations with additional sustenance

---

[3] Ibid., p. 80.

and providing an infirmary with a qualified physician to care for them when they were ill. Schindler also took in additional Jews, providing them with jobs and lodging. In January 1945, he learned of a locked goods wagon filled with Jews that was stopped at a nearby rail station. Realizing that the wagon was probably headed for a death camp, he interceded, changing the bill of lading so that it appeared that the wagon was bound for his factory. When the wagon arrived, Schindler saw to it that those Jews who had died in the sealed railway car were given a Jewish funeral, and his wife nursed the remaining Jews back to health.

Later during the war, in order to move "his" Jews to another one of his factories and save them from liquidation, Oskar Schindler made his famous list. Next to the name of each Jew on the list was the description of some spurious skill that made him or her "essential" to Schindler's work. After reviewing the list, the Germans willingly sent these Jews to Schindler's other factory rather than to the death camps.

Going well beyond what was required, and showing himself to be a true humanitarian, at the end of the war Schindler obtained truckloads of textiles from German warehouses. He used these to provide the Jews under his care with new clothes to wear back into freedom. Oskar Schindler himself fled to Argentina after the war, later returning to Germany, where he died in 1974. He is buried in Israel.

Raoul Wallenberg

An equally amazing story, and one that shows what creativity and courage can do, is that of Raoul Wallenberg. A member of a famous Swedish banking family, businessman, and diplomat, Wallenberg was able to save roughly 100,000 Jews living in Hungary near the end of the war. He first heard about the Eastern European Jews' plight while living and working in Palestine. Deeply touched by the stories he heard from those who had escaped from Nazi Europe, Wallenberg was glad of the opportunity to help when asked to spear-head Swedish efforts to save Jews still living in Hungary.

Wallenberg's business partner, a Hungarian Jew residing in Sweden, recommended Wallenberg for the position of First Secretary of the Swedish Legation in Budapest with the express mission of starting an operation to save Jews, because he was "a quick thinker, energetic, brave and compassionate." Raoul Wallenberg's efforts to save Jews proved him to be all of these things. He initially set up a number of "Sweden Houses" by purchasing empty buildings in Budapest and declaring them to be officially part of Swedish soil. Jews who could make it to these locations would be safe because they were outside the jurisdiction of Hungarian or German law. In addition, realizing how much emphasis the Nazis put on fancy symbols and bureaucratic documentation, Wallenberg designed a Swedish pass that he could give to Jews, identifying them as Swedish subjects. While these passes were forgeries, they garnered Nazi respect. At first, Wallenberg was able to hand these passes out without Nazi intervention. As the Allies got closer, Adolf Eichmann pushed to complete the process of rounding up all Jews and sending them to concentration camps. Some Jews were sent to the Austrian border on forced marches, and others were put into sealed railroad cars. In both situations, Wallenberg made it a point to be present and hand out as many Swedish passes as possible. In railroad stations, he would

climb to the top of railroad cars and drop the passes into any window or opening. Then he would tell the German soldiers to open the cars because they had mistakenly rounded up Swedish subjects. In this way, he saved thousands of Jews.

Wallenberg is also responsible for saving the Jews in the largest ghetto in Budapest. When he discovered that Eichmann planned to exterminate all the remaining Jews, Wallenberg went to an ally who was a German officer and had him deliver a message to the German general responsible for this effort. Wallenberg's message was that if the extermination took place, he would personally make sure it was later blamed entirely on the general. Whether it would have been possible to do this or not, clearly the general knew that the war was almost over and that Wallenberg could be a threat to him. The order was lifted.

At the end of the war, when the Russians entered Hungary, Raoul Wallenberg left the city with them, either by his own choice or because he was under arrest. What happened to Wallenberg afterward has never been clearly determined. The Russians maintain that he died in a Russian prison either of natural causes or at the hands of the state.

Other Righteous Gentiles
Wallenberg and Schindler are the best known of the Righteous Gentiles, in part because they were able to help such large groups of people. However, there were many, many others who helped protect Jews during the Holocaust, often at great danger to themselves and their families. In Eastern Europe, which had a long history of anti-Semitism and where most civilians were happy to turn Jews over to the authorities, some families hid Jews on their farms while others provided them

with certificates of baptism so that they could hide in plain sight as Christians.

Still others smuggled food into the ghettoes and children out of the ghettoes, placing them in Christian orphanages where they would be safe from the Nazis. As of 2003, the country with the largest number of individuals honored by Yad Vashem is Poland, where 5,632 people are documented as having helped to save Jewish lives.

In Western and Northern Europe, the situation was very different. Here the Nazis found the greatest resistance to their authority and their policy toward the Jews. While Germany was able to invade and conquer part of France, other sections remained free for much of the war. France had a strong religious history, and here the Church and devout Christians saw it as their Christian duty to help those who were in trouble. Priests helped hide Jews, and there was an underground network called the *Circuit Garel* (or the Garel Circuit, named after a French Jew involved in the underground), made up of Christians and Jews who helped protect Jewish children about to be rounded up and deported.

The only train driver to ever refuse to drive a deportation train was also French. His name was Leon Bronchart, and he was later denounced to the Gestapo.[4] In the French countryside, there were many small villages, one of which was Le Chambon-sur-Lignon, a Huguenot (French Protestant) village. Remembering their own persecution at the hands of French Catholics, the villagers followed their minister's lead and hid many children in a boarding school, and in their own homes.

Norway and Denmark were able to save almost all their Jews from Nazi atrocities by working together and resisting German orders. Soon after the Germans invaded Norway, they began to destroy synagogues just as they had on *Kristallnacht* in Germany. Here, too, a strong Christian presence combined with deep religious convictions helped Jews as Church leaders spoke out against the desecration of synagogues and made it known that they would not tolerate such actions. In 1942, seven bishops resigned to protest what the Nazis were doing. Ordinary Norwegians smuggled Jews across the border to Sweden, a neutral country that had offered aid to Jews in Norway and Denmark.[5]

In Denmark, the whole country from the government down to the common people, worked together to save all seventy-two hundred Danish Jews from the Nazis. This cooperative effort was born of a conviction that it was the right thing to do and that Danes would not allow German invaders to control their lives.

When the Danish government learned that the Germans were planning to deport Danish Jews to concentration camps, the country went into action. Economic and social organizations sent written protests to the Germans. King Christian X, the king of Denmark, voiced his strong feelings against the deportations and publicly supported the Jews. The Danish police refused to cooperate with the Germans and forbade them from breaking into apartments, making it impossible for the Nazis to round up Danish Jews. Finally, Danes and Jews worked together until all Denmark's Jews crossed the Swedish border to safety.[6]

---

[4] Martin Gilbert, *The Righteous: The Unsung Heroes of the Holocaust*, New York: Henry Holt and Co., 2003, p. 261.

[5] Ibid., pp. 250–254.
[6] Ibid., pp. 255–258.

All of these individuals helped Jews who did not have the ability to fight back themselves. It is heart-breaking to speculate how many more Jews might have been saved had a sovereign State of Israel already existed. It is partly because of the Holocaust that many western nations realized that a country of their own was not just a national whim on the part of a handful of Jews residing in Palestine, but a necessity if Jews were to continue to survive in the modern world. So, in 1948, after much lobbying on the part of Palestinian Jews and Jews elsewhere, the United Nations passed the resolution giving Israel the right to exist.

CONNECTING TO OUR TRADITION

Chapter 17 of the Book of Exodus describes the battle between Israel and Amalek, who came upon the Israelites from behind, striking first the women and children. With God's help the Israelites were victorious, but the story concludes with Moses saying, "Adonai will have war with Amalek from generation to generation." From this verse, the rabbis believed that Amalek would rise again. Haman, in the story of Esther, is considered to be a descendant of Amalek. Some in the modern age view Hitler as the most modern incarnation of Amalek. Modern history has taught us the importance of not just blotting out Amalek, but also remembering Amalek, as the Torah commands. We need to remember those who have no one to remember them. We need to remember so that history will never repeat itself. With all this in mind, the Jewish people have added a modern observance to the calendar—Yom Ha-Sho'ah, a day of remembrance for the Holocaust.

DID YOU KNOW?

Of all the countries invaded by Germany, Denmark alone protected and was able to save every one of its Jewish citizens.

IMPORTANT TERMS

Nuremberg Laws   Righteous Gentiles
Genocide   *Circuit Garel*
Nazi Party

Names, Places, Events

St. Louis   Herschel Grynszpan
Mein Kampf   Ernst vom Rath
Sudetenland   Adolf Eichmann
Nuremberg Trial   King Christian X
Kristallnacht   Wannsee Conference
Warsaw Ghetto   Simon Wiesenthal
Oskar Schindler   Le-Chambon-sur-Lignon
Raoul Wallenberg

DISCUSSION QUESTIONS

- How might things have transpired differently had there been a modern State of Israel in existence in the 1930s and 1940s?
- Could something like the Holocaust happen again? Why or why not?

ACTIVITIES

Nuremberg Law Web (S, A)
Have the class read the Nuremberg Laws or a simplified version. Discuss the impact these laws might have on everyday life. As a class, create a bulletin board web with the text of the Nuremberg Laws at the center. Add and connect other acts, laws, and events that grew from these restrictions.

Interview with Herschel Grynszpan (S, A)
Have an adult or teen leader come to the classroom as young Herschel Grynszpan. He can discuss why he was living with his uncle in Paris, the events leading up to his murder of Ernst vom Rath, and his feelings about *Kristallnacht*. After the visit, discuss Herschel Grynszpan's act of terrorism. Is terrorism ever appropriate? Have the students think of modern acts of Jewish terrorism. What was the difference between what Herschel Grynszpan did and the acts of sabotage that were carried out by the underground during the war?

Warsaw Ghetto Uprising Investigation (S, A)

Provide the class with a variety of primary sources related to the Warsaw Ghetto Uprising. Have the students read and discuss the texts, and then use them to develop an outline of what happened during this significant example of Jewish resistance. The outline might focus on what led up to the Warsaw Ghetto Uprising, who was involved, how the Jews worked together as a community, what other communities were involved, and the ultimate outcome.

Paper Clips (S, A)

Show the class the film *Paper Clips,* about middle school students in Tennessee who collected millions of paper clips in order to conceptualize the number of people killed during the Holocaust. Following the movie, engage your students in a discussion about the project and the values behind it.

TIMELINE (all dates are CE)

1889
Adolf Hitler born in Austria

1908
Oskar Schindler born in Austria-Hungary

1912
Raoul Wallenberg born in Sweden

1923
Hitler writes *Mein Kampf* in prison

1933
Hitler becomes chancellor of Germany

1933
(April) Boycott of Jewish shops

1935
Nuremberg Laws are established, stripping Jews of citizenship

1938
(March) Germany annexes Austria

1938
Buchenwald Concentration Camp opened

1938
Germany annexes the Sudetenland

1938
Kristallnacht

1939
Hitler invades Poland

1942
Wannsee Conference

1943
Warsaw Ghetto Uprising

1946
Nuremberg Trial

1962
Adolf Eichmann found guilty of war crimes by an Israeli court and hanged

1974
Oskar Schindler dies and is buried in Israel

RESOURCES
Books and Articles

Blech, Benjamin. *Eyewitness to Jewish History.* Hoboken, NJ: John Wiley & Sons, 2004.

Daniels, Fred. *Shadows in Twilight: A 1940–1945 Testimony.* Jerusalem: Gefen, 1992.

Gilbert, Martin. *The Holocaust: A History of the Jews of Europe During the Second World War.* New York: Henry Holt, 1986.

Gilbert, Martin. *The Righteous: The Unsung Heroes of the Holocaust.* New York: Henry Holt and Co., 2003.

Hallie, Philip P. *Lest Innocent Blood Be Shed.* New York: Harper Perennial, 1994.

Sachar, Howard M. *The Course of Modern Jewish History.* New York: Vintage Books, 1990.

Internet
Visit www.behrmanhouse.com/booklinks for links to Web sites that offer additional resources for this chapter.

CHAPTER TWENTY-FIVE
THE STATE OF ISRAEL

WHAT'S THE BIG IDEA?
Covenant
Jews have traditionally understood that they were God's chosen people, singled out for a special covenant that promised them the Land of Israel. For the Jews of the Diaspora, this covenant between God and the Jewish people was central to religious practice and tradition. With the birth of Zionism in the nineteenth century, it appeared to many Jews that the covenant might be realized in their lifetime. Yet, just as their biblical ancestors had to overcome many obstacles before entering the Promised Land, so, too, their modern counterparts faced difficult challenges in obtaining a land of their own.

BACKGROUND INFORMATION
As various forms of Zionism took hold throughout Jewish communities in Eastern Europe (see chapter 23), waves of immigrants began to make *aliyah* (literally, "going up" or emigrating) to Palestine. These pioneers did not arrive in an empty land waiting to be redeveloped; rather, like Joshua and the Israelites, many arrived in areas already settled by others. How were they to turn this land into a homeland for the Jewish people? Some Zionists believed that the answer was purchasing and working the land, while others believed the answer lay in gaining rights to the country through political means. History would show both were right, and neither way was without its perils.

Britain Supports a Jewish Homeland
During his lifetime, Theodor Herzl tried to gain political support for a Jewish home-land. His first efforts included entering into a dialogue with the Ottoman leaders who controlled Palestine in the early twentieth century. With the outbreak of World War I, many maps changed as borders shifted and new governing powers took over, with Great Britain in control of significant parts of the Middle East. While Jewish immigrants continued to enter Palestine, purchase land, and develop Jewish culture in the Holy Land, others turned their efforts to garnering political support from the British for a Jewish homeland in Palestine.

Balfour Declaration
Chaim Weizmann, an ardent Zionist who would become Israel's first president, was a chemist. During World War I, he invented TNT for the British, which helped the Allies win the war. Partly in gratitude for his help, the British Parliament voted to support a Jewish homeland in Palestine. In November 1917, the Balfour Declaration, a letter from Lord Arthur James Balfour to Lord Rothschild—both members of Parliament—made public the British government's decision to support a Jewish homeland. The letter reads as follows:

Foreign Office
November 2nd, 1917

Dear Lord Rothschild,

I have much pleasure in conveying to you, on behalf of His Majesty's Government, the following declaration of sympathy with Jewish Zionist aspirations which has been submitted to, and approved by, the Cabinet.

His Majesty's Government views with favor the establishment in Palestine of a national home for the Jewish people, and will use their best endeavors to facilitate the achievement of this object, it being clearly understood that nothing shall be done which may prejudice the civil and religious rights of existing non-Jewish communities in Palestine or the rights and political status enjoyed by Jews in any other country.

I should be grateful if you would bring this declaration to the knowledge of the Zionist Federation.

Yours,
Arthur James Balfour

Mandate for Palestine

Five years after the Balfour Declaration, the new League of Nations, an international political body formed after World War I to help keep peace in the world, issued a Mandate for Palestine that put the Balfour Declaration into effect. Significantly, it recognized that Palestine had been the Jewish homeland in the past and was to become so again, thus affirming the Jews' natural right to this land based on the history and covenant put forth in the Bible. The League of Nations also instructed the British to help Jews settle the land and immigrate to Palestine.

While the Balfour Declaration tried to protect the interests of Palestine's non-Jewish residents, the Mandate did not refer to the Arabs already living there. Clearly, the British and the League of Nations had different agendas, which would come into conflict with each other and with those of the Arabs and Jews living in Palestine then and in the future.

Both the Balfour Declaration and the Mandate recognized the right of Jews to settle in Palestine. Both also approved the creation of a quasi-government that would administer the Jews in Palestine and work with the British, while the British government would continue to hold the real power. British soldiers in the area were charged with keeping the peace, and no provisions were made to create a Jewish military force.

The Beginnings of the Arab-Jewish Conflict

Hebron Massacre of 1929
As increasing numbers of Jews arrived in Palestine with each wave of immigration, struggles with the local Arab population increased as well. These conflicts were largely economic in nature, but presented themselves as familiar anti-Semitic sentiments. Arab landowners could no longer get cheap Arab labor because the Jewish workers and settlers had helped increase the wages and standard of living for Arab workers. The Arab landowners incited the lower classes to riot against the Jews, with similar results as the Cossack pogroms in Russia (see chapter 22). In Palestine, this form of anti-Semitism led to the Hebron Massacre of 1929, in which many Jews were killed while the British stood idly by.

Irgun and Haganah
The Hebron Massacre convinced some Jews that since the British had failed to protect them, they needed a more effective way to protect themselves. Ze'ev Jabotinsky, a rival of David Ben-Gurion (discussed later in this chapter) and organizer of Jewish defense efforts as well as the Revisionist Zionist movement,

created Israel's first military organization. The Haganah (literally, "defense") and its underground military, the Irgun (short for *Irgun Tzv'ei Le'umi,* or "national military organization"), eventually grew into an army that, after the birth of the modern State of Israel, would become the Israel Defense Force (IDF), or *Tzahal* (an acronym for *Tz'va Haganah L'Yisrael*).

The Haganah began as an underground military organization to help defend Jews against Arab attacks. Originally a loose organization of local defense groups, its structure changed following the Hebron Massacre of 1929, when the Jewish community realized it needed a real army with better organization and training. Some of the more significant changes to the Haganah included efforts to recruit more members, to provide those members with comprehensive training, and to increase the underground production of arms.

The British government never officially recognized the Haganah, though they sometimes worked together on matters of intelligence. However, as Britain's policies regarding immigration changed and fewer Jews were allowed to immigrate legally, the Haganah and the British army more often found themselves in open conflict.

The Peel Commission
Tensions between Arabs and Jews continued with heightened violence between 1936 and 1939. Britain, which still controlled the area, sent a royal commission of inquiry to Palestine to investigate the situation and propose a solution. The commission, headed by Lord Robert Peel and known as the Peel Commission, suggested that since Arabs and Jews could not peacefully coexist, the country should be partitioned between the two groups. Land and people could be

exchanged simultaneously so that the size of each area would be similar. From Mount Carmel to south of Be'er Tuvia along the coast, the Jezreel Valley, and the Galilee would belong to the Jews. The Arabs would control the hill regions, Judea and Samaria, and the Negev. Britain would continue to control an area between Jaffa and Jerusalem. While this plan, had it been put into effect, might have ended the Jewish-Arab conflict, neither side was wholly supportive of the compromise, and the plan was ultimately abandoned by the British.

Britain Changes Its Mind
The White Paper
Frustrated by the continuing tensions among Jewish and Arab residents of Palestine, and having failed to find a solution acceptable to either side, the British looked for other ways to control the situation. Since Jewish immigration was one source of Arab dissatisfaction, Britain decided to restrict Jewish immigration to Palestine. On May 17, 1939, Great Britain issued the White Paper, which would allow only seventy-five thousand Jews to enter Palestine over a five-year period.

The White Paper basically revoked the Balfour Declaration by stating that "His Majesty's government declares unequivocally that it is not part of their policy that Palestine should become a Jewish state."[1] The timing of the White Paper could not have been worse. Palestine had been one of the few countries allowing Jewish refugees from Eastern Europe as Hitler worked to annihilate them, and now this avenue of escape was closed, too. The Haganah responded to the White Paper by creating

---

[1] Benjamin Blech, *The Complete Idiot's Guide to Jewish History and Culture,* New York: Alpha Books, 2004, p. 303.

underground routes by which they could now smuggle Jewish refugees into the country, creating yet another area of tension between Jews and British.

The Exodus

In 1947, after the end of World War II and eight years after the publication of the White Paper, a ship carrying Jewish refugees from Europe tried to enter Palestine illegally. Seventeen miles from shore, while still in international waters, five British destroyers and one cruiser opened fire on the ship *Exodus,* seriously damaging the vessel. The damaged ship was towed to the port of Haifa, and its passengers were forced to board another ship, which took them back to displaced persons camps in Europe, provoking a storm of international criticism.

UN Decision

Later the same year, Great Britain decided to give up its mandate in Palestine as it became increasingly obvious that they could not effectively administer the area. The British government turned to the United Nations (the international body that had replaced the League of Nations after the end of World War II), asking them to develop and implement a plan that would resolve Jewish-Arab issues and allow Britain to withdraw from the area. The UN, after intense debate, voted to create a Jewish state in Palestine. World opinion in the aftermath of the Holocaust played a significant role in this decision, as did the lobbying of prominent Zionist leaders. The UN's plan called for partitioning the country into two states, similar to the suggestion the Peel Commission had.

On May 5, 1948, the modern State of Israel was born. Jewish leaders chose to call their new country Israel, the name given to the patriarch Jacob by God, and by which Jews had referred to their homeland throughout the centuries. It was the first time in thousands of years that the name "Israel" had been used officially as the name of the country. While Jews celebrated in the streets of Palestine, many Arabs fled and others prepared to attack in order to reclaim what they viewed as their territory.

Israel: The Formative Years

David Ben Gurion

Born in Poland, David Ben-Gurion immigrated to Palestine in 1906. When he arrived as part of the Second Aliyah, Ben-Gurion worked on a kibbutz. He believed that the Bible gave the Jewish people ownership of the Land of Israel and that the Balfour Declaration only recognized something that already existed. Ben-Gurion wanted Israel to give the Jews a new position in the world, similar to that of other national groups with a country and a culture uniquely its own. After honing his leadership skills and perfecting his Zionist vision on the kibbutz and with the Haganah, Ben-Gurion became Israel's first prime minister. Ben-Gurion lived out the ideals he shared with other Zionists and worked for those values throughout his entire life.

The War of Independence

Although the United Nations as a whole voted Israel into existence on November 29, 1947, all the Arab states had voted no. While the Jews were happy to be able to claim even part of Eretz Yisrael as their own, the Arabs would not accept the partition plan. Over the next six months, Arab soldiers came into Palestine from neighboring states and attacked Jews. Once the Jewish state was officially born on May 14, 1948, all the surrounding Arab states attacked. The War of Independence had begun. The new Israeli government had to obtain materials quickly and organize a defense. World Jewry and the money they provided were instrumental in making Israel's defense possible.

Prime Minister David Ben-Gurion believed that every inch of soil the Jews had been granted by the Partition Plan was critical; nothing could be given up. Holding on to the Land was the goal of the Israel army, and its soldiers had two significant advantages: personal knowledge of the land and passionate dedication to the cause for which each soldier fought.

In addition, throughout the country private security forces were maintained by various *kibbutzim* to protect the residents until the army could reach them. Although the army was largely successful, today one can still see rusted, burned-out carcasses of makeshift army vehicles along the highway between Tel Aviv and Jerusalem and elsewhere in the country. These stand as a testament to the battles fought and as a memorial to the lives lost by men and women who died trying to get supplies through to the population under attack.

Thinking they had the element of surprise when they attacked, the Arabs had not expected much resistance. Israel, however, had anticipated such attacks and showed the Arab states it would not easily be overrun. On June 11, 1948, the Arabs accepted a UN-brokered truce of one month. While the war continued after the truce, it was much clearer that Israel would win.

Ben-Gurion's choice was now whether to accept the land Israel had been granted and had fought so hard to defend, or whether to try to win more land for Israel. The decision was made to move into the Negev, which was still controlled by Egypt, and take it if possible. The Israeli

army succeeded. Only once the Negev was in Israel's hands did Ben-Gurion agree to an armistice. Israel now had new boundaries, achieved by armed conflict. They had won the war. Arab Palestinians—those residents of Palestine before 1948—were in a sense the real losers. Since the Arab states had rejected the Partition Plan and lost the war, the "Palestinians" didn't actually have sovereignty over any of the lands granted by the plan. They were still under the jurisdiction of the original Arab nations who had ruled them in the first place: Egypt, Jordan, Syria, and Lebanon.

Fearing for their lives, despite Israeli assurances, many Arabs fled the area after the War of Independence. In some cases, their fears were enflamed by Arab League propaganda. In addition, many Arab states encouraged them to leave, promising to return them to the area after the defeat of Israel in the near future.

Unfortunately, these Palestinian refugees were not welcomed by Israel's Arab neighbors either; in fact, the Egyptian and Jordanian governments refused to allow them to settle in their countries. Therefore, many had no choice but to join others in abysmal refugee camps, administered by the United Nations, mostly along the borders with Israel. Many of their descendants continue to live in these refugee camps, where poverty, unrest, and dissatisfaction smolder and periodically erupt in terrorist acts.

Once Israel became its own sovereign nation, Jews from all over the world were welcome to immigrate. This open-door policy was wonderful in theory, but the reality put great pressure on the resources of a nascent country. Israel's population tripled in nine years as countries in the

Middle East and Eastern Europe saw the opportunity to rid themselves of unwanted Jews who, in many instances, also wanted to leave.

Israel built transitional housing camps made up of huts and tents for the new immigrants. Agencies were established to help provide basic necessities, teach the immigrants Hebrew, and train those without job skills. Although these efforts taxed the limited resources of the new country, the new arrivals also provided much-needed manpower for agricultural settlements and recruits to the Israeli army. What Israel learned during these early years about the absorption of immigrants has continued to serve it well as new waves of immigration have continued to enter the country up to the present day.

Other Wars

The Suez Canal and the Sinai Campaign
During the years following the War of Independence, Israel continued to build its country, developing ways to meet the needs of new immigrant groups and solidifying its military and political base in the region.

Nearby, in Egypt, the political world was also changing. Gamal Abdel Nasser was a wounded veteran of the Palestine war (as the War of Independence was known in Egypt) who took control in Egypt after King Farouk was ousted. He had greater ambitions than controlling just Egypt, and made alliances accordingly. In 1956, using weapons provided by the Soviet Union, Nasser seized the Suez Canal, which connects the Mediterranean and Red Sea, providing an important shipping route. He went on to form an alliance with Syria and Jordan, in case of war with Israel. Ben-Gurion and the Israeli government realized it was only a

matter of time before Egypt would attack Israel. On October 28, 1956, Israel mobilized its forces and marched into the Sinai Peninsula in a preemptive strike, taking the Egyptian army by surprise.

When the dust cleared, Israel controlled the Sinai Peninsula and the Gaza Strip. While Ben-Gurion was willing to return the Sinai to Egypt, he refused to move out of Gaza for national security reasons. While now within its borders, Gaza created a huge security issue for Israel, because its UN-monitored refugee camps now stood within its national borders. (After several decades, Israel finally vacated the Gaza Strip in the summer of 2005, turning it over to the Palestinian Authority.) Once the war ended, Israel received a commitment from the United States to help protect its shipping interests in the Gulf of Aqaba on the Red Sea, which was critical to Israel's economy.

The Six-Day War
After the Sinai Campaign (as the 1956 war was known), Israel's borders with Egypt were relatively quiet; the same could not be said, however, of its borders with Syria to the north. Border skirmishes between Syria and Israel became more common as Syrian guns on the Golan Heights shot on *kibbutzim* below, interrupting their work in the fields and killing or wounding kibbutz members.

The situation came to a head in 1967 after a major battle in which Israel shot down six Syrian MiG aircraft. In the aftermath of this situation, Russia provided misinformation to Egypt about Israel's intentions to attack. Although Nasser realized that Russia's reports were not accurate, he chose to attack in order to relieve political pressures at home. At the same time, he closed the Straits of Tiran to Israeli shipping, putting economic pressure on the young country. While the world told Israel not to be the first to strike, but to wait for an attack by the Arabs, Israel decided to act preemptively. On June 5, the Israeli air force smashed the Egyptian air force on the ground. Then Israel's ground forces attacked. Tricked into believing that Egypt was victorious, Syria, Jordan, and Iraq also entered into the war. Still, Israel managed to defeat all its enemies and reunify Jerusalem, which had been under Jordanian rule since 1948.

The Yom Kippur War

Six years later, the Arab world tried to destroy Israel again. This time, they chose to strike on Yom Kippur day, assuming that the whole country would be at synagogue and unable to defend themselves. However, Israel was again victorious. As in other wars in the Middle East, the UN was of little help and appeared in their actions, and inactions, to support the Arab states more than Israel.

The Struggle for Peace

Having proved itself in a series of wars, Israel managed to gain a semblance of peace. Two significant peace treaties were also signed by Israel and Egypt and by Israel and Jordan in the last decades of the twentieth century. These treaties, however, did nothing to resolve the issue of Palestinians living in Gaza and the West Bank. These territories, with no sovereignty of their own, proved to be a breeding ground for Palestinian unrest.

Two significant *intifadas,* or uprisings, took place in which Palestinians sent suicide bombers to attack Israelis on their streets and in public places. The Israeli government has continued to struggle with protecting its people, especially in the face of world opinion, which has often taken the side of the Palestinians. The early

years of the twenty-first century have seen the construction of a security fence between Israel and the Palestinian territories and the withdrawal of Jewish settlements and military personnel from the Gaza Strip. Only history will tell how well Israel will overcome these last obstacles to its dream of a peaceful homeland for all Jews.

CONNECTING TO OUR TRADITION

Traditionally, Jews pray three times a day for the ingathering of the exiles back to Zion. The modern State of Israel makes this ingathering a real possibility. Ever since 1948, Israel has been a haven for persecuted Jews from such divergent places as Russia, Ethiopia, and Yemen.

Many Jews who do not suffer from persecution have also chosen to make *aliyah* (literally "to go up," or immigrate to Israel). The question today is not "Is there a Jewish homeland to which one can return?" but "Will there be enough space for all those Jews who wish to return?"

IMPORTANT TERMS
Aliyah
Mandate
Zionism

Names, Places, and Events

Palestine	Ze'ev Jabotinsky
Balfour Declaration	Haganah
Chaim Weizmann	Peel Commission
Lord Arthur James Balfour	White Paper
	The *Exodus*
Lord Rothschild	Yom Kippur War
League of Nations	Six-Day War
United Nations	Gaza Strip
Mandate for Palestine	West Bank
	Ze'ev Jabotinsky
Hebron Massacre of 1929	Irgun

DISCUSSION QUESTIONS

- Prior to the establishment of the modern State of Israel, Jews living in the Diaspora continued to hope and pray for a return to the Holy Land. In an age when a modern State of Israel exists, what does it mean for us to pray for a return to Zion, even if we have no plans to make *aliyah*?

- Do you think the creation of the modern State of Israel by Jewish men and women fulfills God's covenant with the Jewish people? Why or why not?

- What obstacles to entering the Promised Land faced our biblical ancestors? What obstacles faced Jews trying to create a modern homeland in the twentieth century? How were these similar or different?

- How did the early history of the State of Israel lay the foundation for contemporary conflicts?

ACTIVITIES

Interview with David Ben-Gurion (E, S)

Invite a parent, teacher, or other adult volunteer to come to your class as David Ben-Gurion. Ask Ben-Gurion to share basic information about his life and then allow the students to ask questions. After the visit, have students design postcards illustrating an event from Ben-Gurion's life. This activity can serve either as an introduction to or as a closing activity for the study of the modern State of Israel.

Museum Exhibit: David Ben-Gurion, A Modern Moses (S, A)

Have students research David Ben-Gurion's life and many leadership roles. Videos, computers, books, and articles can be used as resources. Make a chart. On one side, have the students recall elements of Moses's story from birth through death. On the other side, have the students come up with similar elements from Ben-Gurion's life (born in a foreign country, travels to a new country, becomes a leader of the Jewish people, leads Jewish people through battles). Divide the class into groups. Each group can work on a different part of the exhibit, which will show the similarities and differences between the biblical experience and the modern experience. Invite parents and/or other classes to view the exhibit.

The Exodus (S, A)

Show your class the early sections of the film *Exodus* (1960). Provide information about the White Paper as background. Have the students write newspaper articles from different perspectives (Jewish, British, European, American) about the *Exodus*.

Israeli History Obstacle Course

(Family or Camp Program)
After the class has learned some Israeli history, divide students into teams of Jewish pioneers. You may want to give the teams the names of *kibbutzim* from Israel's early history. Each team has to work its way through the obstacle course, beginning with arrival in Palestine (a cooperative activity requiring the group to cross the "water" on three planks without leaving anyone behind) and ending with signing the Declaration of Independence (everyone in the group reads and signs a copy of the document).

Along the way, students may have to participate in a game of tug-of-war with "British soldiers," help build a "sandbag" wall around a kibbutz, create a celebratory cheer about Israeli independence, and other activities that reflect the ups and downs and obstacles early Zionists faced in creating the State of Israel. At the end of the event, discuss the obstacles along with the history they represented, and the ways that the students had to work together.

Book Discussion (S, A)

To help students understand the tensions between Jews and the British during the mandate period, have them read and discuss Eli Wiesel's *Dawn*.

Cultural Soup (E, S, A)

Have small groups of students research some of the different immigrant groups that entered Israel in the years after the War of Independence. Plan an event for parents or other classes at which the students share aspects of the food, clothing, and customs of these groups. Discuss the effects these immigrant groups had on the young country.

DID YOU KNOW?

- A Jewish chemist, Chaim Weizmann, invented TNT during World War I.
- A very young Paul Newman was in the movie *Exodus,* which was based on the story of this ship.
- It was easier for Israel to call up reservists and other military aid for the Yom Kippur War because announcements of the attack and need for defense were made at synagogues already filled with Jews observing the holiday.

TIMELINE (all dates are CE)

1906
    David Ben Gurion arrives in Palestine
1917
    Balfour Declaration
1922
    Mandate for Palestine
1920
    Haganah founded
1929
    Hebron Massacre
1937
    Peel Commission
1939
    White Paper

1947
    British fire upon and turn away the *Exodus*
1948
    Creation of State of Israel
1948
    Haganah becomes Israel Defense Force
1956
    Sinai Campaign
1967
    Six-Day War
1973
    Yom Kippur War
2005
    Gaza disengagement

RESOURCES

Books and Articles

Bard, Mitchell G. *Myths and Facts: A Guide to the Arab-Israeli Conflict*. Chevy Chase, MD: American-Israeli Cooperative Enterprise, 2001.

Blech, Benjamin. *The Complete Idiot's Guide to Jewish History and Culture*. New York: Alpha Books, 2004.

Blech, Benjamin. *Eyewitness to Jewish History*. Hoboken, NJ: John Wiley & Sons, 2004.

Sachar, Howard M. *The Course of Modern Jewish History*. New York: Vintage Books, 1990.

Sachar, Howard M. *A History of Israel from the Rise of Zionism to Our Time*. New York: Alfred A. Knopf, 1996.

Wiesel, Elie. *Dawn*. New York: Bantam, 1982.

Internet

Visit www.behrmanhouse.com/booklinks for links to Web sites that offer additional resources for this chapter.

North American Jewish Experience

CHAPTER TWENTY-SIX
JEWS IN THE NORTHEAST AND CANADA

WHAT'S THE BIG IDEA?
Acculturation

Judaism and the Jewish people have survived through centuries of change, but they have not remained the same. America has provided the Jewish people with opportunities that they have not had any place else besides the historic and modern State of Israel. This is due in part to the early involvement of Jewish settlers in shaping the United States of America. Perhaps even greater than the influence of Jews on America has been the influence of American religion, culture, and politics on American Judaism.

BACKGROUND INFORMATION
Jews Help Settle the Northeast

In 1654, the sailing ship *Sainte Catherine* arrived in New Amsterdam harbor with twenty-three Jews of Spanish-Portuguese descent aboard. This small Jewish group had made its way from Recife, Brazil, and had asked to settle in the Dutch colony. Peter Stuyvesant, the governor of New Amsterdam, did not look favorably on the idea of Jews in his colony and initially denied their petition.

The new immigrants were forced to remain on board the *Sainte Catherine* until their request could be considered by the directors of the Dutch West India Company, who oversaw the colony. Since approximately one-third of its directors were Jewish, permission was ultimately given for the Jews to settle in New Amsterdam with the restriction that they would not be allowed to pray publicly in the colony. This initial group of Jewish settlers would help shape the Jewish experience in America by paving the way for further Jewish settlement, securing rights for Jews in the New World, and establishing Sephardic Jewish traditions as the dominant form of Judaism in North America for many years.

While Jews were allowed to live in New Amsterdam, there were many colonies in the Northeast in which Jews initially could not settle, including Massachusetts, Connecticut, Maryland, and New Hampshire. Even in the colonies where non-Christians could live, Jews had to work for the rights of citizenship. Asser Levy, who was part of the original twenty-three who settled in New Amsterdam, petitioned for the right to stand guard in that city. Although he was initially turned down, his request was ultimately granted in 1655. This opportunity opened the way for greater Jewish participation in society that eventually culminated in full citizenship a century later.

The Jews who settled in New Amsterdam, along with others who came later in the seventeenth century, were of Spanish-Portuguese descent and brought Sephardic customs of worship with them. Since the synagogue had always played an important role in the Jewish community, not only as a place of worship but, also as an institution that enforced Jewish law and custom, all Jews who settled in New Amsterdam came under the influence of the Sephardic community, whether or not they were of Sephardic background. The Mill Street Synagogue, also known as

Congregation Shearith Israel, built in 1730 and later known as the Spanish-Portuguese Synagogue, was the first North American synagogue. Even in 1740 when there were more Ashkenazic than Sephardic Jews in the community, the synagogue continued to be organized around Sephardic customs.

Revolutionary War

By the beginning of the Revolutionary War, Jews had been living in the American colonies for over one hundred years. Many made their living by providing services and merchandise to their communities through commerce, shipping, and fur trading. These Jewish merchants felt the impact of the taxes and tariffs imposed by England on items such as tea, paper goods, and other necessities, so it is not surprising that their names would be found on many of the early petitions that protested these unfair British taxes.

During the Revolutionary War, American Jews could be found on both sides of the conflict. While some Jewish merchants supported the revolutionaries, others who had benefited from their business relationships with England, or who hoped to keep the rights they had under British rule, sided with the English. Those Jews who supported independence helped the war effort in many different ways. Some were sutlers, suppliers of goods to the local militias.

Approximately one hundred Jews fought on the side of the patriots including Hart Jacobs, who petitioned for the right not to fight on Shabbat. Others, like Haym Solomon, helped provide financial backing for the war. Solomon helped raise needed funds for the Revolutionary War and loaned money to both individuals and groups involved in the war effort,

including James Madison and the Continental Congress.

When the Revolutionary War was over and America had won its right to exist independently of Great Britain, Americans turned their thoughts to setting up a new government and writing a Constitution. This important subject was no less in the minds of American Jews, who were concerned that they might lose some of the rights they had enjoyed under British rule.

Even more important, they saw the opportunity to gain rights that they had not had in the past. With this goal in mind, Jonas Phillips, a Philadelphia businessman, wrote to the delegates of the Constitutional Convention asking them to ensure that government officials would not be required to take any religious oaths in order to be sworn into office. Even without Phillips's prompting, the Constitutional Convention had already included Article VI, stating that religious oaths were not required in order for individuals to assume political positions in the federal government.

Also important to the Jewish community was the First Amendment to the Constitution, which gave freedom of religion to all Americans. This amendment put into national law what many Americans had already acquired in their individual states, and what was centuries ahead of its time for much of the rest of the world.

As the United States came together as a country with a new constitution that guaranteed equal rights to Christians and non-Christians alike, change was also affecting the Jewish community. During the Revolutionary War, many synagogues had disbanded or been displaced by events related to the War. Now these synagogues were reestablishing themselves, and others were forming. In the past, all Jews in a community had belonged to one synagogue that regulated all religious matters. As American Jews began to think of themselves as Americans and became more and more involved in their secular communities, they began to think about their synagogues in different ways.

Ashkenazic Jews, who were quickly becoming a majority in the Jewish community, wanted to worship in synagogues that reflected their particular customs and traditions. In an equal society, it was harder for the synagogue to enforce Jewish laws and traditions. This new way of thinking led to the establishment of a new breed of independent synagogues. Where once the synagogue was the community, now there was a community of synagogues.

During this time, many Jewish communities also began to reevaluate the internal structure of their synagogues. As synagogues reexamined or wrote new rules and regulations, they did away with those that seemed undemocratic, such as special seating for prominent families. They also began to use the term "constitution" or "Declaration of Rights" for their governing documents instead of the earlier *haskamot,* or agreements. These synagogue changes were just one more way that the Revolutionary War and the establishment of the United States as an independent country had an impact on the lives of American Jews.

To show their appreciation for the many opportunities they were finding in America, and to prove themselves loyal citizens, many synagogues sent letters on behalf of their communities to George Washington upon his inauguration as president of the United States of America. The most famous of these letters was that sent to the President by the Touro Synagogue in Newport, Rhode Island. George Washington responded to the synagogue's letter with the assurance that the U.S. government would continue to protect the rights of all American citizens. He went on to quote the prophet Micah: "Everyone shall sit in safety under his own vine and fig tree, and there shall be none to make him afraid" (Micah 4:4).

With the Constitution guaranteeing political rights and religious freedom, and the new president promising that these rights would be upheld, one would think that the Jews wouldn't have anything to worry about in America. Yet, the truth was that many of the rights outlined in the U.S. Constitution were to remain rights on paper only for many years.

Individual states still had their own state constitutions that could and often did deny Jews and others the rights outlined in the national Constitution. For example, it was not until 1826 that Jews could hold political office in Maryland, because until that time elected officials had to swear upon their faith as a Christian that they would uphold the laws of the State of Maryland. Since Jews could not do this without lying, they could not hold elected office (see chapter 20 for more information about such restrictions in Great Britain). In 1826, after a long struggle, the Maryland legislature finally passed what became known unofficially as the "Jew Bill," which revoked this oath. In the following years, other states followed suit.

Jewish Life in the United States

Jews in America began to realize how lucky they were to live in the United States and how much America could offer their brothers and sisters who were being persecuted in other parts of the world. One such person was Mordecai Manuel Noah, a Jewish journalist, politician, and writer. He had spent time in North Africa and knew firsthand how difficult life was for Jews outside America. When he returned to the United States, he conceived the idea of starting a colony in America to which all persecuted Jews could go and live in peace. He chose an island near the Niagara River in New York as the location for his colony, which he called Ararat, after the mountain where Noah's ark came to rest following the Flood. While the colony was dedicated on September 2, 1825, Noah's idea never found much support, and nothing remains of the colony today but an engraved foundation stone.

While forward-thinking Jews like Mordecai Manuel Noah looked for ways that America could help foreign Jews, others were concerned with the state of Jews in America, specifically with their Jewish education. By the 1830s German Jews had begun to arrive in the United States in increasing numbers. They brought with them different customs from their Sephardic coreligionists and were often less likely to practice their Judaism.

At the same time, there were few trained rabbis or Jewish educators in the United States. Rebecca Gratz, a well-known Philadelphia philanthropist and charity worker, along with other Jewish women in her community, decided that something needed to be done about the education of Jewish children in their city. In 1838, these women started the first Jewish Sunday school in the United States. The school was modeled on Christian Sunday schools, many of which had sprung up at the end of the eighteenth century. The instruction at this school was primarily oral and included an opening prayer, Bible readings, the singing of Hebrew hymns,

and the memorization and recitation of catechism, a summary of religious doctrine often in the form of questions and answers, from a volume called *Pyke's Catechism*. This last text was a Christian textbook in which Gratz and her fellow teachers had blacked out all the Christian references, since no Jewish textbooks existed at the time.

Civil War
As issues of states' rights and slavery came to a head, the United States entered another war, this one a Civil War between the North and the South. Once again, Jews found themselves taking sides on the issues that divided the country. Prior to the Civil War, rabbis in the North, for the most part, either spoke out against slavery or kept silent on the issue, and during the war these rabbis supported the Union's position and the war effort.

Approximately six thousand Jews fought in the Union army. With this many Jewish soldiers, the Union army and the Jewish community soon came into conflict over the issue of chaplains. The original law required that any army chaplain was to be elected by field officers and company commanders, and that he had to be a Christian minister.

One Pennsylvania unit that had many Jewish soldiers chose to elect a Jew as its chaplain. Since this choice was counter to the law governing chaplaincy requirements, the secretary of war nullified the election. The Jewish community sent a communication to President Lincoln protesting the regulations on the grounds that they required a religious test as qualification for an office under the U.S. government, which was unconstitutional. President Lincoln responded to the group and promised to find a way to enact a law that was broad enough to include Jewish chaplains. In 1862 the chaplaincy law was reworded to include the phrase "some religious denomination," instead of "some Christian denomination." This regulation is still in place today and there are many rabbis who serve as military chaplains in the U.S. armed forces.

While the United States was reconstructing itself after the Civil War, the Jewish community was dealing with its own internal divisions. Beginning as early as the 1820s, American Jews were reforming their Judaism to fit more comfortably into American society and culture. Some synagogues had incorporated the use of organs, added English to their services, and/or shortened the worship service in general (see chapter 28 for more details). By the middle of the century, other pressures had come to bear on the Jewish community. Some Jews chose not to practice Jewish customs or had settled in areas where it was difficult to keep kosher or belong to a synagogue. This was also a time of Christian reawakening, and missionary groups worked to convert Jews to Christianity. Many Jewish leaders felt it was time to modernize Jewish practice to better fit with the contemporary world and especially the unique nature of Jewish life in America.

The idea of modernizing Jewish practice coincided with the arrival in America of a number of European-trained Jewish leaders who brought with them the ideas of the new Reform Judaism developing in Germany (see chapter 21 for more information). One of these was Rabbi Isaac Mayer Wise. Born in Bohemia, Wise immigrated to the United States in 1846. While he wanted to reform Judaism, he also believed that all Jews in the United

States should feel a sense of unity. Toward these ends he helped form the Union of American Hebrew Congregations (UAHC) in 1873 (now known as the Union for Reform Judaism—URJ) as a central organization of all synagogues, with the goal of unifying all of its member congregations.

One of the UAHC's first projects was to raise money to start a college that would train American rabbis. Two years later, in 1875, the Hebrew Union College (HUC) was founded in Cincinnati, Ohio. The first American-trained rabbis were ordained at Hebrew Union College in 1883. Their ordination was an important historic event, first, because it proved that the American Jewish community could now train and hire rabbis at home without being forced to look for religious leadership overseas, and second, because of the elaborate dinner that was served on the occasion.

Wealthy Jews in Cincinnati along with the UAHC helped sponsor a celebratory dinner on the occasion of the ordination of HUC's first rabbis. Rabbis, delegates of the UAHC, and Christian leaders were invited to this affair. The first course consisted of littleneck clams on the half shell, a food that was clearly not kosher. While this menu selection did not faze many of the diners who had long since given up the dietary laws, a number of rabbis walked out of the dinner in outrage.

The following courses also included a number of dishes that were *treife* (not kosher). Due to the nature of the menu, this event has become known as the "*treife* banquet." It was never clear how the nonkosher foods came to be part of the dinner, and Wise and his supporters denied any prior knowledge of the menu. Others believe that it was the fault of the caterer or delegates who wished to force the issues of reform.

While the *treife* banquet did not cause the split of American Judaism, it did underscore the differences between those American Jews who wished to continue to reform Judaism and those who took a more traditional approach. These differences became clearer in 1885 when Kaufman Kohler, a leading Reform rabbi, called a meeting of Reform congregations in Pittsburgh. At this meeting, the rabbis outlined their beliefs and put them in writing as guidelines for the Reform movement.

The Pittsburgh Platform, as it came to be called, was a clear break with traditional Judaism. Two of its most significant points were (1) that Reform Jews would only accept as binding the "moral laws" of Judaism, rejecting all rituals and laws that were not adapted to a modern view of the world; and (2) that Jews no longer considered themselves as a nation, but rather as a religion, and as such did not seek to return to Palestine or to recommence sacrificial worship.

In the face of the *treife* banquet and the Pittsburgh Platform, those Jews who were concerned about the state of Judaism in America but were not comfortable with the many changes the reformers were making, split into two camps. One counter-approach was a broad-based inclusive coalition of traditional Jews who sought some changes in Jewish life, but not a total abandonment of Jewish ritual. This group would eventually become the Conservative movement, and in 1887 they established the Jewish Theological Seminary in New York to train more traditional American rabbis. The second counterapproach to Reform Judaism was a

more narrowly defined and exclusive Orthodoxy that believed that the only way to solve the problems of Judaism in America was to return entirely to ritual and tradition. In 1902 this group, represented by sixty European-trained rabbis, formed the *Agudath Ha-Rabbanim* (Union of Orthodox Rabbis, or the "OU"). The OU favored ordaining rabbis at its Rabbi Isaac Elchanan Theological Seminary in New York, which had opened in 1897 and was based on a traditional European yeshiva model.

Thus, by the beginning of the twentieth century, American Judaism had unalterably changed from one united Judaism into smaller divisions, all of whom felt that their way of adapting to the freedoms of American life were the best.

Do Not Separate Yourself from the Community

Once American Jews felt that their own position in society was safe, they began to organize to help Jews in other parts of the world. In this way, they were carrying out centuries-old Jewish values related to *k'lal Yisrael* (the community of Israel). They would also become caught up in many of the social concerns of their day and play an important part, along with their Christian neighbors, in changing the nature of work in America.

In 1840, American Jews organized themselves for the first time to protest what became known as the Damascus Affair. The French consul in Damascus had accused Jews of murdering a Capuchin monk as part of a Jewish ritual. This was the revival of old blood libel charges with which Jews around the world were all too familiar (see chapter 13). The Syrian authorities had arrested a number of Jews and removed approximately sixty children from their homes in order to put pressure on their parents to confess to the crime. While this tragic affair had nothing to do with American Jews directly, they decided to act. The American Jewish community came together to organize protest rallies in many cities and urged President Martin Van Buren to take action on behalf of the Syrian Jews.

The outrage expressed by American diplomats, along with pressure from other Jewish communities in Europe, helped gain the release of the prisoners. This model of community rallies and political pressure would be used by numerous Jewish organizations in seeking help for persecuted Jews worldwide up until the present day. In the early twentieth century, two Jewish organizations were established specifically with the goal of speaking out for Jewish rights. These were the American Jewish Committee (founded in 1906) and the American Jewish Congress (founded in 1917).

American Jews did not just aid their brothers and sisters living abroad, but also helped less fortunate Jews and non-Jews living at home. In the late nineteenth century and into the early twentieth century, millions of immigrants arrived in America, many of whom were Jews. Immigrants had to endure a difficult journey before they arrived in America, and once here they found the streets were not paved in gold. Going through the entry point of Ellis Island and finding a place to live and to work were all tasks made more difficult for people who did not speak the English language. In 1909, the Hebrew Immigrant Aid Society (HIAS) was established to help new Jewish immigrants with such things as food, housing, transportation, and emergency funding.

Many of the Jews helped by HIAS helped settled in an area of New York City known as the Lower East Side. It was a closely packed residential and business district in which immigrants from many parts of the world lived crammed together in small, dark, and unsanitary tenement apartments. As the plight of the lower classes came to the attention of wealthier Americans, individuals, particularly women, and religious organizations determined to improve the lives of poor immigrants while at the same time helping them acclimate to American society.

American Jewish women were very involved in this movement. One was Lillian Wald, a nurse from a German Jewish family in Cincinnati, Ohio. The Henry Street Settlement House, which continues to help immigrant families today, was founded by her. There, she held classes to teach immigrant mothers how to care for their families, fought for laws that would protect children in the workplace, and demanded that playgrounds be built for children.

Immigrants in New York and elsewhere often worked in terrible conditions for long hours, six days a week. Since factory workers were paid very little, whole families, including children, often had to go to work. There were no laws that prevented employers from hiring children, nor were there laws limiting work hours or ensuring safety precautions. On March 25, 1911, 146 sewing machine operators were killed when a fire broke out at the Triangle Shirtwaist Company in New York City. The men and women, primarily of Italian and Jewish background, tried to escape, but found that the doors had been locked by their bosses who did not want them to leave without permission. This tragedy helped focus attention on many labor issues, strengthening the labor unions.

Labor unions had existed before the Triangle fire and were a means for workers to organize and demand better conditions. Many of the early union organizers and supporters were Jewish. The first labor union in America was the American Federation of Labor (AFL), organized in 1886 by Samuel Gompers, an English-born Jew. Four years later, Jews involved in the garment trade in New York formed the International Ladies Garment Workers Union (IGLWU), and David Dubinsky, also a Jew, served as its president from 1932 to 1966.

Another union, the Amalgamated Clothing Workers of America, was founded by Sidney Hillman, a former rabbinical student from Lithuania. One notable Jew who spoke out against the terrible working conditions of factory employees was Louis Brandeis, who would become better known as a justice of the Supreme Court and the person for whom Brandeis University is named.

Jewish Influence on American Culture
During the twentieth century, American Jews began to influence the way Americans viewed themselves and the world through the media of film and music. Without any specific plan, many of the Jews drawn to these industries were to have a large impact on the American psyche.

Early in 1900, a few Jewish businessmen began to notice that a new form of entertainment—silent movies—was attracting a lot of working-class people in their free time. Two businessmen, Adolph Zukor and Carl Laemmle, decided to open theaters of their own. Instead of the small

movie houses where spectators had to stand, which had been the norm, Zukor and Laemmle built beautiful theaters that included seating for moviegoers. The theaters that Zukor and Laemmle built would eventually lead others to construct movie palaces in major cities across the country.

From exhibiting movies, Jews eventually became involved in the distribution and production of films. By the end of World War I, many Jews were involved in the film industry at all levels. Three of the major film studios established between World War I and World War II were owned and operated by Jewish business-men. Louis Mayer and Samuel Goldwyn formed Metro-Goldwyn-Mayer (MGM), which was known for movies with patriotic themes that made viewers feel good about being American.

Warner Bros. was founded by brothers Jack and Harry Warner, and in 1927, Warner Bros. released the first feature film with sound. Interestingly, the movie, *The Jazz Singer,* also had a Jewish theme, telling the story of a cantor's son who becomes a famous vaudeville singer. A third major studio, Columbia Pictures, was also run by a Jew, Harry Cohn. Together, these three movie studios shaped the film industry of their time and a significant part of American culture.

Jews in the film industry were not alone in their influence on American culture; they were joined by coreligionists involved in the music industry. Music has always been an important part of any culture, whether a national anthem, holiday song, or love song. Music becomes part of a person's memories and his or her view of the world. For many people, "White Christmas" is the quintessential Christmas song, yet it was written by Irving Berlin, an American Jew. Berlin was a cantor's son who came to his adopted country at the age of five and got his start in music as a singing waiter in a saloon. He later went on to write many popular tunes including "White Christmas," Easter Parade," and "God Bless America." Other American Jews also influenced popular culture with their American-themed music. George Gershwin wrote jazz and a great folk opera, *Porgy and Bess,* and Aaron Copland's uniquely American classical music and operas included *Appalachian Spring, Billy the Kid,* and *Fanfare for the Common Man.*

Civil Rights Movement

Although the history of Jews in America had not been devoid of anti-Semitism, by the 1960s American Jews felt comfortable and had achieved equal rights. From this perspective, many Jews (and others) began to realize that not all Americans were so fortunate. Though freed from slavery during the Civil War, African-Americans still struggled against racism. In the South, this racism was institutionalized through segregation of schools, businesses, and public transportation. While many southern rabbis were afraid to get involved with civil rights issues because they feared that their involvement would foster anti-Semitism, rabbis and other Jews in the North played a significant role in the Civil Rights Movement.

For some Jews in the North, supporting African-American rights was nothing new. When the National Association of Colored People (NAACP) was founded in 1910, a number of its original members were Jewish, and Jews continued to be involved in the organization. In the 1950s, when issues of African-American rights began to be addressed at a national level, a

number of Jewish organizations got involved. The American Jewish Congress, the Anti-Defamation League, and the American Jewish Congress submitted *amicus curiae* briefs to the U.S. Supreme Court advocating an end to school segregation prior to the 1954 *Brown v. Board of Education* decision.

The Jewish involvement in these early issues of civil rights was based on the universal Jewish experience of persecution and discrimination, and the deeply held belief that no other group should have to suffer these societal ills. Relying on their experience of gaining rights for themselves in America, Jews got involved in many aspects of the Civil Rights Movement. Jews took part in civil rights marches including those to Washington, D.C. in 1963 and from Selma to Montgomery, Alabama in 1965. Approximately thirty Reform and Conservative rabbis participated in the march from Selma to Montgomery during which Rabbi Abraham Joshua Heschel, a professor at Jewish Theological Seminary, helped lead the march arm in arm with the Reverend Dr. Martin Luther King Jr.

Many Jews also went South to help register African-Americans to vote. Michael Schwerner and Andrew Goodman were two such Jewish college students who, along with civil rights worker James Earl Chaney, went to Mississippi to help register African-American voters. They were kidnapped by the Ku Klux Klan and killed by a lynch mob; their bodies were later found by the FBI. By acts of violence such as this, racists in the South hoped to put an end to the efforts of the Civil Rights Movement. However, Jews and African-Americans together persevered to make a difference in American society and history.

Canadian Jews

The first Jews came to Canada approximately one hundred years after Jews first arrived in the United States, and yet there are many similarities between the Jewish experiences in these two countries. Jewish entry into both countries was delayed by feelings of anti-Semitism that were common in both France and Holland at the time. While the few Jews who arrived in New Amsterdam in 1654 were eventually able to get support from Holland to override Peter Stuyvesant's desire to deny them entry on religious grounds, the French forbade anyone who wasn't Catholic to settle in their colony of Canada.

The first Canadian Jews had to wait until 1760 and arrived as part of the British regiment under General Jeffrey Amherst, which captured Montreal and won Canada for the British. This regiment included four Jewish officers, the most prominent of whom was Lieutenant Aaron Hart who eventually settled in Canada with his family. Hart's son, Ezekiel, would play a

The Jewish community in Canada grew very slowly, with most Jews concentrated in Montreal. However, growing anti-Semitism in Russia in the 1880s caused a rise in Jewish emigration and a large increase in the Jewish population of Canadian cities. Many of these Jews were poor, having come to Canada with little or nothing. Canadian Jews, wanting to do something to help their coreligionists, created immigrant aid organizations similar to those in the United States. The Hebrew Philanthropic Society, created by Abraham De Sola, was one such organization. It was formed in order to provide relief to Jews who were poor or sick.

By the beginning of World War I, 100,000 Jews called Canada home. Most still lived

significant role in Canadian government and helped to eliminate the requirement for elected officials to take an oath of office "on my faith as a Christian." More than twenty years after this land-mark change, on June 5, 1832, Canadian Jews were extended full political rights, twenty-five years before Jews in England.

Unlike in the United States, very few Canadian Jews were merchants or landowners; rather, most made a living by trading furs or serving in the British army. This meant that early Jewish settlers were often scattered at great distances from each other. But as soon as a few Jews settled close together, they sought to develop a community with a synagogue at its center. In 1768, the Jews of Montreal built Shearith Israel Spanish and Portuguese Synagogue, the first synagogue in all Canada. Like the first synagogue in the United States, it followed Sephardic traditions, since most of its members could trace their lineage back to Spain or its colonies.
in large cities like Montreal and Toronto. By this time, many Canadian Jews owned stores and worked in the textile industry, helping to build the Canadian economy along the way. As the Jewish community grew and prospered in the 20th century, it built organizations to provide economic, social, and religious services. In 1919, the Canadian Jewish Congress was formed to represent the entire Jewish community of Canada, and, of course, to help fellow Jews who had immigrated to the country.

Canada, like the United States, saw a rise in anti-Semitism during the years between the World Wars. This anti-Semitism led to immigration restrictions, which in turn made it even more difficult for Jewish refugees fleeing the Holocaust to find a safe haven anywhere in North America.

As one civil servant put it when asked how many Jews Canada would take after World War II, "none is too many." Despite such feelings, Canada did relax its immigration restrictions after the war, and many Holocaust survivors made new lives for themselves within its borders.

By the end of the 20th century and the beginning of the 21st century, Canada (with 350,000 Jews) could claim the title of the fourth largest Jewish community in the world. Jews of many different religious movements and national origins live together, creating vibrant Jewish communities throughout Canada.

Conclusion
For over 350 years, Jews have lived in America and made it their home. The relationship between America and the Jewish people has been a unique one in world history and one that has served both parties well. By seeking and securing equal rights for themselves, Jews have opened the door for other minority groups to do the same. By providing religious freedom, the United States has given Jews the opportunity not only to practice their religion, but Judaism in any form to which they are attracted. By removing social and political barriers, America has given Jews the opportunity to enter any field or business on an equal footing with all other Americans. This openness in turn has provided America with cutting-edge science discoveries, business opportunities, and great entertainers.

The foundation laid by our ancestors has given us all something to build upon, and we continue to walk in their footsteps when we work for the betterment of all citizens, take advantage of the opportunities afforded us, and continue to preserve and protect our Jewish faith and culture.

CONNECTING TO OUR TRADITION
The Jews who settled in the Northeast brought with them the values that had allowed generations of Jews to survive throughout Europe. In America, these values found new outlets and sometimes helped shape the growth of America. One of these values was helping others, both within and outside the Jewish community. Jewish involvement in labor unions and the Civil Rights Movement grew out of this important philosophy.

TIMELINE (all dates are CE)

1654 Twenty-three Jews from Recife, Brazil, arrive in New Amsterdam

1686 British grant freedom of religion to those living in the British colonies

1730 Synagogue opens on Mill Street in New York

1760 First Jews arrive in Canada with the British Army

1825 Dedication of Ararat colony on Grand Island in New York

1832 Canada extends full political rights to Jews

1838 Rebecca Gratz, of Philadelphia, organizes the first Jewish Sunday school

1840 American Jews organize to protest the Damascus Affair

1873 Union of American Hebrew Congregations is formed

1875

Hebrew Union College is founded

1886

Jewish Theological School is
founded

1897

Yeshiva University is founded

1906

American Jewish Committee is
founded

1911

Triangle Shirtwaist Company fire
in New York

1917

American Jewish Congress is
founded

1919

Canadian Jewish Congress
founded

1922

Jewish Institute of Religion is
founded

1927

The Jazz Singer is the first feature-
length film with sound

IMPORTANT TERMS
Sephardic
Ashkenazic
Revolutionary War
Tariff
Haskamot
Army Chaplain

Names, Places, and Events

Sainte Catherine	*Agudath Ha-Rabbanim*
Asser Levy	Damascus Affair
Hart Jacobs	Adolph Zukor
Haym Solomon	Carl Laemmle
Congregation	Louis Mayer
Shearith Israel	Jack and Harry
Rebecca Gratz	Warner
Mordechai Manuel	
Noah	

Ararat	Harry Cohn
Isaac Mayer Wise	Irving Berlin
Treife banquet	George Gershwin
Jew Bill	Aaron Copland
Pittsburgh Platform	General Jeffrey Amherst
Dutch West India	Lieutenant Aaron Hart
Company	Ezekiel Hart
Pyke's Catechism	Canadian Jewish Congress
Hebrew Union	Abraham De Sola
College	Hebrew Philanthropic
Jewish Theological	Society
Seminary	Union of American
	Hebrew Congregations

DID YOU KNOW?
- In 1776, Hart Jacobs, a Jewish soldier in the Continental army, petitioned for and was granted an excuse from fighting on Friday nights because it was Shabbat.
- On July 4, 1788, at a parade in Philadelphia marking the ratification of the U.S. Constitution, kosher food was served at a separate refreshment table for members of the Jewish community.
- The U.S. Constitution granted Jews full citizenship for the first time since the Roman emperor Caracalla had done so in 212 CE.
- Monticello, the home of Thomas Jefferson and now a national landmark, was purchased and preserved by Uriah Phillips Levy, a Jewish naval officer who fought in the War of 1812.
- Two Jewish teenagers, Jerome Siegel and Joe Shuster, created the *Superman* comic strip in 1939.

ACTIVITIES
Character Interview (E, S)
Invite someone to come to the classroom to play the part of an American Jewish historical figure, such as Rebecca Gratz or Asser Levy. (Make sure students are familiar with the appropriate period of history prior to the visit.) Ask students to

focus their questions on such issues as how being an American affected his or her life or Judaism, or how he or she helped shape American history as a Jew. Make sure to have students write letters to the character thanking him or her for coming to visit, and saying what they found most interesting about the character's experience.

Document Reading (S, A)

As an introduction to this activity: (1) Discuss why synagogues have by-laws and what types of rules and regulations might be included. (2) Explain that after the Revolutionary War, many synagogues were reestablished and wrote new rules and regulations.

For this activity, break the class into small groups and provide students with a copy of the Declaration of Synagogue Rights from 1790 and a copy of the Declaration of Independence. Each group should also receive a list of questions about the documents they are examining. Some questions for the Declaration of Synagogue Rights from 1790 might include: (1) What kind of document is this? (2) According to this document what rights do members of the synagogue have? (3) How might these rights have differed from previous synagogue rules?

After examining the Declaration of Synagogue Rights, ask the students to examine the Declaration of Independence. Some questions for this examination might include: (1) What language is similar between the Declaration of Independence and the Declaration of Synagogue Rights? (2) What language is different? (3) Based on these two documents, how do you think the Jewish community felt about America becoming an independent country? (4) How did changes in American history influence the Jewish community?

Wax Museum (E, S)

Have students research famous American Jews from different historical periods and different careers. Research can focus on how being Jewish influenced what these famous Americans did and/or how they influenced American history and culture. In order to share their research, each student will write a short script narrating the biography of the famous American they researched. At a special program, the students will dress up as their research subject and become an exhibit at a "wax museum." As parents or students from other grades tour the exhibit, the students will present their script.

Alphabet Soup Game (E, S)

To introduce or review the many different Jewish organizations that were created to help the Jewish community, have your class play the Alphabet Soup Game. *Making the Game:* Have the students design a board game on a piece of poster board or inside a file folder. The board should have a track that goes around the perimeter of the poster board or folder. For a little variety, the board can have some twists in it, like a Candyland game board. At irregular intervals, squares on the board should be marked "Jewish Organizations." The students will also make game cards with eight or more spaces on them and game pieces with the names of Jewish organizations, for example, American Jewish Congress, HIAS, Anti-Defamation League, and short descriptions of those organizations.

Playing the Game: Each player or team is given a game marker and a game card. Students place their markers on the "Alphabet Soup" square, which is the start of the game. They roll a die to see how many squares they will move their markers. When a player lands on a "Jewish Organizations" square, he or she drawsa game piece from the pile in the center of the board and places it on the game card. The object of the game is to collect all four types of institutions and match them with the appropriate descriptions by placing them on the game card.

Jewish Jeopardy (E, S)
This game can be used to review information about any period of American Jewish history.

Buy a large piece of poster board and several library card pockets. Glue the library pockets onto the board in rows of five across and five down. Create (or have your students create) five different categories for your game with several questions written on index cards for each category. If reviewing the whole chapter, categories might include the American Revolution, the Civil War, and Jews and Entertainment. Narrower categories could be designed if using the game to review a particular time period within American Jewish history.

RESOURCES
Books and Articles
Abella, Irving and Harold Troper. *None is Too Many: Canada and the Jews of Europe, 1933–1948*. New York: Random House, 1983.

Finkelstein, Norman H. *Heeding the Call: Jewish Voices in America's Civil Rights Struggle*. Philadelphia: Jewish Publication Society, 1997.

Isaacs, Ronald H., and Kerry M. Olitzky. *Critical Documents of Jewish History*. Northvale, NJ: Jason Aronson, 1995.

Leiman, Sondra. *America: The Jewish Experience*. New York: UAHC Press, 1994.

Libo, Kenneth, and Irving Howe. *We Lived There Too*. New York: St. Martin's Press/Marek, 1984.

Marcus, Jacob R. *The American Jewish Woman: A Documentary History*. New York: Ktav, 1981.

Rosenberg, Roy A. *Everything You Need to Know About America's Jews and Their History*. New York: Plume, 1997.

Rosenberg, Shelley Kapnek. *Challenge and Change: History of the Jews in America*. Springfield, NJ: Behrman House, 2004.

Sarna, Jonathan D. *American Judaism: A History*. New Haven, CT: Yale University Press, 2004.

Internet
Visit www.behrmanhouse.com/booklinks for links to Web sites that offer additional resources for this chapter.

CHAPTER TWENTY-SEVEN

SOUTHERN JEWS

WHAT'S THE BIG IDEA?
Acculturation

Judaism and the Jewish people have survived through centuries of change, but they have not remained the same. At different times, and in different places, Jews have adapted to the cultures within which they found themselves. Jews in the American South had the opportunity to participate in a relatively open society. In turn, they adapted some of the ideas they found in the surrounding Christian culture and shared their skills with the people in their new home. Some of these adaptations would profoundly affect American Judaism and help lead to changes in the American South.

BACKGROUND INFORMATION

Although the charters of a number of southern colonies prohibited the settlement of Jews, a few Jews had settled in the South as early as the late seventeenth century. The largest group of Jews to make their home in the South prior to the Revolutionary War was a community of forty-one German and Spanish-Portuguese immigrants who arrived in Savannah in 1733.

Slowly, others followed them from Europe, the Caribbean, and the northern colonies. Many were professionals or merchants who settled in growing port cities, and as in other parts of America, began establishing Jewish communities with synagogues, Jewish cemeteries, and *mikva'ot* (ritual baths). Jews helped establish trade with the North and

Europe, and some, such as the Charleston merchant Abraham Seixas, were involved in the slave trade, which would become one of the distinguishing characteristics of antebellum southern life. By 1800, Charleston would have the largest Jewish population of any American city, with one out of every fifteen Charlestonians being Jewish.

However, not all Jews lived in the cities of the South. The great majority of Jews came South as peddlers and merchants. Living in small towns or traveling from farm to farm or plantation to plantation, their experience was very different from that of Jews living in Charleston or Savannah. Being few and far between, these Jews might rarely see another Jew or have access to a Jewish community with a synagogue, *mohel* (ritual circumciser), or Kosher butcher. Engaged in commerce with their Christian neighbors, some Jews felt it necessary to adapt their Jewish traditions to a Christian society by conducting business on Saturday or eating nonkosher foods.

While generally allowed to pursue their livelihood in cities or small towns, own land, and sometimes hold office, many Jews in the South continued to feel like outsiders in an almost exclusively Christian environment. Perhaps for this reason, many Jews adapted outwardly to prevailing customs and views, and sometimes even adapted their Jewish practices along the way. At the same time they took pains to keep from assimilating completely into the larger culture.

The Beginnings of Reform Judaism in America

In 1824, forty-seven Charleston Jews, led by Isaac Harby, petitioned the leaders of Kahal Kadosh (K-K) Beth Elohim for major changes in the Shabbat service. They wanted to use English, add new prayers that reflected contemporary American life, and shorten the service. In short, they wanted their worship services to be more like those they saw at the surrounding Protestant churches.

When the leaders of the synagogue refused to consider the petition, the reformers left K-K Beth Elohim and established the Reformed Society of Israelites for Promoting the True Principles of Judaism According to Its Purity and Spirit. This organization existed for approximately ten years before most of its members drifted away.

In 1838, the issue of reform was revisited when a fire destroyed K-K Beth Elohim and the congregation had to consider rebuilding. Thirty-eight members of the synagogue petitioned for the inclusion of an organ in the new building. This idea reflected a major break with Jewish tradition, which prohibited the playing of musical instruments on Shabbat for fear that one might have to repair an instrument.

The Great Organ Controversy, as it came to be known, split the congregation. When the issue was finally brought to a general meeting, the members voted to install an organ in the new building. Penina Moise, a member of the congregation and an early Jewish American poet, wrote the first hymn played at the dedication ceremony. Her hymns, based on the psalms, were similar to those sung at local churches and were collected in the first Jewish book of hymns published in America. These changes from Orthodox *minhag* (tradition) helped open the way for other changes, and eventually helped lead to the development of the Reform movement in America.

The Civil War

While Jews in the South may have been divided over how much Jewish practice should be adapted in their new homeland, that very home was soon to be divided along geographical, philosophical, and economic lines in the Civil War. Jews would take sides in this war, much as their Christian neighbors would—sides that divided families and friends. Yet, for many Jews in the South, the Civil War would also be a reminder that however much they had adapted to the southern way of life, they were still outsiders.

In 1862, the Jews of the South faced one of the most sweeping anti-Jewish orders in American history (General Order Number 11) when General Ulysses S. Grant expelled all Jews from Kentucky, Tennessee, and Mississippi. Grant, angered by the smuggling of cotton from these areas into the North by a few Jewish traders and others, blamed the entire Jewish community in this region for the problem.

Some Jewish traders had to walk many miles to evacuate the area. In other areas, long-term residents were given just twenty-four hours to leave. The Jewish community in the North organized protest rallies and sent telegrams to President Lincoln condemning Grant's order. Barely a month after issuing General Order No. 11, General Grant revoked it at President Lincoln's insistence and Jewish families were able to return to their homes.

The Jews affected by General Order Number 11 were not the only ones to become scapegoats during the Civil War. In 1861, Confederate president Jefferson Davis appointed Judah Benjamin, a southern lawyer and senator, to be attorney general of the Confederacy. Benjamin also later served as secretary of war and secretary of state. Not only was Judah Benjamin the first Jew to hold a cabinet-level office in an American government, but also the only Confederate Cabinet member who did not own slaves.

As the Confederacy took a beating because it did not have the resources necessary to win against the Union, Davis allowed Roanoke Island to fall into Union hands. Benjamin took the blame and resigned. Anti-Semitism was an unpleasant fact—North and South—during the Civil War years, and Benjamin was falsely defamed as having weakened the Confederacy by transferring its funds to a personal bank account in Europe.

The Jew Store

Jews in the South not only helped change the image of Judaism in America, but also helped make a mark on small-town life. Graduating from a peddler's pack to a store of their own, many Jewish men and their families spread out across the South setting up dry goods stores that sold work clothes and school clothes, sheets and towels, yard goods and notions. While these stores might have names that reflected who their owners were, such as Bronson's Low-Priced Store, such an establishment was often referred to by other members of the community as "the Jew Store."

The Jews who established such businesses were often the first Jews to move to a small town. They might serve as the first

introduction many southerners had to Jews at all. While not always given a warm welcome, many store owners were eventually accepted into the community, in part because of the importance of what their store provided to the town's residents.

In some cases, the Jew Store also tested cultural boundaries. By providing low-cost general stores, the Jewish proprietor might market not just to working-class whites, but also to the poor black residents of the town. A few of these businesses went as far as employing black clerks to wait on customers.

As much as the town might need the business and goods provided by the Jew Store, they also might find they needed the owner. In keeping with the Jewish tradition of supporting one's community, Jewish merchants often came to the aid of their towns during hard times. Whether it was finding money to keep an important business open during the Depression or raising money for community chest projects, small southern towns often found they could depend on their Jewish merchants.

Holding an unusual place in society, that of a white businessman but still outside the Protestant mainstream, Jewish merchants could also sometimes politically unite the white and black segments of the community behind important issues. For example, in 1950, "Mutt" Evans, a Jewish merchant in Durham, North Carolina, was asked to run for mayor by the Citizens for Good Government Committee because he was the only person all political factions could agree on. Both the black and white communities trusted him. Despite some anti-Semitic propaganda during the campaign, Evans was eventually elected mayor of Durham.

Trial and Lynching of Leo Frank

Even as Jews in the South were outwardly adapting to prevailing customs and views, they knew that just under the surface of many of their neighbors was a deep-harbored anti-Semitism that at the least kept them at arm's length, and at the worst could have deadly consequences.

In 1913, Leo Frank was convicted of murdering Mary Phagan, a thirteen-year-old employee of the Atlanta pencil factory that Frank managed. The young girl had picked up her wages from Frank on the morning of April 26 and never returned home. Her body was later discovered in the factory basement, and Frank had been the last one to see her alive. Rumors that Mary had been sexually assaulted further inflamed the case. False testimony by factory workers and important evidence that was hidden by Georgia's solicitor general helped further build a case against Leo Frank.

In August 1913, the jury found Frank guilty of murder and the judge sentenced Frank to death despite the fact that Frank had clearly not been given due process in his trial. Georgia's governor, after reviewing evidence and letters, commuted Frank's sentence to life imprisonment. Later that same month, a group of twenty-five men stormed the prison, kidnapped Frank, and hanged him from a tree in Mary Phagan's hometown of Marietta, Georgia. "In 1986, the Georgia Board of Pardons and Paroles finally granted Leo Frank a posthumous pardon, not because they thought him innocent, but because his lynching deprived him of his right to further appeal."

CONNECTING TO OUR TRADITION

Throughout the centuries, Judaism has evolved to deal with new situations. This was equally true for Jews in the American South. From the first Jews who settled in the South in the seventeenth century through the merchants of the early twentieth century, Southern Jews have tried to adapt to the surrounding culture in their lifestyle and traditions. These adaptations provided a new model for American Judaism and unique types of businesses. Despite these adaptations, Southern Jews were not truly able to assimilate until quite recent times because of an underlying anti-Semitism that often coexisted with other forms of prejudice in many southern communities.

IMPORTANT TERMS
Reform
Minhag
Jew Store
Antebellum South
General Order Number 11
Mikveh, mikva'ot

Names, Places, and Events
The Great Organ Controversy
Isaac Harby
Abraham Seixas
Leo Frank
Judah Benjamin
Penina Moise

DISCUSSION QUESTIONS
- What is the difference between adaptation and assimilation? Is one better than the other? Why or why not?
- How were Jews influenced by the white southern Christian culture around them?
- How did Jews have an impact on the towns and cities where they lived?
- (If you have also studied the Dreyfus trial) What are the similarities or differences between the Dreyfus trial and what happened to Judah Benjamin? How do the different events reflect the mood and culture of the communities in which

the Jews of the times lived? How do events such as these impact the ability of Jews to adapt or assimilate?

- Have Jews influenced the history or culture of your community? How have Jews in your community adapted to the surrounding culture?

ACTIVITIES

Game: Jewish Jeopardy (E, S)
Jewish Jeopardy is a standard and easily manipulated game that can used for many units of study in endless ways.

Buy a large piece of poster board and several library card pockets (or cut off the tops of invitation-size envelopes). Glue the library pockets onto the board in rows of five across and five down. Create (or have your students create) five different categories for your game with several questions written on index cards for each category.

For example, if this game is "Jewish Life in the South," the categories could be Name That Person (with answers like "The name of the Jewish senator who later went on to be the secretary of war of the Confederacy"), Jewish Geography ("The city in which you would have found the first organ placed in a Jewish synagogue"), Events ("General Order Number 11 forced Jews in certain southern states to do this").

Community Research (S, A)
If your institution is located in the southern United States, have your students research the development of the Jewish community in your town or city. You and your students might visit local landmarks (the first synagogue in your town, the Jewish cemetery), interview older members of the community and tape the interviews to begin an oral history archive,

and/or do research at a historical society. The students can use the information gathered from this research to compare and contrast their community to what they have learned about the Jewish experience in the South. This information can be shared with parents and/or other classes through skits or an exhibit.

Biography (E, S)
Assign each student to research an important historical figure, for example, Judah Benjamin or Penina Moise, dress up as his or her character, and address the class. Provide your class with research questions to get them started, such as: How did this person adapt to living in the South? What kind of impact did he or she have on the community? Do you think this person adapted his or her Judaism or assimilated? Would you nominate this person into a Jewish Heroes Hall of Fame? Why or why not?

Debate: The Great Organ Controversy (S, A)
Have the students debate whether K-K Beth Elohim should introduce an organ and organ music into its new building. Divide the students into small groups. Each group represents different parts of the congregation who were for or against the organ, or had mixed feelings. Give each group background information about K-K Beth Elohim and the organ contro-versy. Have the students study the material and put together their arguments. Have a mock debate. Appoint someone to be the president and someone to be the secretary of the congregation to moderate and record the debate. At the end of the debate, share with the class what actually happened at K-K Beth Elohim.

DID YOU KNOW?

The first synagogue in America to install an organ was in Charleston, South Carolina.

TIMELINE (all dates are CE)

1697

Four Jews made citizens of South Carolina

1733

James Oglethorpe founds colony at Savannah, Georgia; receives forty-one Jewish settlers

1749

K-K Beth Elohim established in Charleston, South Carolina; third-oldest synagogue in America

1790

George Washington replies to letters of congratulations from Jews of Charleston, South Carolina, and Richmond, Virginia

1824

Society of Reformed Israelites established in Charleston, South Carolina

1838

The first synagogue in America installs an organ

1913

Trial and lynching of Leo Frank

RESOURCES
Books and Articles

Bauman, Mark K. *The Southerner as American: Jewish Style.* Cincinnati, OH: American Jewish Archives, 1996.

Brilliant, Richard. *Facing the New World: Jewish Portraits in Colonial and Federal America.* New York: Jewish Museum, 1997.

Evans, Eli. *Judah P. Benjamin: The Jewish Confederate.* New York: Free Press, 1988.

Evans, Eli. *The Provincials.* New York: Free Press Paperbacks, 1997.

Libo, Kenneth, and Irving Howe. *We Lived There Too.* New York: St. Martin's Press/Marek, 1984.

Matas, Carol. *The War Within: A Novel of the Civil War.* New York: Simon & Schuster, 2001.

Suberman, Stella. *The Jew Store.* Chapel Hill, NC: Algonquin Books, 1998.

Internet

Visit www.behrmanhouse.com/booklinks for links to Web sites that offer additional resources for this chapter.

CHAPTER TWENTY-EIGHT
JEWS OF THE WEST

WHAT'S THE BIG IDEA?
Building Community

Throughout our history, Jews have moved from place to place. In the mid-nineteenth century, many American Jews chose to leave Jewish centers on the East Coast to seek a new life in the Far West. While this move differed from many forced moves in our past, one thing remained the same, the need for community. The Jews who moved to the Far West sought out other Jews and established communal institutions that would support a Jewish way of life.

BACKGROUND INFORMATION

In the mid-nineteenth century, American Jews in the East and South began to move to the Far West along with thousands of other Americans. For these Jews, the move was not forced but chosen. American Jews sought to improve their wealth, their health, or their Jewish character by moving to an area of America where opportunities abounded.

The California Gold Rush attracted individuals who were eager to get rich quickly. Jews joined the gold rush as prospectors and as merchants serving them. Levi Strauss, an enterprising young clothing manufacturer, was one of these merchants. He moved to San Francisco in 1853, began to sell denim overalls, and the rest—as they say—is history.

As they had done in countless other places throughout their history, Jews started new communities by establishing

Jewish organizations. The challenge in the West was that often very few Jews lived in any given town or city. Whereas in other times and places Jews relocated as a large group, in the mid-nineteenth century the Jews moving westward often went as individuals or in small family units.

As a community of Jews grew, the types of Jewish institutions its members were able to build changed. In very small towns or cities lacking a substantial Jewish population, Jews would still try to hold High Holy Day services in a rented hall, even if they did nothing else during the year.

In communities where there were one hundred or more Jews, organizations such as cemeteries and benevolent societies would be established first, in addition to small prayer groups, or *minyanim*. These organizations helped support Jewish life through worship and culture, and often assisted the people themselves when their plans of fame and fortune fell through.

The Far West offered other opportunities besides great wealth. The dry air and mountain climate of places like Denver, Colorado, were thought to be beneficial to one's health, particularly to those suffering from tuberculosis and other respiratory illnesses. The wide-open spaces offered pioneers the opportunity to buy land and become farmers, supporting themselves through the honest work of their own hands.

Such opportunities also gave rise to two unique types of organizations: the Jewish hospital and the Jewish agricultural colony.

The Scourge of Tuberculosis

Tuberculosis prevailed in the overcrowded, unsanitary environment of many of the East Coast's growing cities. It was believed that dry, fresh air could cure tuberculosis, so doctors often sent patients out west to cities like Denver to "take the cure." Jewish patients may have hesitated at first to leave their families and communities to travel into the unknown territory of the "Wild West."

The Jewish community of Denver soon solved this problem by establishing two Jewish tuberculosis hospitals and other support organizations. One of these hospitals offered kosher food to its patients, and both provided other services (such as High Holy Day worship) that Jews would expect, as well as the company and comfort of other Jewish patients and doctors. Both hospitals were supported by the Jewish community, allowing patients with little money to come to Denver.

These hospitals also treated non-Jews; in fact, the first patient who entered National Jewish Hospital in 1899 was a non-Jewish tuberculosis patient from Minneapolis. These hospitals, in turn, enhanced the growth of the Denver Jewish community since many of the patients remained in Denver once they recovered.

Back to the Land

It wasn't only the physical health of its people that concerned the Jewish community, but also their condition and safety. In the mid-nineteenth century, a growing group of Jews abroad and in America believed that the only way for Jews to leave oppression behind was for them to get back to the land. The thought was that such an opportunity would give rise to a new kind of Jew (remember, most governments in Europe forbade Jews to own land, and so the ability to own and to farm land was a totally new possibility). Jews who were inclined to homestead could then develop skills that could be used to rebuild a Jewish homeland in Palestine as well.

Between 1811 and 1915, forty Jewish agricultural colonies were founded in the United States as part of an international Back to the Soil movement. These colonies sought to remedy the problems of overcrowding and disease that Jews faced in the major port cities on the East Coast, particularly New York. Often these groups were sponsored by Jewish organizations in the eastern United States as a way to help fellow Jews migrating out west, where there was plenty of land to go around.

The Clarion Colony, founded in 1911 about a hundred miles away from Salt Lake City, Utah, was one of these enterprises. The founder, Benjamin Brown, along with twelve founding families, each invested three thousand dollars in the colony. The money, a substantial amount in the early twentieth century, was used to purchase land, equipment, and animals, and the members of the community were expected to build their own houses, school, and farm buildings and to work the land.

Unfortunately, the colony closed down in 1915 when the members were unable to bounce back from hardships including crop damage due to storms and the death of some of the original members. Like the Clarion Colony, many Back to the Soil communities failed because the colonists lacked farming skills, were not prepared for the hardships of farming, and could not support themselves financially.

Conclusion

The growth of the American Far West led to the establishment of many new Jewish communities, which gave rise to the development of many Jewish communal organizations. Some of these institutions were unique to the special needs and challenges faced by the Jews who moved west, while others could be found in any Jewish community in America or abroad.

CONNECTING TO OUR TRADITION

The development of Jewish communities in the Far West demonstrates the importance of the following key Jewish values:

"All Jews are responsible for each other." —Talmud, Sanhedrin 27b
The Jewish community in Denver felt an obligation to help poorer Jews when they established two Jewish tuberculosis hospitals. This in turn brought many new Jews to the area.

"Do not separate yourself from the community."—Pirkei Avot 2:5
This Mishnaic quote by Hillel emphasizes the importance of being part of a community. Wherever Jews went in the

Far West, they sought to establish and participate in Jewish communities.

"If I am only for myself, who will be for me?"—Pirkei Avot 1:14
Hillel again emphasizes the need for Jews to not only look out for themselves, but also look out for others. While some of the organizations established by the Jewish community, such as the Hebrew Benevolent Society, only helped Jews, other institutions, such as the tuberculosis hospitals in Denver, benefited people of all backgrounds.

IMPORTANT TERMS
Back to the Soil movement
Hebrew Benevolent Society
Minyan

Names, Places, and Events
California Gold Rush
Clarion Colony
Jewish Consumptives Relief Society
National Jewish Hospital
Levi Strauss

DISCUSSION QUESTIONS
Have students interview each other, teachers in the school, or the principal, about issues related to relocating or about Jewish communities, using some of the following questions:

Questions related to relocating:
* Have you ever had to move?
* Have you ever had to leave your friends, family, and home to go some place else?
* How did it feel?
* What were some of the reasons that made you choose to move?
* What did you look for in your new community?

Questions related to Jewish communities:

- What kinds of Jewish organizations are in your community?
- How do these organizations help support the community?
- If you were starting a new Jewish community, what organizations would you start first? Why?
- Why did agricultural collectives in Israel thrive, but those in the American West did not?

ACTIVITIES

Name That Institution (E, S)

Making the Game: Have the students design a board game on a piece of poster board or inside a file folder. The board should have a track that goes around the perimeter of the poster board or folder. For a little variety, the board can have some twists in it, like a Candyland game board.

At irregular intervals, squares on the board should be marked "Jewish Institutions of the Far West." The students will also make game cards with eight spaces on them and game pieces with the names of Jewish organizations, for example, synagogue, Hebrew school, Hebrew Benevolent Society, and short descriptions of those organizations.

Playing the Game: Each player or team is given a game marker and a game card. Students place their markers on the "Welcome to the West" square, which is the start of the game. They roll a die to see how many squares they will move their markers. When a player lands on a "Jewish Institutions of the Far West" square, he or she draws a game piece from the pile in the center of the board and places it on his or her game card. The object of the game is to collect all four types of institutions and match

them with the appropriate descriptions by placing them on the game card.

Time Travel (E, S)

In order to have students compare and contrast the types of Jewish organizations found in small, medium, and large communities in the Far West, invite the class to travel back in time. They will visit three different Jewish communities in the Far West: a small mining town, a medium-size town, and the large city of San Francisco.

For this activity the students will rotate through three learning centers, each representing one of the communities. At each learning center, they will examine pictures of institutions in the community and read newspaper articles, letters, or journals. Each student will have a Time Travel passport that will be stamped at each center when he or she has completed the activity there.

When the groups are done, the activity will end with a short discussion and debriefing. Some discussion questions might include: What were some Jewish institutions found in the Far West? What kinds of services did they provide to members of the Jewish community? Which could be found in any size community? Which could only be found in large cities? Why do you think there was a difference between the kinds of institutions found in small towns and large cities?

Character Interview (E, S)

Have a person come to the classroom to play the part of a Jew who has moved west to go to a tuberculosis hospital. This person will talk about his or her experience and the students will also have a chance to ask questions. After the interview, have the students write letters to the character thanking him or her for coming to visit, hoping he or she feels better, and saying what they found most interesting about the character's experience.

Biography (E, S)

Assign each student to research an important figure from the time period, for example, Levi Strauss, dress up as their character, and address the class. Offer research questions such as: What brought this person to the Far West? What kind of contribution did he or she make to the Jewish community? To the larger community? What can we learn about being part of a Jewish community from this person? Would you nominate this person into a Jewish Heroes Hall of Fame?

Clarion Colony Debate (S, A)

Students imagine they are living in the Clarion Colony in 1915, just before its failure. Hold a debate to determine whether the colony should continue or not. Divide the students into small groups, each representing a separate family living in the Clarion Colony.

Give each group background information about the Clarion Colony and about their family. Have the students study the material and prepare their argument for or against continuing the colony. Have a mock debate with the teacher (or in older groups, a student) acting as head of the colony who calls the meeting to order and moderates the discussion. At the end of the debate, share with the class what actually happened at the Clarion Colony. (This activity would also be good for family education.)

How to Succeed in Business (E, S)

Log on to the Levi Strauss Co. Web site. Learn about Levi Strauss's original store in San Francisco. What was life like for Levi Strauss when he started the business? How did Levi Strauss and his company emulate Jewish values of social responsibility? How many pairs of jeans per year does the Levi Strauss Company sell today?

DID YOU KNOW?

- Today, National Jewish Medical and Research Center in Denver, Colorado is the number one respiratory hospital in the nation.
- The Jewish cemetery with the highest elevation in the United States is located in Leadville, Colorado. Founded in the 1880s, the Hebrew Cemetery is located at 10,350 feet above sea level.

TIMELINE (all dates are CE)

1848
    Beginning of the California Gold Rush

1853
    Levi Straus moves to San Francisco

1893
    Completion of the National Jewish Hospital for consumptives

1911
    Establishment of the Clarion Colony in Utah

1915
    Clarion Colony closed by the State of Utah

RESOURCES
Books and Articles

Levinson, Robert E. *The Jews of the California Gold Rush*. Berkeley, CA: Judah L. Magnes Museum, 1994.

Libo, Kenneth, and Irving Howe. *We Lived There Too*. New York: St. Martin's Press/Marek, 1984.

Rischin, Moses, and John Livingston, eds. *Jews of the American West*. Detroit, MI: Wayne State University Press, 1991.

Rochlin, Harriet, and Fred Rochlin. *Pioneer Jews: A New Life in the Far West*. Boston: Mariner Books, 1986.

Uchill, Ida Libert. *Pioneers, Peddlers, and Tsadikim: The Story of the Jews in Colorado*. Denver: University Press of Colorado, 2000.

Wenner, Anita. *A Curriculum Guide: Early History of Jews of Colorado*. Denver: Central Agency for Jewish Education and Rocky Mountain Jewish Historical Society, 1998.

Internet
Visit www.behrmanhouse.com/booklinks for links to Web sites that offer additional resources for this chapter.

CHAPTER TWENTY-NINE

JEWISH RELIGIOUS LIFE IN TWENTIETH-CENTURY AMERICA

WHAT'S THE BIG IDEA?
Jewish Culture and Thought

Despite repeated devastation to Jewish communities over the centuries, a creative, rich Jewish culture and religious life have always continued to flourish. The flexible and resilient nature of that religious system has enabled Jews to successfully respond to and thrive in new environments and circumstances. America in the twentieth century provided the perfect environment for Jews to explore new ways of expressing themselves Jewishly.

BACKGROUND INFORMATION

As Jews have come to feel part of American society, they have turned their energy to creating new ways to express themselves culturally and religiously. While the foundation for some of these changes had been laid earlier, much of this growth took place in the second half of the twentieth century as Americans were experiencing a new spiritual revival and sense of ethnic pride.

Reconstructionism

In 1889, Mordechai Kaplan came from Lithuania to America with his family. This young man would eventually have a significant impact on American Judaism. Ordained at the Conservative Jewish Theological Seminary, Kaplan was influenced by what he saw happening in the Jewish community between World War I and World War II: Jews were becoming increasingly assimilated, moving away from Jewish ritual, and

becoming more secular. In 1934, while still teaching at JTS, Rabbi Kaplan wrote *Judaism as a Civilization,* which set forth the philosophy that later evolved into Reconstructionism. The main tenet of this philosophy places Jewish peoplehood at the center of Judaism. It was extremely controversial for four reasons: (1) it redefined God in terms of process (that is, it was willing to consider the idea that God is not an actual being); (2) it negated the idea of Jewish chosenness; (3) any beliefs that were in conflict with what people knew to be true or right could be eliminated; and (4) there was a willingness to alter or discard *mitzvot.*[1]

Reconstructionism continued as an offshoot of the Conservative movement through much of the twentieth century. In 1969, the Reconstructionist Rabbinical College opened in Philadelphia. With the establishment of its own institution to train rabbis according to its own philosophy, Reconstructionism became a fourth wing of American Judaism. By this time, Reconstructionist Judaism's impact could also be seen elsewhere as other movements adopted the ideas of Judaism as a civilization with its own distinctive art, music and culture, and the synagogue center where people could meet not just for religious life but for many different activities.

The Reconstructionist movement has also led the way in creating opportunities for

---

[1] Jonathan Sarna, *American Judaism: A History*, New Haven, CT: Yale University Press, 2004, p. 245.

all Jews to become full participants in the community. In 1922, Judith Kaplan, daughter of Mordechai Kaplan, was the first girl to have a bat mitzvah. With this ceremony, Kaplan introduced the idea, which would later become part of Reconstructionism, that women should have a more important role in Jewish worship. Today, girls and women in many Jewish communities become *b'not mitzvah*. Seventy-one years later, in 1993, the Reconstructionist movement made another landmark decision when they were the first in Judaism to declare homosexual and heterosexual lifestyles equal as "ways of being which offer fulfillment."[2]

By the beginning of the twenty-first century, the Reconstructionist movement included 103 affiliate congregations with sixteen thousand households. While these numbers make the movement the smallest, it provides an alternative for many American Jews.

Habad

While the period after World War II saw many American Jews assimilating and looking for a more secular way to experience their Judaism, there was also a resurgence of Orthodox Judaism in America. With the destruction of much of the Eastern European Jewish community during World War II, many Hasidic Jews, survivors of the Holocaust, immigrated to America during the postwar period. This group helped add numbers to and revive the American Orthodox community.

However, this immigration is only part of the reason for the growth of Orthodoxy in America in the late twentieth century. The 1960s and 1970s saw a growing number of

young people, raised in observant families, turn to observant Judaism. Many of these "returnees," or *ba'alei t'shuvah*, were influenced by the counterculture or antiestablishment atmosphere prevalent among young people of this period. They were looking for different ways to live their lives and experimented with Shabbat observance and other aspects of Orthodox Judaism. For many, this was a temporary change, but others continued to live as Orthodox Jews. A number of groups reached out to these Jewish seekers, but the group that has been the most involved in Jewish outreach and has had the most significant impact on American Judaism is Habad (commonly spelled Chabad) Lubavitch.

Lubavitch Hasidism began in the eighteenth century in the town of Lubavitch in Russia. Habad is a Hebrew acronym for *hochmah* (wisdom), *binah* (comprehension), and *da'at* (knowledge). According to Habad, "The movement's system of Jewish religious philosophy, the deepest dimension of G-d's Torah, teaches understanding and recognition of the Creator, the role and purpose of Creation, and the importance and unique mission of each Creature. This philosophy guides a person to refine and govern his and her every act and feeling through wisdom, comprehension, and knowledge." This philosophy is tied to a belief that Jews, through their own efforts and actions, can help bring the coming of the Messiah.

The Lubavitch movement has been led by seven rabbis. Rabbi Menachem Mendel Schneersohn, known simply as the Rebbe, arrived in America in 1941 and was declared the seventh Lubavitcher Rebbe in 1950. He built a community and organization that has gone out to educate Jews throughout the world about Judaism using a variety of techniques and media.

[2] Ibid., p. 323.

Emissaries, or *shliḥim,* of the community set up institutions around the world modeled on a Ḥasidic lifestyle. Their goal is to educate Jews to do more *mitzvot* in order to hasten the coming of the Messiah. In addition, the Lubavitch started using the Internet and computer technology as early as the 1980s and 1990s in order to reach a larger number of Jews.

The Lubavitch community faced a crisis in the early 1990s as Rabbi Schneersohn became very ill. Throughout its history, Ḥabad Lubavitch had relied on a line of succession for its rabbis, but Rabbi Schneersohn had no children and had not named a successor. After the Rebbe's death in 1994, Ḥabad leadership decided that Schneersohn would be the last Rebbe. This development led some within the group to believe Schneersohn was the Messiah, which in turn led to a philosophical split within Ḥabad. Although some predicted that the group would fall apart without the Rebbe's leadership, the movement has continued to grow and bring Jewish education and a Ḥasidic lifestyle to growing numbers of Jews throughout the world.

As of this writing, there are four thousand full-time emissary families who help direct thirty-three hundred institutions that are spreading the message of Ḥabad Lubavitch to Jews throughout the world. Increasing numbers of American Jews who are looking for a more traditional Jewish lifestyle have found a community with Ḥabad.

Not all Jews are happy to see *shliḥim* move into their communities. For some American Jews, the *shliḥim* and the very observant Orthodox form of Judaism they represent can be seen as a threat. This may be particularly true for parents who watch their adult children become *ba'alei t'shuvah.* It is often difficult for parents to understand why their children have rejected the Judaism they grew up with for a more observant life—which in some cases the parents themselves have rejected. An observant life may also run counter to the dreams these parents had for their children. So while Ḥabad may help provide Jewish continuity and an alternative way to experience Judaism for many American Jews, it has also caused a certain amount of conflict and division within the Jewish community.

Havurot and Jewish Renewal

In 1968, a group of students in Massachusetts who wanted to "reimagine" Judaism founded Ḥavurat Shalom Community Seminary. These students could trace their philosophy to two different cultural streams—one American and one Jewish. In choosing the Hebrew word *havurah,* which means "fellowship," the students were looking back to the separatist religious fellowships that were formed in the days of the Pharisees.

Later the Reconstructionists used the term for small groups that met within congregations for prayer and study. In their desire to reimagine Judaism, the students who founded Ḥavurat Shalom Community Seminary were also connected to a new trend in American Judaism. Whereas during the post–World War II years the focus of the Jewish community had been on perfecting the world through *tikkun olam* (perfecting the world) and social action, the 1960s and 1970s saw a focus on perfecting one's own soul.

The Ḥavurat Shalom Community Seminary did not endure as a seminary, but eventually became a "commune congregation." Many other similar groups developed in America, comprised mostly of those who were seeking religious renewal but did not want to be part of an organized Jewish movement. The *Jewish Catalog,* published in the 1970s, and its successors, helped bring Jewish ritual and the ideas of the *Havurah* movement into the mainstream of Jewish life. *Havurot* began to spring up in communities all over America including within some Reform and Conservative synagogues, which developed *havurot* for study and religious life within the congregation.

An outgrowth of both the *Havurah* movement and Lubavitch Hasidism, Jewish Renewal took the ideas of the *havurot* and went further. Jewish Renewal traces its roots to the work of Rabbi Shlomo Carlebach and Rabbi Zalman Schachter-Shalomi, both of whom were ordained as Lubavitch rabbis. The emphasis of Jewish Renewal is on direct spiritual experience and the mystical teachings of kabbalah.

Kabbalah (literally, "to receive" or "to accept" in Hebrew) is an ancient Jewish mystical tradition that scholars believe dates to the Middle Ages or even earlier. (See chapter 16 for more information about kabbalah.) Its central writing, the *Zohar,* helps teach how one can reach the spiritual world through interpreting the hidden meanings of the Torah. Originally meant to be studied only by those who had already studied and come to understand other basic Jewish texts, during the late twentieth century kabbalah became popular among Jews and non-Jews when many American celebrities became involved in kabbalah. Places like the Kabbalah Center in Los Angeles, as well as a plethora of books on the subject, have

also helped spread interest in this mystical tradition.

Jewish Renewal does not consider itself to be a separate Jewish movement, but operates on many levels and sometimes within the more formal Jewish movements. Some of the spiritual elements that were first used by the *Havurah* movement and Jewish Renewal later found their way into Reform, Conservative, and Orthodox synagogues: meditation, music, dance, and healing.

Feminism and Egalitarianism

While the 1960s and 1970s saw a spiritual revival in America, they also saw a new consciousness among American women about their own place within society. With the Women's Rights movement, American women wanted to help one another gain equality in jobs, politics, and society in general (as did a small number of egalitarian-minded men). Many of the leaders of this movement were Jewish and also voiced criticism of women's place in Judaism. Each of the major Jewish movements in America would be affected by the changes that were taking place in American society.

For centuries, most Jewish women were not permitted to participate in the synagogue as equals to their fathers, husbands, and brothers. While men were counted as part of a minyan for worship, could lead services, were permitted to read from Torah, and could become rabbis, women were not allowed to fill any of these roles. In 1971, a group of young Conservative women, knowledgeable in Jewish tradition and influenced by the Women's Rights movement, formed *Ezrat Nashim* to help change the role of women in Conservative Judaism. The organization's name refers to the women's section of the synagogue, but can also be understood as "assistance of women." The following year, they went to the Rabbinical Assembly and demanded a more equal role in Jewish life.

Perhaps the women of *Ezrat Nashim* were also influenced by what was happening in the Reform Jewish community. Beginning in the 1960s, the Reform sisterhoods had been calling for the ordination of women as rabbis within the Reform movement. Already, many women involved in the youth movement had begun taking classes at Hebrew Union College, but they were denied the privilege of enrolling in the college as rabbinical students. In 1968, Sally Priesand became the first female rabbinical student at Hebrew Union College, where she was ordained in 1972, making her the first female rabbi in the United States. Two years later, in 1974, Sandy Eisenberg Sasso was ordained as the first Reconstructionist rabbi. Due to the tension within the Conservative movement between those who allied themselves more closely with Jewish tradition and law and those who felt that the modern era called for change, it took the Conservative movement another eleven years to ordain its first female rabbi, Amy Eilberg, in 1985.

As women became more involved in congregational life, they also became more aware of the predominantly male language of the worship service. Many women (and men) now urged their congregations toward the use of more gender-sensitive language, while others helped develop new prayers and rituals to mark a woman's life cycle. The question now arose whether there were times when it was appropriate for women to pray on their own, separate from men. From these questions grew special Rosh Hodesh

prayer and study groups, and women's seders.

Within the Orthodox movement, the questions raised by the women's movement often divided congregations. Was it appropriate for women to pray separately? Could women be called to the Torah in a group of only women? Could women don prayer shawls or dance with the Torah at Simhat Torah? In trying to find answers to these difficult contemporary questions, many looked to the area of education for women. Gradually, there began to be higher-level Jewish educational opportunities for women within the Orthodox community. Soon some women became known for their scholarship and became role models for other women; however, most of these women did not have any expectations of ordination.

CONNECTING TO OUR TRADITION
The openness of American society has allowed Jews to take their Judaism in new directions. Some Jews who might not have found what they were looking for within more traditional models of Judaism could stay within the community by leading new initiatives and exploring new avenues. At the same time, the value of "not separating yourself from the community" has become both an opportunity and a challenge as different ways to express one's Jewish identity continue to develop and evolve.

IMPORTANT TERMS
Reconstructionism
Hasidism
Havurah
Jewish Renewal
Ba'al t'shuvah/ba'alei t'shuvah
Women's movement
Ezrat Nashim
Kabbalah

Names, Places, and Events

Rabbi Mordechai Kaplan

Judith Kaplan

Rabbi Menachem Mendel Schneersohn

Judaism as a Civilization

Jewish Catalog

Shlomo Carlebach

Rabbi Zalman Schachter-Shalomi

Rabbi Sally Priesand

Rabbi Sandy Eisenberg Sasso

Rabbi Amy Eilberg

DISCUSSION QUESTIONS

- How has the flexibility of Jewish culture and thought helped Judaism remain relevant today?
- What are some modern cultural trends that might eventually have an impact on Jewish life?

DID YOU KNOW?

Reconstructionism is the only Jewish movement to have developed totally in the United States.

ACTIVITIES

Compare and Contrast (S, A)

Divide the class into small groups. Provide each group with copies of a few pages from your synagogue's prayer book and those from some of the groups described in this chapter. Ask the students to compare and contrast these different documents. Which are the most similar? Which are the most different? What differences in language do you find? What are some themes found in each? What can we learn about the different expressions of Judaism that the books represent?

OR

Divide the class into small groups. Provide each group with copies of one of the prayers (Hebrew and English translation) from the synagogue's prayer book and the equivalent prayer (Hebrew and English translation) from *The Book of Blessings: New Jewish Prayers for Daily Life, the Sabbath, and the New Moon Festival* by Marcia Falk. Ask the students to compare and contrast these different documents. How is the language in the prayers the same? How is it different? What are some themes found in each? Which version are you most comfortable with? Why?

Field Trips (S, A)

Arrange to take your class on a field trip to services at a Reconstructionist synagogue, Ḥabad, and/or a *havurah*. Make arrangements to speak with a knowledgeable person from the group before and/or after the service so that students have the opportunity to ask questions. Prior to the field trip, provide your students with information about the service in which you will participate. After the field trip, discuss with the students what they experienced, what was new to them, what was similar to what they are used to, and anything that might have made them uncomfortable.

Research Project (S, A)

Provide the students with names of different Jewish movements currently found in the United States. Have the students use the Internet, magazine articles, and books to research these movements. Some questions on which the students might focus are: (1) What are the central beliefs of this movement? (2) Has this movement influenced other streams of Judaism? If yes, how? (3) Does this movement reflect other changes or trends in American society? If so, how?

Community Research (S, A)

Using your community's Jewish newspaper and other resources, have the class research which Jewish movements are represented in your community. If possible, invite some members of these different movements to come and speak to your class. A final project could be to have your students write up a newspaper for their parents with articles based on interviews and other research.

Ask the Rabbi Panel (S, A)
Arrange to have a panel of rabbis to come and answer student questions about the different Jewish movements. Each rabbi can give some brief background about his or her own movement. Then the panel can answer questions that the students may have prepared in advance or which come up during the panel discussion.

RESOURCES
Books and Articles
Ellenson, David. "350 Years: Religious Revival in a Land with No Medieval Past, Judaism Flourished." *Forward,* July 16, 2004.

Falk, Marcia. *The Book of Blessings: New Jewish Prayers for Daily Life, the Sabbath, and the New Moon Festival.* New York: Beacon Press, 1999.

Fishkoff, Sue. *The Rebbe's Army: Inside the World of Chabad-Lubavitch.* New York: Schocken Books, 2003.

Kaplan, Mordechai. *Judaism as a Civilization.* Philadelphia: Jewish Publication Society, 1994; reprint of 1934 ed.

Leiman, Sondra. *America: The Jewish Experience.* New York: UAHC Press, 1994.

Sarna, Jonathan D. *American Judaism: A History.* New Haven, CT: Yale University Press, 2004.

Strassfeld, Michael, and Richard Siegel. *The First Jewish Catalog.* Philadelphia: Jewish Publication Society, 1973.

Strassfeld, Michael, and Sharon Strassfeld. *The Second Jewish Catalog: Sources and Resources.* Philadelphia: Jewish Publication Society, 1976.

Strassfeld, Michael, and Sharon Strassfeld. *The Third Jewish Catalog: Creating Community.* Philadelphia: Jewish Publication Society, 1980.

Discography
Carlebach, Shlomo. *Days Are Coming.* Sameach Music, 1999.

Carlebach, Shlomo. *HaNeshama Lach.* Sameach Music, 2002.

Carlebach, Shlomo. *HaNeshama Shel Shlomo.* Sameach Music, 1997.

Carlebach, Shlomo. *Live.* Israel Music, 1996.

Carlebach, Shlomo. *L'kvod Shabbos.* Sameach Music, 2003.

Carlebach, Shlomo. *Rabbi Shlomo Carlebach Sings—Shlomo Live 1962.* Sameach Music, 2002.

Carlebach, Shlomo. *Shlomo Carlebach at the Village Gate.* Vanguard Records, 1995.

Internet
Visit www.behrmanhouse.com/booklinks for links to Web sites that offer additional resources for this chapter.

AUTHORS' BIOGRAPHIES

Julia Phillips Berger, RJE has worked as a congregational educator and a history museum educator. Julia received her master's degree in History Museum Studies from the Cooperstown Graduate Program in History Museum Studies in Cooperstown, NY. As the Director of Education and Public Programming at a historic site in Ohio, Julia developed tours for children and adults, and worked with the local Board of Education to develop an interdisciplinary field-trip partnership with the public schools.

She returned to school to earn her Master's Degree in Jewish Education from the Rhea Hirsch School of Education at Hebrew Union College-Jewish Institute of Religion in Los Angeles. Julia presents workshops on the subject of teaching Jewish history at educational conferences, has published articles in Jewish education journals, and contributed a chapter on teaching Jewish history to *The Ultimate Jewish Teacher's Handbook* (A.R.E. Publishing).

Sue Parker Gerson lives in Denver, CO, where she works for the Colorado Agency for Jewish Education, directing the local Florence Melton Adult Mini-School and serving on its faculty. Sue has worked as a religious school principal and teacher of children, teens, and adults in a wide variety of formal and informal settings in Colorado, New York and New Jersey. Sue received her master's degree in Jewish History from the Jewish Theological Seminary, and her principal's and teacher's licenses from the Board of Jewish Education of Greater New York. *Teaching Jewish History* emphasizes her professional passions for Jewish education and history, and is her first book.